D1588332

PROUST'S
WAY

PROUST'S WAY

A
FIELD GUIDE
TO
In Search of
Lost Time

ROGER
SHATTUCK

ALLEN LANE
THE PENGUIN PRESS

ALLEN LANE
THE PENGUIN PRESS

Published by the Penguin Group
Penguin Books Ltd, 27 Wrights Lane, London W8 5TZ, England
Penguin Putnam Inc., 375 Hudson Street, New York, New York 10014, USA
Penguin Books Australia Ltd, Ringwood, Victoria, Australia
Penguin Books Canada Ltd, 10 Alcorn Avenue, Toronto, Ontario, Canada M4V 3B2
Penguin Books (NZ) Ltd, Private Bag 102902, NSMC, Auckland, New Zealand

Penguin Books Ltd, Registered Offices: Harmondsworth, Middlesex, England

First published in the USA by W. W. Norton & Company Inc. 2000
First published in Great Britain by Allen Lane The Penguin Press 2000
1 3 5 7 9 10 8 6 4 2

Printed and bound in Great Britain by The Bath Press, Bath

Cover repro and printing by Concise Cover Printers

A CIP catalogue record for this book is available from the British Library

ISBN 0–713–99478–9

In Memory of
H. Francis Shattuck, Jr.
(1920–1997)

CONTENTS

LIST OF DIAGRAMS

A SENSE OF LIFE

Two impulses propel this book—one affirmative and one corrective.

Each chapter affirms different ways in which Proust's superficially forbidding novel *In Search of Lost Time* welcomes us to a world of vivid places and intensely human characters. And those chapters taken together affirm the philosophical and moral profundity of the book, kept in motion by a narrative structure as simple and as sturdy as that of a suspension bridge. Perhaps I shall win a few readers to my conviction that the *Search* is the greatest and most rewarding novel of the twentieth century, outdistancing its closest rivals, Joyce's *Ulysses*, Thomas Mann's *The Magic Mountain*, and Faulkner's *Absalom, Absalom!* But no literary sweepstakes will be mounted here. I undertake an exploration of the bounty of literature in all its forms.

The corrective impulse that also carries this book appears primarily in Chapters V and VI and addresses two misapprehensions firmly lodged in prevailing opinion about Proust and his work.

First, even though the seven volumes of the *Search* deal with motifs of time, the past, and recollection, the novel is not primarily about memory and sentiments concerning the past. The famous episode of the madeleine cake and the cup of tea introduces a series of reminiscences to which Marcel, the protagonist, attaches great significance. But the reminiscences provide stepping-stones on a path that will lead beyond their uncertainty to more essential and more durable mental states. Marcel finally outgrows involuntary memory in a way that allows him, against all odds and expectations, to find himself and his vocation.

The second corrective turns to another stereotype applied to Proust by popular journalists and cartoonists and even by scholars. They portray him as the ultimate aesthete, the impeccably barbered and tailored dandy reclining on a chaise lounge, sipping a cup of tea, and closing his heavily lidded eyes in exaltation. One is meant to glimpse, symbolically arrayed behind him, the founders and devotees of this tradition of artistic refinement: the philosophers Shaftesbury and Kant; the Romantic poets Schiller, Coleridge, Gautier, and Poe, who enunciated the doctrine of art for art's sake; the great figures of Flaubert and Baudelaire, who linked art for art's sake to a darker realism; the French schools of Symbolism and Decadence; and the associated Anglo-Irish branch of Ruskin, Pater, Wilde, Yeats, and Joyce. Posed as the culmination of this two-century aesthetic heritage, Proust has become something of a cult figure.

The nearly identical titles of two intelligent critical works on Proust reveal how far scholars can go toward accepting the aesthetic interpretation of Proust's work. Barbara Bucknall entitled her study *The Religion of Art in Proust* (1969). Leon Chai entitled his book *Aestheticism: The Religion of Art in Post-Romantic Literature* (1990) and devoted the crowning chapter to Proust. These two books, like the popular caricature of Proust as decadent dandy, combine sound insights with lingering elements of distortion. In Chapter VI, I try to adjust our understanding of Proust as an artist more closely to the evidence than is the case with the stereotype of the ultimate aesthete. The protagonist of the *Search* does not retreat to a monastery devoted to the religion of art. He returns to society in a last attempt to test the integrity of his literary calling. This time, he finds his way. The novel does not subside into passivity and coterie art, as does the decadent hero, Des Esseintes, in Huysmans' *A rebours*

(*Against Nature*, 1884). The *Search* creates a four-dimensional society and a stringently critical perspective on the snobbery and superficiality of that society. Proust was more a social critic than a decadent.

READING PROUST BEARS many resemblances to visiting a zoo. The specimens he collected from the remotest corners of society amaze and amuse us in their variety. Their extremes of color and shape, size and locomotion, temperament and response also cause a certain apprehension. And before long we realize that this is no ordinary zoo, where the creatures exhibited are confined in cages. The tables have been turned on us. The specimens roam free in a vast park. We drive through it confined to our vehicles, scorned by some animals, pursued and harassed by others. Ours is the alien presence, at least until we have remained long enough to adapt to the environment and to provoke no stir. Then we may begin to wonder why anyone set out to create this vast narrative landscape, and how we were ever induced to enter a zoological territory so challenging.

Now that I have lived with *In Search of Lost Time* for several decades, I believe I can offer an answer to both questions. The novel opens (like the *Tanach* or Old Testament and *Alice in Wonderland*) with a fall—a mental collapse backward and downward in time and space, an initial rite of passage, which carries the unidentified narrating consciousness to a critical point of near annihilation. We come to this sentence on the third page: "I had only, and in its simplest form, the feeling of existence, as it must flutter in the deepest recess of an animal" (I 5/i 4). All history and part of evolution have disappeared. The story almost sputters out at the start—and then catches again with increasing force, which plunges us headlong into places and people and their actions.

What draws us to a zoo is the sheer sense of life, both shared and utterly alien, animating those beautiful and grotesque animals. The melodramatic fact of their existence makes us newly attentive to our own. Similarly, the amazing caricatures of human beings that roam the open zoo of Proust's novel—Aunt Léonie, the servant Françoise, the glowering Baron de Charlus—reawaken us to our own existence. Marcel, the boy who grows to manhood in these pages, spends the early part of his life absorbed in his own sensations, which give him a powerful sense of life concentrated upon himself. Nothing is more precious than this physical, organic, inward sense of his own existence as himself in the world's zoo. Yet, after every move to an unfamiliar place and a new bedroom, Marcel must build this sense of himself all over again. At the same time, he yearns to escape from the caul of this confined, self-absorbed existence and to reach out to other human creatures. He wants to know and to touch what is not part of him. He yearns to live beyond himself.

The pendulum-like motion between solitude and sociability also strikes the reader in the rhythm of Proust's style. He is famous for the dimensions of his sentences. Their coilings and uncoilings encompass the extended landscape of the protagonist's mind. Readers are less likely to notice the short, one-line sentences even against the ground of lengthier constructions. On the one hand, Proust is constantly tempted to fit his endlessly expanding, introspective universe into one proliferating, carefully built sentence whose syntax will articulate an order of subordination and temporality and causation holding all its parts in place. In discussing Flaubert and Nerval, Proust insists many times on the beauty of syntax as an organizing principle. On the other hand, Proust knew the advantages of terseness. "It's you." "Here's why." "I dared not move." He can be as laconic as Hemingway and the Gospels. His opening sentence does not fill out a line. The bulk of the novel is made up of what grammarians call *hypotactic* style, where syntax records a wide range of connections and relations among the elements of our experience. Proust also relies, but fleetingly, on *paratactic* style—setting simple sentences side by side without transition and connectives, a style associated with primitive writing and with ultramodern writing, as in Gertrude Stein and some passages of James Joyce. Hypotaxis tends to hold the world together in a comprehensive order. Parataxis tends to fragment the world into small parts among which we can move swiftly and freely.

Proust did not seek to tear his world apart, a tendency present in a large segment of modern literature. He tried to convey to his readers the richness and the cohesiveness of his inner life. The organizing power of syntax served him faithfully, along with metaphor and his sense of the comic. Without the consolidating force of his hypotactic style, Proust could never have brought onstage and kept track of so many contrasting characters to people this zoo of a narrative.

PROUST GREW TO maturity during the fin de siècle period when Paris was the cultural capital of Europe. French literary and artistic culture, swept up since midcentury by the second wave of Romanticism, had separated into two rival camps: Naturalism and Symbolism. Even though there was a great fund of poetry and imaginative élan in his temperament, the naturalist Zola championed the cause of systematic, almost scientific observation of the real world and devoted his novels to the objective study of all levels of society, including the lowest. His opposite number, Stéphane Mallarmé, though by no means an irresponsible dreamer, used his rarefied poetic diction to explore highly subjective moods and tableaux existing almost beyond the reach of language.

The reason why Edmund Wilson's early essay on Proust in *Axel's Castle* (1931) has shown great staying power is that Wilson portrays Proust as at first drawn to by the subjective aesthetics of Symbolism and as gradually yielding to the objective discipline of Naturalism. But the two terms from literary history will not really serve us. The greatest authors cannot be contained within the confines of one school or movement. (The same can be said of James Joyce, for different reasons, as Wilson shows in another fine essay.) As Proust tentatively incorporated other people into his solitude, he also incorporated convincing descriptions of the material and social worlds into his preoccupation with elusive currents of thought and feeling. This indefatigable invalid embraced all aspects of existence.

The chapters of this book evolve gradually from elementary pointers for beginning readers to comprehensive arguments about the structure and the moral tenor of Proust's novel. The final chapter, on continuing disputes about the *Search*, closes with an exploration of how Proust reconciles reason and imagination, intelligence and sentiment. That remarkable synthesis reinforces the sense of life that flows through his tentacular sentences.

Forget the cork-lined room and the dallying aesthete. Proust lived in this world and wrote about it with fervor.

N.B. As is specified in the Acknowledgments (page 271), sections of this book draw on and revise my earlier books on Proust. Other sections incorporate uncollected writings along with extensive new materials.

BIOGRAPHICAL RÉSUMÉ ON PROUST

1871   Proust born July 10 during the Paris Commune. Brother born two years later.

1880   First asthma attack.

1882–90   Studies at Lycée Condorcet. Military service. Brief university study.

1890–1907   Social climbing. Publishes stories and essays in literary reviews and newspapers. Influence of Robert de Montesquiou. *Les Plaisirs et les jours* published in 1896. Discovers Ruskin's work and translates two of his books. A first novel remains unfinished. Father and mother die (1903, 1905).

1908–13   Intense work on a new draft of his novel; "finished" in 1912. First volume published in 1913. Second in preparation.

1914–22   Constant writing and poor health. World acclaim after the Goncourt Prize is awarded to second volume in 1919. Two more volumes published before Proust dies on November 18, 1922.

1923–27   Appearance of remaining three volumes.

NOTE ON EDITIONS
AND TRANSLATIONS

References to Proust's *A la recherche du temps perdu* and *In Search of Lost Time*, given in the form (III 1032/vi 507), cite first the most widely owned reader's edition in French, and second, after the slash, the currently available translation in the United States:

> I–III refers to *A la recherche du temps perdu*. Texte édité et présenté par Pierre Clarac and André Ferré. Bibliothèque de la Pléiade. Paris: Gallimard, 1954. 3 tomes.
>
> i–vi refers to *In Search of Lost Time*. Translated by C. K. Moncrieff and Terence Kilmartin, revised by D. J. Enright. New York: Modern Library, 1992. 6 volumes.

The British edition of *In Search of Lost Time* (Vintage, 1996), also in six volumes, contains the same translation with a different pagination.

The translations used here are based on Moncrieff, *Remembrance of Things Past* (Modern Library, 1923–32), and revised by me.

Dependable reader's editions of the novel in French are available also from Garnier-Flammarion, Bouqins, and Folio. Proust scholars who may have bought the new four-volume Pléiade edition (1987–89) will

find a Table de Concordance at the end of each volume allowing them
to collate my references with these volumes. I discuss the merits of this
new Pléiade edition at the opening of Chapter VIII, where I also examine translations of the *Search* in English.

Three more Proust volumes are cited in the references under the following abbreviations:

*CSB Contre Sainte-Beuve précedé de Pastiches et mélanges et suivi de
Essais et articles*. Edition établie par Pierre Clarac et Yves Sandre. Bibliothèque de la Pléiade. Paris: Gallimard, 1971.

JS Jean Santeuil précedé de Les plairirs et les jours. Edition établie par
Pierre Clarac et Yves Sandre. Bibliothèque de la Pléiade.
Paris: Gallimard, 1971.

OAL On Art and Literature, 1896–1919. Translated by Sylvia
Townsend Warner, with an introduction by Terence Kilmartin. New York: Carroll and Graf, 1984.

PROUST'S
WAY

THE WORK AND ITS AUTHOR

AMONG THE HANDFUL OF LITERARY CLASSICS PRODUCED IN this century, Marcel Proust's *In Search of Lost Time* is the most oceanic—and the least read. Joyce and Kafka, Faulkner and Camus sell hundreds of thousands of copies. Proust sells barely in the thousands. His substantial reputation as an extreme case of something—long-windedness, psychological vivisection, the snobbery of letters, salvation by memory—rests not on wide readership but on a myth of uniqueness that often hides his true attractions. In an era when the significance and the privileged status of the work of art are being both questioned and reinforced, this ultimate monument to the artistic vocation, banked high on all sides by interpretation and biography, refuses to sink back into the sands of time.

Obstacles and Inducements

The inordinate length of Proust's novel (three thousand pages) goes a long way toward explaining the wariness of readers. Balzac's one-hundred-volume printout of all French society comes in separate packages; the links between the volumes serve as a special reward for the persevering. The first two sections of Proust's novel, "Combray" and "Swann in Love," can stand separately and have earned many admirers. Yet true believers insist that there is no substitute for the cumulative effect of the whole work. Understandably, many readers hesitate to make the investment of time and attention required to assimilate even a fraction of the whole.

Compounding the challenge of sheer magnitude and of an extended plot, there is Proust's style. His transcontinental sentences contribute to the appearance of a motionless plot. The original French is no easier than the translations. How can one follow a story line through such labyrinthine prose? One reason why true believers are right to insist on a full reading is that you cannot distinguish the plot if the first sections are all you have to go on. Proust's first critics were at a terrible disadvantage; they had to interpret the whole from a few parts. As a result, Proust had to serve as the sole qualified guide to his own uncompleted work. He devoted endless letters and several newspaper interviews to rebutting his critics and explaining episodes still to come. Gradually, Proust's description of his work has been validated by several generations of critics. But for fifteen years his work appeared piecemeal in the face of enormous odds against comprehension. It looked at first like a conspiracy against readers.

Furthermore, the plot remains close to a romantic stereotype. Will the young protagonist of the *Search* succeed in becoming a writer? God save us from another story about a sensitive young artist trying to find his way! Poems about writing poetry, novels about becoming a novelist, literature preoccupied with the life of literature—what form of narcissism could annoy a discriminating reader more than this aesthetic self-absorption? Proust takes several measures to reduce the damage of the outworn plot. He turns our annoyance at the posing young artist into indulgent laughter. He postpones the most crucial episodes of discovery of his vocation of art until the end of the story. And he fills the twenty-five hundred intervening pages with scenes and sensations and characters so vivid that we are sustained by this immediacy of experience. The protagonist records and animates so much of his physical and social milieu for us that we mostly forget about the overarching question of literary vocation. It's always there, but shrouded, out of sight.

These objections to plot and style in Proust's novel often arise from partial reading and incomplete understanding. Many of them can be traced to remarks by early commentators, some of whom were sympathetic. Edmund Wilson, one of the first and most perceptive of American critics, deeply admired Proust's work; yet he called the *Search* "one of the gloomiest books ever written." In this instance his critical acumen failed him. Proust's novel earns its place in literature as a great comic tale, punctuated with smiles and guffaws. Henry James produced a petulant formula: "inconceivable boredom associated with the most extreme ecstasy which it is possible to imagine." It is hard to read the sentence as anything but a mixed verdict. The volume of "tributes" a dozen English writers devoted to Proust in 1923 sows even more confusion. Joseph Conrad finds intellectual analysis at its most creative, but "no reverie, no emotion." Three pages later, George Saintsbury insists on a "constant relapse upon—and sometimes self-restriction to—a sort of dream element." Had they read the same author? Arnold Bennett wrote more in outrage than in tribute and could not excuse "the clumsy centipedalian crawling of the interminable sentences." There is Aldous Huxley's description (though not in this same volume) of Proust as a hermaphrodite, toadlike creature spooning his own tepid juice over his face and body. On the centenary of Proust's birth, in July 1971, the *New York Times Book Review* assigned its front page to the novelist William H. Gass for a discussion of Proust's work. Gass's rancorous article adds little to Bennet's comments. ". . . there is no special truth in him. . . . Proust writes a careless self-indulgent prose, doesn't he? . . . Epithet follows epithet like tea cakes in flutes of paper. . . . It is a style that endangers the identity of the self in its reckless expressions of it."

The fact that many of these critics contradict one another does not discredit them collectively or individually. But it does mean that we must beware of incomprehension and prejudice. The most persistent negative judgments of Proust can be reduced to two. First, Proust's work is boring because of slackness in both style and construction. Second, the moral universe of Proust's work never breaks free from the attitude of a spoiled, sickly, adolescent snob, born to wealth on the fringes of high culture and high society. To these criticisms one could add two more that are less frequently voiced.

Clausewitz described war as the continuation of policy by other means. Like many authors, Proust often treated writing as a continuation of life by other means. The word can conquer where the flesh is weak. Having discovered this path, Proust became one of the great megalomaniacs of literature, unwilling (in part because of his semi-invalid condition in later years) to relinquish any small hold he could gain over other people by writing. In his letters he often mixed honey with acid. He dominated his mother with interbedroom memoranda and his friends with pitiful pleas for help. He sought to hypnotize his readers and to command the world from his sickbed. This sensitive weakling sought power and won it.

The last stricture is closely related. From Proust's writings, as from an electric generator, flows a powerful current always ready to shock not only our morality but our very sense of humanity. He frequently undermines individual character as the source of anything coherent and reliable in our behavior. Love and friendship, honesty and sexuality crumble into mockeries of human relationships. Except for Marcel's immediate family, no one in the *Search* escapes the curses of selfishness, self-contempt, and snobbery. Few grounds for human dignity survive Proust's touch. The inhumanity of artistic creation seems to triumph over everything.

Quite deliberately I have begun with harsh and seriously distorted versions of Proust's stature. I shall rebut these charges in the course of time. Meanwhile, I feel it is wise not simply to affirm his innocence but to ask for a far more illuminating verdict: *guilty—but not as charged*. For Proust had the power to modify, as he went along, the laws under which he wrote and under which he asks us to read. Neither the novel form nor "human nature" remains unchanged after he has passed. The problem is to detect and measure the shifts. Snobbery, megalomania, boredom, aestheticism, and instability of character do indeed loom large in the world

Proust creates. The first task of the critic is to prevent the uninitiated reader from reacting against these elements before one understands the role they are assigned in a remarkably coherent work of art.

No single theory or approach will make Proust easily and quickly available to all inquiring minds. The very resistance of his work to simplification and analysis constitutes its most evident general characteristic. Beyond this feature, however, we discover endless contradictions in the *Search*. Walt Whitman lived at peace with the fact that he contradicted himself. He said that he contained multitudes. Proust asks the next question. How much of one's multitudinous self can a person reveal or embody at one time? The first answer is plain common sense: it all depends. It depends on many things, from chance and volition to memory and forgetting. The second answer is categorical. No matter how we go about it, *we cannot be all of ourselves all at once*. Narrow light beams of perception and of recollection illuminate the present and the past in vivid fragments. The clarity of those fragments is sometimes very great. They may even overlap and reinforce one another. However, to summon our entire self into simultaneous existence lies beyond our powers. We live by synecdoche, by cycles of being. More profoundly than any other novelist, Proust perceived this state of things and worked as an economist of the personality. In himself and in others he observed its fluctuations and partial realizations. Through habit and convention we may find security in "the immobility of the things around us" (I 6/i 5). Yet this appearance of stability affords only temporary refuge. We yield with excitement, apprehension, and a deeper sense of existence to the great wheeling motion of experience. On a single page Proust refers to that endless shifting process as both "the secret of the future" and "the darkness we can never penetrate" (II 67/iii 81, 82). He also has a word for it: our lot is "intermittence," the only steady state we know. One of the early titles for his novel was "The Heart's Intermittences."

As in life itself, the scope of action and reflection encountered in the *Search* exceeds the capacity of one mind to hold it all together at one time. Thus the novel embodies and manifests the principle of intermittence: to live means to perceive different and often conflicting aspects of reality. This iridescence never resolves itself completely into a unitive point of view. Accordingly, it is possible to project out of the *Search* itself a series of putative and intermittent authors. Precisely that has happened. The portraitist of an expiring society, the artist of romantic reminiscence, the narrator of the laminated "I," the classicist of formal structure—all these figures have been found in Proust, approximately in that order of historical occurrence. All are present as discernible components of his vision and his creation. His principle of intermittence anticipates such veerings of critical emphasis. It is in the middle of a literary discussion that his Narrator observes, *"On ne se réalise que successivement"* (III 380/v 511). It really means: one finds, not oneself, but a succession of selves. Similarly, Proust's work is still going on in our gradual discovery of it.

The Life of an Enfant Nerveux

If forced to make the distinction, most of us would indicate a deeper and more lasting interest in people than in works. We ascribe greatness or goodness more readily to an individual person, accountable for the actions of an entire life, than to a deed detached from its context of individual agency and motivation in a person's life. One could with good reason interpret the history of Western civilization as a sustained attempt to divert us toward a concern with good works, both ethical and artistic. Religion and aesthetics have developed along curiously parallel paths. Yet fundamentally our attention directs itself toward men and women, their temperaments and their lives. Only a lifetime provides an adequate unit of significance and value. (We have also cultivated a powerful materialist doctrine: the tendency to judge a person not by what one is or does, but by what one owns.)

It is not surprising, therefore, that the biography of so curious a figure as Proust should exert a fascination equal to that of his literary work. I suspect that more readers have read through George D. Painter's biography of Proust than have reached the end of the *Search*. Furthermore, Proust's work lies in very close proximity to his life. On two occasions toward the end of the novel, when he supplied a first name for his Narrator-hero, Proust used his own, Marcel (III 75, 157/v 91, 203). Writers' lives are neither holy ground nor useless appendages. Without some knowledge of Proust's biography, we would remain blind to a whole section of countryside surrounding his work and lending meaning to it.

Proust's life began with the Paris Commune of 1871 and ended in fame and exhaustion four years after World War I. In those fifty-one years he lived two closely interlocking careers. Beginning very early, this sensitive, gifted young man with something slightly exotic about his soft manner and dark look carried out a brilliant escape from his bourgeois background and from the professional career expected of the eldest son of a prominent Paris doctor. He accomplished this feat by ingratiating himself with the wealthy and sometimes aristocratic families of his schoolmates at the Lycée Condorcet. By the age of seventeen, exploiting his talents as a mimic and conversationalist, he was visiting literary salons and learning his way in society. In his midthirties, soon after the death of both his parents, his first career as a somewhat eccentric man of the world gave way to another activity: literature. Up to that point Proust's writing had served his social ambitions or had been kept hidden. He now reversed the poles of his existence. For the last fifteen years of his life, his social connections and his worldliness furnished the raw material of his writing.

It was a shift, never a clean break. Proust claimed that he wrote parts of his first book at the age of fourteen (*JS* 902), and there is little reason to doubt him. Just a month before he died, suffering terribly and aware of how much remained to be done on the final volumes of his novel, he dragged himself out of bed to go to a party given by the Comte and Comtesse de Beaumont. The overlap of careers was extensive. Nevertheless, the general movement of Proust's life pivots on an obscure point, somewhere between 1905 and 1909, in which north and south changed places. He became a convert—a convert to true faith in himself as the novelist of his own conversion.

Such a schematic version of Proust's life keeps things simple and clear. It glosses over minor conflicts of fact and major conflicts of interpretation. There are good reasons for us to seek a closer knowledge of how Proust became a convert to his own calling. The most systematic and the least satisfactory explanations of Proust's life are pseudomedical. Son and brother of prominent doctors, Proust was himself a contributor to this line of thought. Inevitably he had heard that the terrors and upheavals of the Commune (his father was almost shot by accident) had affected his mother's pregnancy. Sickly at birth, he nevertheless survived. Nine years later came his first serious attack of asthma; he received all the attention he could want, and his condition stabilized during youth and early manhood. The attacks recurred in his midtwenties, at about the time he was coming to terms with his homosexuality. Mostly from his own testimony we know that he was prone to hypochondria and was fascinated by voyeurism and certain forms of sadomasochism. Psychoanalysts have produced resounding terms to apply to the roots of his condition. When Serge Béhar speaks of "infantile neurosis developing into cenesthopathy in the adult," he is affirming a diseased condition of the organic sensation of existence and well-being. Perhaps: but this ground is as treacherous as it is fascinating. And I wonder if the technical vocabulary really improves on the term Proust's family applied to him very early and which he cites frequently in *Jean Santeuil: un enfant nerveux*.

It is significant that all psychological studies of Proust accept his identification of the determining childhood scene: the good-night kiss described near the opening of the *Search*. But to what extent is it part of Proust's biography? To what extent is it fiction? In the earlier *Jean Santeuil* version of the scene, the little boy revels in the power and freedom he finds when he finally triumphs over his mother's refusal to leave her guests and come to his room to kiss him good night. The same scene in the *Search* emphasizes a strong aftertaste of disappointment over the fact that his mother and father give in to his importunings. Their capitulation, the Narrator states, undermines what little willpower the boy has to control his moods. No one has gone further than Proust himself in probing the complete significance of this scene. But we cannot for that reason read it unquestioningly as autobiography.*

Heredity provides another way of explaining Proust's temperament and behavior. George Painter seems to accept the "facts" of Proust's "hereditary neurasthenia" and calls attention to a similar condition in a paternal aunt who became a recluse. André Maurois lays great emphasis on the mingling of two parental strains: French-Catholic and Jewish. One cannot readily attribute contrasting character traits to these two races or religions as true genetic strains. On the other hand, the marriage did combine two contrasting cultures. In Proust's sensibility one soon detects the jostling opposition between city and country, between cosmopolitan Paris and provincial, semipastoral Illiers/Combray. His father never lost the brusque manners of a village grocer's son. Dr. Proust was the first of a long line of farmers and tradesman to leave Illiers. Mme Proust, fifteen years younger than her husband, was the highly educated, art-loving daughter of a wealthy stockbroker. Her brother was a bachelor and ladies' man; her mother had connections in elegant society and in the world of literature and the arts. Proust practiced neither Judaism nor Catholicism yet remained close to both faiths. The tidal move-

---

*In a volume of provocative psychoanalytic studies, *L'Arbre jusqu'aux racines*, Dominique Fernandez interprets the whole of the *Search*, and this sequence in particular, as an elaborate feint on Proust's part to distract our attention from his jealousy of his younger brother and disappointment in his father, and from the overpowering domination of his mother. Thus, according to Fernandez, Proust masks the true origins of his homosexuality and protects the myth of the happy family. Many of Fernandez's points are persuasive, but he has a distressingly narrow belief in "precise psychological causes" from which all human behavior will "necessarily flow." Those causes reduce a novel to an excrescence of a psychological case history. I cannot accept this tight determinism on any level of life or literature. Proust's novel makes revelations that transcend his particular case and cannot be read back into it. There, in fact, lies the principal justification for calling it a novel. Fernandez also argues that *Jean Santeuil* is a better and more courageous book than the *Search* because it reveals more about Proust's neurosis than the final novel does. Though Fernandez argues his premise very resourcefully, his conclusion does not follow.

ment of the *Search* arises not from a contrast of races or religions but from a geographical and intellectual exchange between city culture and country culture. We glimpse it first in the "two ways" that polarize the child's world of Combray, and later in the contrast between Combray itself and Paris.

Whatever Proust's medical and psychological condition may have been, and whatever his heredity, he found his own path into the Parisian life of *la belle époque*. He had an agile mind, a prodigious memory (especially for poetry), and a hypersensitive discernment of other people's feelings and reactions. Despite frequent illnesses during his teens, he was healthy enough to excel in school, especially in philosophy. The philosophy teacher Darlu, who tutored him privately for a year, made a profound impression on him and introduced him to the idealist analysis of the contrast between appearance and reality. Very early, Proust fixed on reading and literature as the locus of his interests. He apparently experienced puppy love a number of times. In the most intense instance, his parents discouraged his desires for Marie de Benardaky, insisting that she was socially too far beyond his reach. Taking advantage of a law discriminating in favor of the rich and educated, Proust volunteered at eighteen for one year of military service. Though he did not distinguish himself as a soldier, he made several good friends among the other privileged young men and later called that year the happiest of his life.

One of the favorite pastimes in that leisured self-conscious society was a modified game of truth or consequences played by filling in an elegantly printed questionnaire. Some families kept albums containing these questionnaires along with other mementos of their friends and relatives. In Proust's case we have two such documents, one written at thirteen and the other at twenty. Despite the artificial circumstances, Proust's answers furnish two unmatchable probes of these early years of the slow bloomer. Where possible, I quote both sets of answers.

What is for you the greatest unhappiness? To be separated from maman
(13). Not to have known my mother and grandmother (20).
In what place would you like to live? In the land of the Ideal, or

rather of my ideal (13). In the place where certain things I want would come to pass as if by enchantment—and where tender feelings would always be shared (20).

Your ideal of earthly happiness? To live near all my loved ones, with the charms of nature, lots of books and musical scores, and, not far away, a French theater (13). I'm afraid it isn't high enough, and I'm afraid of destroying it by telling it (20).

For what faults do you have the greatest indulgence? For the private life of geniuses (13). For those I understand (20).

Your principal fault? Not to know how, not to be able, to will something [*vouloir*] (20).

What would you like to be? Myself, as people I admire would like me to be (20).

Your favorite quality in a man? Intelligence, the moral sense (13).

Your favorite quality in a woman? Tenderness [*douceur*], naturalness, intelligence (13).

Your favorite occupation? Reading; daydreaming; poetry (13). Loving (20).

Your present state of mind? Annoyance [*ennui*] over having thought about myself to answer all these questions (20).

Even for Proust's hothouse milieu, these are precocious answers, steeped in literary attitudes, and displaying the capacity to speak the truth within certain limits of coyness and insecurity. No bumbler wrote these apothegmatic lines.

At twenty this young sensitive had to face the painful question of what he would do with himself. For close to fifteen years he temporized and spent his days and nights essentially in the provinces of his mind looking for the capital. He entered the university and took a degree in law and another in philosophy. He also qualified by competitive examination for an unsalaried library position, and then never started work. For several years his best efforts went into two complementary activities: writing short stories and literary sketches for newspapers and symbolist reviews, and cultivating the elegant families of the friends he had made at school and during military service. He memorialized his success in both lines with the publication of his first collection, *Pleasures and Days* (1896). It was an overly elegant edition illustrated by a salon hostess, Madeleine Lemaire, with a preface extorted from Anatole France. It looked like the work of a dilettante with powerful connections, even though it does not read that way.

The strongest presence in Proust's life at this juncture was Comte Robert de Montesquiou-Fezensac. Fifteen years older, he had everything Proust thought he wanted. The Count was descended from the model for D'Artagnan of *The Three Musketeers* and could claim most of European nobility as relatives by blood or marriage. Immense wealth enabled him to cultivate an aesthetic manner and way of life remarkable enough to have already inspired one notorious book, Huysmans' *A rebours*. He was also a published poet of some note and flaunted his homosexuality with enormous style. Proust fawned on him for several years before he could pull away, and the fascination never disappeared entirely. When Montesquiou mentioned his young friend once in print, Proust had to fight a pistol duel with a critic who seized the occasion to ridicule him as "one of those small-time fops in literary heat." No one was hurt.

It was during this time that the Dreyfus affair exploded in November 1897. Proust, aged twenty-six and fully committed to his Jewish heritage, joined the Dreyfus cause from the start. He helped get Anatole France's signature for the Petition of the Intellectuals, attended every session of Zola's trial, and was active in support of Colonel Picquart, the second hero of the affair. This public behavior placed Proust in the opposite camp from much of his family (his father knew practically every minister) and most of his society hostesses. He recorded the harrowing tension and the human consequences of these events in sections of the novel he had been working on in spurts and fragments for some four years. *Jean Santeuil* provides scenes from the sad yet charmed life of a young man who can never pull himself together and is forever protected from above. After some eight hundred pages without form or continuity, Proust abandoned the manuscript in apparent dissatisfaction.

He was still in the provinces. His next discovery was John Ruskin, the English art critic and social thinker. Between 1899 and 1905 Proust spent much of his time reading him and making "pilgrimages" to the sites in France and Italy about which Ruskin had written. He went on to translate two of Ruskin's books (with the help of his mother and an English girlfriend) and to write prefaces that grew until they almost swallowed the works they were intended to present. Proust performed a dance with Ruskin similar to the one he had performed with Montesquiou. For a time Ruskin's combination of aesthetic sensitivity, scholarship, and social thought won his deep admiration. Later he found Ruskin guilty of a false idolatry of art and of a masked moralism. This long encounter with Ruskin was deeply profitable for Proust. He was able to clarify his own ideas on art and to acknowledge to himself that fiction was still his goal. In December 1902, at the peak of his Ruskin absorption, he wrote to Prince Antoine Bibesco: ". . . a hundred characters for novels, a thousand ideas keep asking me to give them substance, like those shades that keep asking Ulysses in the *Odyssey* to give them blood to drink and bring them to life, and that the hero pushes aside with his sword."

At thirty, Proust was already a deeply eccentric man, and still living at home on an allowance. His preferred schedule of rising in the afternoon and going to bed at dawn estranged him from his own family. The events of the next few years came perilously close to paralyzing him. His younger brother, a doctor following in their father's footsteps, married in 1903 and set up on his own. At the wedding, Marcel was a grotesque semi-invalid figure in several overcoats and mufflers. A few months later their father died, and Mme Proust devoted herself for two years to caring for Proust's asthma and hay fever, and helping him translate Ruskin. She also organized dinners for his friends in their apartment. Then, after a short illness, Mme Proust died in 1905. Her son lay for almost two months in sleepless seclusion in the apartment, and then spent six weeks in a private clinic. After this, his nocturnal and neurotic behavior became more pronounced than ever.

The shift I have mentioned in Proust's career took place over the next four years—not a single event or development, but a gradual convergence of forces already at work. He began to withdraw slowly from his salon life and saw his friends in restaurants late at night. He could now have homosexual affairs by hiring young men as chauffeurs or secretaries. Composing a series of literary pastiches increased his conviction that he must find his own style and his own form. Meanwhile, his writing was becoming more and more autobiographical. In 1908 his drafts of a projected critical essay, *Against Sainte-Beuve,* kept turning into personal narrative whenever he let them take their course. If Proust had any revelation, it must have been the discovery that he could accommodate his irresistible autobiographical impulse in the novel form. During a lull in his writing in January 1909, he apparently had an unexpected and compelling surge of memory over a cup of tea into which he dipped some dry toast. When he described the incident in the preface he was writing for *Against Sainte-Beuve,* a number of similar reminiscences came to mind. Some missing element had fallen into place, and now it seemed as if he were at work on a wholly new book. Yet it was really the same one—the book begun in *Pleasures and Days,* tried again and laid aside in *Jean Santeuil,* tried once more in the anecdotal pages that open the preface to Ruskin's *Sesame and Lilies,* carried on in *Against Sainte-Beuve.* Endowed with a new plan but no firm title, this transmuted work took possession of him during the spring of 1909 and filled the rest of his life. By August he wrote proudly and optimistically to Mme Emile Strauss, one of his hostesses, "I have begun—and finished—a whole long book." About the same time he gave a few details to Alfred Vallette, a possible publisher for it. "I'm finishing a book which, in spite of its provisional title, *Against Sainte-Beuve: Recollections of a Morning,* is a genuine novel and an indecent novel in some of its sections. The book ends with a long conversation on Sainte-Beuve and aesthetics."

We should probably be grateful that Vallette refused Proust's novel then, for it was many years and thousands of pages away from having finished. But at least it was begun, and already getting out of control.

These developments were the signal for Proust to modify his life of indecision and distraction. In the fall of 1910 he announced to his friends a kind of withdrawal and retreat, referring mysteriously yet resolutely to the long work ahead of him. His caginess about the title and plan of his novel made it sound like a scientific discovery or a military secret. In 1910 he sealed himself into the bedroom of his new apartment by lining it with cork, and sent out irregular reports on the page count he had reached. A few close friends like Georges de Lauris and Reynaldo Hahn, sworn to confidence, were allowed to read the oilcloth-covered notebooks. They gave him the encouragement he needed. Of course, Proust did not retire completely from Parisian life as he had known it. He kept up with his friends and, at intervals, muffled in outlandish clothes, dropped in on an elegant hostess just as her party was breaking up. He even went occasionally to a music hall or an art gallery, and he listened to concerts and plays by subscribing to a service that allowed members to hear live performances over the telephone. But from 1910 until his death in 1922, his novel took precedence over everything else. The tide had turned. His forays into the outer world and the bulk of his letters were either means of obtaining information for his writings or attempts to arrange the proper publication and reception for his work. For the latter purpose he pulled every string, used every connection, and called in every outstanding debt available to him. Yet four publishing houses refused his book. After a cursory look, André Gide turned it down for Gallimard as too snobbish and amateurish. He later changed his mind. Grasset, a new house, finally published it, at the author's expense, in 1913. All Proust's advance work was barely sufficient to launch this first of two projected volumes. By the time Gallimard published the second volume after the war, the manuscript had grown irrepressibly, frighteningly, like a carnivorous vine that would finally entwine and devour its owner.

The remainder of Proust's life takes on a mythological quality. His nocturnal, bedridden, disorderly work habits appear heroic. In his private life he mixed low-grade hedonism with deliberate psychological and moral experiment. What looks degrading to some of us may be edifying to others. This man of shrewd medical insight mercilessly punished his frail body and refused proper advice, even from his brother. He followed what he told Louis de Robert was his "only rule": "to yield to

one's demon, to one's thought, to write on everything to the point of exhaustion." When he was awarded the prestigious Goncourt Prize in 1919
for the second volume of the novel, *A l'ombre des jeunes filles en fleurs,* the
event barely ruffled the waters in his special universe of nurture and devotion. His work had become a living being, making demands of its
own. "For me it had turned into a son. The dying mother must still submit to the fatigue of taking care of him" (III 1041–42/vi 522). He knew
he had given birth.

The last decade of Proust's life displays an outward life gradually
abdicated in favor of a work—both the inward process and the material product. Yet there is nothing reluctant or tragic about his abdication.
It does not resemble the two great royal departures that would occur
shortly thereafter, when a Spanish king bowed to republicanism and an
English king chose love of a commoner over royalty. With surprising
confidence Proust simply decided in favor of the dense tropical growth
he felt within him. For he discovered that it was at last assuming a shape
it had not exhibited earlier. Throughout his life, Proust composed in a
discontinuous fashion. Except possibly in the earliest short stories, he did
not start at the beginning of a narrative and follow it through to the end.
Observations and incidents and characters came to him in disparate fragments often directly based on his day-to-day experience. His notebooks
seem to be in total disarray in spite of the dazzling insights they carry. In
reading *Jean Santeuil,* still virtually a notebook, one rarely receives the
sense of a direction in which events are moving. It drifts to a standstill.
The prose pieces Proust wrote for the abandoned essay-novel, *Against
Sainte-Beuve,* display this desultory quality to an even greater extent. He
seems totally at sea.

But after 1909 he has a chart and a course. The "very exacting composition" Proust lays claim to in a letter to Louis de Robert in 1912 was
the major new element that had entered his work and claimed his energies. In the *Search* he holds his characters and his story in an iron grasp.
Lengthy digressions and hernia-like extensions of a single scene or sentiment do not mean that he has lost track of where his characters are
going and what they have already been through. Considering its length,

its unfinished condition, and the handicapped circumstances in which he wrote the novel, it contains extraordinarily few repetitions and inconsistencies. The overall design and the narrative links rarely waver.

The other major shift in Proust's writing after 1909 concerns the narrative voice in which he wrote. With a few revealing exceptions, *Jean Santeuil* employs the third person to designate a "hero" very close to Proust in biographical and psychological terms. The opening pages of *On Reading,* and the preface to *Against Sainte-Beuve* use the *I* without feint or dissembling to represent Proust as a real person and signatory. In none of these passages has he found his true discursive pitch and pace. Somewhere in the early stages of the *Search,* however, when he still thought it was *Against Sainte-Beuve,* a double reaction occurs. It is both a fusion and a fission attacking the *I*. First of all Proust calls in the scantily veiled third person of *Jean Santeuil* along with his various uses of the first person. He combines them into the *je* of the *Search*—equally narrator and character, a double personage in one pronoun. At the same time Proust takes himself, his life, and his character, and divides them up among a number of characters in the novel: Charlus, Bloch, Swann, as well as Marcel and the Narrator, both of whom say *I*.

This fission-fusion process explains why it is so unsatisfactory to keep asking if Marcel or the Narrator represents Proust. There can be no doubt that the *Search* embodies a version—both revelation and disguise—of Proust's life. The links are too evident to discount, from the setting and action to details like the Narrator having translated Ruskin's *Sesame and Lilies.* But Proust's disclaimers are equally powerful. He insists that his book be read as a self-contained story and not as autobiography masquerading as fiction. It would be foolish to insist on one of these approaches to the exclusion of the other. Toward the end of the novel one comes upon an odd passage that makes a tiny step toward reconciliation. There is nothing like it elsewhere in the *Search.*

In this book, in which every fact is fictional and in which not a single character is based on a living person, in which everything has been invented by me according to the needs of my demonstration, I must

> state to the credit of my country that only Françoise's millionaire rel-
> atives, who interrupted their retirement in order to help their needy
> niece, are real people, existing in the world. (III 846/vi 225)

Here, I believe, Proust is pointing out to us a kind of vestigial navel
cord, a detail which proves that his vast work does not coincide with ac-
tuality but was born from it. Images of slow gestation and final parturi-
tion do greater justice to the novel's origins than concepts of literal
imitation or of complete autonomy.

In Proust's final years the autobiographical nature of the *Search* seems
less significant than the literary nature of its author's life. He prepares
us for this perspective with the much quoted line in which he attacks the
failure of Sainte-Beuve's critical method to take into account what true
wisdom should have told him: ". . . that a book is the product of a different self from the one we display in our habits, in society, in our vices"
(*CSB* 221–22/*OAL* 99–100). This may be as close as we can come to
gospel. But there is a further question. Need we assume that the authorial self has been formed prior to the composition of the work? Valéry
liked to point out that, as the criminal may be the product of his crime,
so the author may be the product of his literary work. What I have said
about Proust's "abdication" points to a sense in which, *as author,* he was
the product of his work in progress. In the cases most crucial to literature, writing is less a record of what has actually happened to someone
than a discovery-creation of what might potentially happen to people,
"author" included. The symbiotic relationship between man and book
grows as much out of aesthetic as out of biographical factors. The development of "the other self" who wrote the *Search* can be traced within
the novel itself, but not in terms of finding keys to characters and identifying incidents transposed from Proust's life. They are incidentals.
Mysteriously and steadily, the *Search* secreted its true author, the literary
creature we call Marcel Proust.

The biographical Proust spent his last three years in bed, in great part
in order to escape the demands of literary celebrity. Surrounded by gal-
ley proofs, manuscripts, and strange potions, he lived his unfinished

book as totally and exclusively as an author can without losing his sense of reality. What kept him sane and even practical was the desire to finish his work and to assure it an enlightened readership. He answered most letters (but not one from an American girl who had read his novel steadily for three years and then rebuked him: "Don't be a *poseur*. . . . Tell me in two lines what you wished to say"), contributed to newspaper surveys on trends and styles, and took time to write two superb essays on his masters: Flaubert and Baudelaire. His remarks about the tonality of tenses and the place of metaphor in their work apply also to his own. An occasional Lazarus-like sortie formed part of the pattern. Shot up with adrenaline and caffeine, he submitted to a ceremonial midnight meeting with James Joyce at a large supper party for Diaghilev, Picasso, and Stravinsky. Neither author had read the other's work. They talked about the only other subject that mattered to them: their health. Another time, Proust let himself be taken to a fashionable 1920s nightspot, le Boeuf sur le toit. He never shed his heavy overcoat and was almost swept into a drunken brawl. Meanwhile, the work never stopped, even during the final months. Most of all Proust feared the affliction that had tortured Baudelaire at the end: aphasia. Yet, beneath the complaints, Proust found a wonderful excitement in the tension between his mission to finish his work and his simple mortality. Three months before the end, he received "a little question" submitted to various prominent persons by the newspaper *l'Intransigeant:* "If the world were coming to an end, what would it mean to you?" Proust knew when to be brief. "I believe that life would suddenly appear wonderful to us, if we were suddenly threatened with death as you propose." Death had long since become his faith, his inspiration. The final complication was pneumonia. He died on November 18, 1922.

An Overdetermined Universe

At intervals throughout the *Search*, Marcel goes to stay in a strange place. Each time it is as if he has to reconstitute from scratch all his perceptions and habits, the whole orientation of his life. Toward the middle of the novel, he visits his close friend Saint-Loup in Doncières, the town where Saint-Loup is doing his military service in the cavalry. What strikes Marcel first on arriving is the "perpetual, musical, and warlike vibratility" (II 70/iii 86) that hangs in the air. For several pages after that, the whole narrative texture is woven out of unfamiliar sounds. He notices Saint-Loup's modified accent. The crackling fire in his friend's barracks room makes Marcel think that someone must be in there while he stands listening in the hall outside the closed door. Once he enters the empty room, the ticking of an unseen clock seems to come from all directions until Marcel has spotted it and given the object and the sound a specific location. And then this acoustical disorientation infects everything, even Marcel's friendship for Saint-Loup and his sense of his own identity in the world. In other words, when his impressions are most vivid, he loses his bearings. Marcel's "auditory hyperesthesia" (II 72/iii 88), which Saint-Loup specifically mentions here as making life difficult for his visitor, serves not to fix the world more clearly in place for Marcel but to send it skittering off toward new patterns and multiple vanishing points. The disconcerting effect of strange sounds throws every element of life into play again, and thus into jeopardy. Even familiar sensations recover significance and urgency.

This dense network of perpetually reconstituted connections among impressions, feelings, meanings, and words constitutes one of the fundamental qualities of Proust's work. He conveys it in the resonance of the prose and in the overall architecture of the action. The superb opening of the book, in which the Narrator puts himself together like Humpty-Dumpty out of fragmentary impressions of waking and dreaming, is baffling at first. Nothing created out of so many elements could be simple. Even when the Narrator fails to achieve this self-creation *ex omnibus* (dialectically the equivalent of *ex nihilo*), the writing itself emits a powerful sense of the links among the things around us and our experiences of them. Proust writes from deep inside the world of Baudelaire's *correspondances,* close to Leonardo's universe where the painter said he saw actual lines connecting objects in a form of visible geometry.

In one respect this sense of the plenitude of relations between things runs counter to a human temper often treated in modern literature. In writers like Kafka and Camus we discern a quality of emptiness that it is hard to describe. For K and Meursault, experience generates very little motivation to undertake anything, to oppose the world or to affirm oneself. They act out of gratuitous impulse or yield to mere circumstance. In Proust the opposite is true. Multiple desires and motivations converge on every action and often impede its execution. Marcel goes to unbelievable lengths to explain to himself the behavior of the women in his life. For them as for him potential motives are often spelled out in a series of either/or propositions. But one motive will never prove to be the correct one and eliminate the others. After two pages of speculation on the character and behavior of one of his oldest friends, Gilberte Swann, Marcel throws up his hands. "None of these hypotheses was absurd" (III 708/vi 26). The mystery of Proust's world arises not from gratuitousness or from the absence of motivation but from the conflictingly overdetermined quality of most actions, and from the adaptability of most actions to a great number of attributions. Until Marcel reaches a wider wisdom, what happens around him is not indifferent but overwhelming.

II

HOW TO READ
A ROMAN-FLEUVE*

Practical Matters

Prospective Proust readers have to make a series of decisions that can be best expressed as questions with tentative answers.

In what language should one read Proust? Anyone who can comfortably read Balzac or Tocqueville or Camus in the original should tackle the *Search* in French. The translation will not turn out to be much easier, and one should at least make the attempt.

A reader whose French is shaky should choose a translation (see Chapter VIII). Yet I know several enterprising individuals who have laid out the French and English versions side by side and developed their own gymnastic method for straddling these two platforms. It required added time, but they also learned a great deal of French.

In either language one has to read with a kind of patient faith that

---

*This chapter is addressed to those seeking guidance for a first reading of Proust. Readers already familiar with the *Search* and looking for commentary on its shape and significance should turn to Chapter III.

Proust is not leading us down the garden path and that he will bring the
sentence, the scene, and the book to a clear conclusion. And so he does.
He tells us himself that he is forever tacking against the wind, and describes a mind "following its habitual course, which moves forward by
digressions, going off obliquely in one direction and then in the other"
(II 816/iv 292). In order to follow this course of advance by indirection,
I believe it is best to approach the reading of Proust as if it were a kind
of long-term cure, or an initiation to unfamiliar mental and physical
movements evolved by another culture. A steady, leisurely pace, without the tension of fixed deadlines, serves best. Certain habits of thought
can thus be laid aside as others are slowly acquired. It may take months,
even years. The *Search* creates a season of the mind outside temporal
limits.

How many of the three thousand pages should one read? How much
food or drink is enough? The reader should probably not decide the
question in advance and should let his appetite guide him. Some will
stop short, scoffing, in the opening pages. Others will continue in absorption to the last page and then start over again. Many more will ask
for a middle way, and they should be shown one. We have Frazer and
Gibbon in one-volume editions. With great profit as a boy I read *Don
Quijote* and *Robinson Crusoe, Arabian Nights,* and *Gulliver's Travels* in
truncated children's editions. Shall we be offered one day a pocket
Proust? *In Search of Lost Time* in three hundred pages? The prospect is
not utterly unthinkable. As in the classics mentioned above, there is in
Proust a deep universal element, an aesthetic consciousness, that may one
day reach many more people than can read his novel. A film might open
the way, though it seems unlikely. Several ambitious projects have already collapsed. (See Chapter VIII.) Roger Cailleux published a novel
in 1949 that describes at length the effect of a reading of "Swann in
Love" on his central character.

Yet such surrogates remain inadequate. Even a sensitive anthology
of set pieces and self-contained reflections cannot represent Proust, for
it conveys no sense of the whole or of the underlying movement. The
resourceful independent reader can now find a way through the maze

and take sensible shortcuts. Recent editions contain useful summaries. On the other hand, reading Proust in an organized course with a competent teacher to set the level of understanding and interpretation and with perceptive students willing to participate in discussions can develop into a very rewarding collective experience. But a term or semester course is too short and often leads to intense frustration at the end.

Though few have ever been proposed in print, there are various ways of reading approximately a third of the *Search* and supplying the missing sections through summaries.* Proust's other writings, though they have various merits, can wait until one has fully assimilated the *Search*.

Are there devices or approaches that can facilitate one's reading? Both in translation and in the original, Proust slows most readers down. His sentences move through long spirals that will not be hastened and deserve to be savored. He offers few paragraph breaks to declare the steps and stages of his thought. In contrast to most nineteenth-century novelists, he does not construct out of short chapters that divide the story into convenient mental mouthfuls. One simply cannot force one's speed and hope to register the prose. Gradually, however, it can come to sound appropriate and effective.

When you look at it closely, no passage in Proust seems typical. The patterns he makes are numerous and contrasting. But it may be helpful to consider one medium-long sentence in order to pick out a few stylistic features that are recognizably his. The sentence quoted below appears in an important juncture at the beginning of *Swann's Way*. Swann

---

*The following is one suggestion, which any Proustian could criticize: *Swann's Way* (the first three-quarters: "Combray" and "Swann in Love"); *Within a Budding Grove* (Part Two: "Balbec"); *The Guermantes Way* (II, Chapter One: "The Grandmother's Death"); *Sodom and Gomorrah* (first thirty pages and the last thirty: "Charlus and Albertine"); *The Captive* (first thirty pages and two hundred pages on the concert at the Verdurins' arranged by Charlus); *The Fugitive* (omit); *Time Regained* (the last two hundred pages: the last reception and reflections on writing). . . .

is an elegant, wealthy Jew, much sought after in the best Parisian society. His worldly milieu has made him both sensitive and blasé. He devotes most of his life to a series of love affairs with women from all
classes who happen to catch his eye. His story begins against this background.

> But, *whereas* each of these liaisons, or each of these flirtations, had
> been the more or less complete realization of a dream inspired by the
> sight of a face or body that Swann had, spontaneously, without effort,
> found attractive, on the contrary, *when* one day at the theater he was
> introduced to Odette de Crécy by one of his former friends, *who* spoke
> of her as a charming woman with whom he might get along, but
> painted her as more difficult than she really was in order to seem to
> have done him a bigger favor in introducing him, *she appeared to*
> *Swann not unattractive certainly but to have a kind of beauty that was in-*
> *different to him, that* did not stir his desire, even inspired a kind of
> physical repulsion in him, to be the sort of woman, as happens to all
> of us in different ways, *who* is the opposite of what our senses ask for.
> (I 195–96/i 275–76) [italics added]

By linking more than a dozen subordinate clauses to both ends of
one principal clause, Proust has composed a difficult sentence. But the
fully articulated syntax and the rhythm it enforces firmly direct the
reading. The emphatic initial *But,* commands attention. Immediately
following, *whereas* projects far out ahead an organizing power that
lasts until it is picked up by *when* and carried on to the central statement. The construction here is more than sturdy than subtle. Why
does Proust write one sentence instead of three or four? What is the
effect?

Had he used several sentences, he would have had to rely on modifiers
and rhetorical devices to bring out the central proposition. Or he would
have had to delete details. In the sentence as written, subordination serves
to arrange a large amount of material around the clause: "she appeared
. . . indifferent to him. . . ." The facts that the introduction took place in

the theater, and that she was not presented as a woman of easy virtue, are minor yet revealing details. Proust uses the nuances and hierarchies of syntax to hold these details in perspective. Furthermore, the very relationships expressed by the connectives (*whereas, when, that, who;* in other contexts he concentrates on causative, concessive, or conditional relations) form an essential part of Proust's subject. This sentence contrives not only to tell us the circumstances under which Swann first met Odette but also to suggest the whole sinuous course of their love affair. Before that interlude, his life followed a recognizable pattern; during it, that pattern is so disrupted as to leave a deep mark on Swann; and at its close (I 382/v 543), he looks back at its surprising beginning (and in effect at this very sentence) to wonder bemusedly how it ever happened. A great number of complex, half-understood circumstances converge on any significant event, and then diverge toward a future of undivulged possibilities. The passage just quoted is one example of how Proust's prose tends to reproduce that plenitude. He wants to make us see that intersection of lines.

One could, of course, go much further. Mallarmé wrote his most ambitious poem, "Un coup de dés," in the form of a single, repeatedly proliferating, meticulously articulated sentence. If a novelist begins to experience both time and meaning as fundamentally continuous, he might well aspire to write one unbroken sentence, paralleling consciousness itself, shadowing or even overshadowing reality. Though tempted by such a course (he once proposed abandoning all chapter and paragraph breaks), Proust pulled back before he abandoned syntax and readability. He shaped the world of his fiction by forming it into high relief in his prose, not by flattening it out endlessly or by cutting it up into little pieces. This same principle of fullness explains his effective use, at long intervals, of a contrasting device: the tersest possible form of declaration, a staccato phrase, an abrupt question. "Dead forever?" "My whole being capsized." I mentioned these two styles in the Introduction. The flowing periods of his prose create extended stretches of lived time. They also set the scene for unexpected and devastating reversals that occur in very few words. We notice the lengthiness more than the brevity, and, indeed, there is more of the former. Both belong to the fullness of his style.

The best way to discover and respond to Proust's expressive voice, as well as the deliberate pacing of his narrative, is to hear the prose, to read it aloud. For he often works by a kind of mimicry at one remove, echoing and aping his characters without abandoning the steady flow of his own thought. The unnamed Norwegian philosopher speaks a totally different French from that of Dr. Cottard or of Odette, and we are allowed to hear each of them. Without an auditory sense of the text, even in its most reflective and interior passages, the visual field of unrelieved print tends to become oppressive. Translations cannot convey the original texture, yet on this score the available versions perform remarkably well. They all bear reading aloud.

Apart from the speech rhythm and inflections stirred up by the prose, there are two other items readers can watch for to help them find their way. Proust frequently employs a recurrent narrative detail or incident as a kind of refrain to orient the course of action. In the "Combray" section, fifty pages of pure description are pinned together by the minute mystery of whether or not Mme Goupil arrived at mass on time. For Swann, the question of who was with Odette the afternoon she did not answer her doorbell becomes the very axis of his life. Marcel develops an imaginary passion for Baronne de Putbus's reputedly sexy maid, whom he has never laid eyes on. He keeps trying to trace her, always without success, in a series of maneuvers that span the latter half of the novel. These colored strands surface just often enough in the narrative fabric to help reveal its pattern.

The other feature a reader would do well to remain on the alert for carries more significance than the narrative refrains. It reveals the unpredictable quality of the action. From time to time in the story, Marcel is told or discovers a small item of information that, when fully grasped and fitted into place, changes his entire perspective on the relationship between important characters or on the nature of human conduct. The aging down-to-earth Marquise de Villeparisis, a girlhood friend of Marcel's grandmother, turns out to be closely related to the aristocratic and inaccessible Guermantes, whom he intensely desires to know. The eminent painter, Elstir, turns out to be the same person as Biche, or Tiche, the ridiculous and vulgar young man in Mme Verdurin's first "little clan." The battle of Méséglise in World War I makes that village famous in world history; yet the Combray church, the incarnation of Marcel's childhood and of French history, is destroyed. A hint is passed in the closing pages that the virtuous Duchesse de Guermantes may not, after all, have always been the most faithful of wives. These tiny shocks profoundly modify the great web of relations and reactions that constitute the substance of the book. One must read Proust as carefully as a detective story in which any detail may become a clue to everything else. Every page tends toward the accumulation of the familiar, the security of habit, in order to establish the sense of location and identity we all need. At the same time every page glows with a blend of excitement and anxiety over the possible introduction of a new element. We half anticipate a break in routine that will disrupt the pattern and launch the whole setting into unpredictable motion. This ambivalent mood, which seems to posit boredom as the inevitable background for excitement, emerges beautifully in "Combray." The *train-train,* or unvarying daily round of events, that characterizes life in Aunt Léonie's house is both tested and reinforced by the "asymmetrical Saturday" (I 110/i 153). On that day each week lunch is served a full hour early to allow Françoise to go to market. The variation, astonishing to everyone, is itself assimilated into the routine. Yet the risk of that established departure from schedule prepares the way for all the dismay and despair to come when this tight little life falls apart.

The Elements of the Story

The biggest help in reading Proust is to have the persons and places of the story clear in one's mind. For this purpose I have arranged the elements in tables and diagrams to accompany the prose exposition that follows.

The *Search* has five major settings (see Diagram I). I mention places
before persons because so much of the action consists of Marcel's gradual and painful accommodation to new settings, and because of the association of character with particularities of place. Albertine *is* essentially
Balbec incarnate and carries always within her the sensuousness of flowers and the mutability of the sea. Furthermore, all geography in Proust,
from ocean to bed to church steeple, is symbolic, even animistic. "The
various places of the earth are also beings, whose personality is so strong
that some people die of being separated from them" (*JS* 534).

I. PLACES

Combray	Paris	Balbec	Doncières	Venice
Church of Saint-Hilaire	Champs-Elysées Gardens	Grand Hôtel	Cavalry Barracks	(Trip planned and canceled)
Aunt Léonie's House	Guermantes' Town House	Elstir's Studio	Pension	Visit with Mother
Swann's Way (Méséglise Tansonville)	Marcel's Family's Apartment	Rivebelle		
The Guermantes Way	Salons	La Raspelière		
Martinville Steeples	Houses of Prostitution			

The first setting is the village of COMBRAY, presumably near
Chartres. (Proust later shifts it eastward into the World War I combat
zone.) Marcel and his parents spend vacations there. Aunt Léonie's house
and the village church are described as if one would never seek to appeal
from their simple reality to a higher realm. Combray embodies the solidarity of family origins as well as the roots of French civilization—
Church, people, royalty. The two "ways" along which Marcel and his
family take their walks divide the countryside, and the universe, into
two irreconcilable and seemingly inaccessible worlds. Marcel will even-

tually penetrate into both: the Guermantes way, or the aristocracy with all its remote mysteries; and Swann's way, a worldly, artistic domain tinged with evil and scandal. After the opening two hundred pages, Combray does not again become the setting of the story except for a brief section in the last volume. Yet it is never out of mind.

PARIS, where most of the novel takes place, is reduced to a few elements. At first everything revolves around the Champs-Elysées gardens where Marcel meets Gilberte Swann as a playmate. Later Marcel and his family move to a new apartment attached to the town house of the Duc and Duchesse de Guermantes. Around this complex of rooms, courtyards, and shops, the streets lead away to two further regions: the various salons to which Marcel is invited, and the houses of ill repute he later stumbles into or visits.

BALBEC is an imaginary seaside resort town in Normandy or Brittany, closely modeled on Cabourg, whose beaches attracted great numbers of French and English summer visitors at the turn of the century. (The Grand Hôtel still stands next to the beach in Cabourg, a massive building with long corridors and a slow-moving, open-cage elevator.) Marcel drives occasionally to Rivebelle, where there is a good restaurant. Elstir's studio is near the beach at Balbec. It is out of this very seascape that "the young girls in bloom" seem to materialize; they arouse Marcel's most enduring desires. A short train ride along the coast brings one to La Raspelière, the estate rented during the summer by the Verdurins.

Inland from Balbec lies the military town of DONCIERES, where Saint-Loup is doing his service in the cavalry. Marcel here makes his first long stay away from his family. On returning to Paris he suddenly perceives his grandmother as a complete stranger, an old lady approaching death.

Early in the novel Marcel's father decides that the family will make a trip to VENICE. Marcel becomes so overwrought with anticipation that the trip has to be canceled. The image of Venice haunts him all his life until he finally makes the journey with his mother long after the desire to do so has passed.

Through these five settings several hundred named characters circulate. Most of them are minor, and their number includes many historical figures who flit by, barely glimpsed on the outer edges of the events. About twenty-five characters carry the central action (see Diagram II).

II. Characters

I	Family	Early Friends	Guermantes	Artists	Others
Marcel	Mother	Françoise	Marquise de Villeparisis	Bergotte	M. and Mme Verdurin
Narrator	Grand-mother	Swann	Saint-Loup	Elstir	Albertine
(Author)	Aunt Léonie	Odette	Charlus	Vinteuil	Cottard
	Father	Gilberte	Duc and Duchesse	La Berma	Jupien
	Uncle Adolphe	Bloch	Prince and Princesse	Rachel	Norpois
		Legrandin	Mlle de Saint-Loup	(Morel)	
				(Françoise)	

From start to finish there is someone in the novel saying *I*. Like the single Martinville spire on the horizon, which separates into two and then three steeples as one approaches it, different voices and different beings step out from behind that first-person singular. Yet the linguistic and semidramatic illusion of their unity inside a single pronoun is one of the principal devices used in the book to weld together the disparate levels of identity and narrative, and to permit rapid shifts among different points of view. The *I* in Proust is an eternal pivot chord. Marcel Muller, the most careful analyst of this aspect of Proust's work, distinguishes seven distinct *I*'s. Let us here be content with two, plus a self-effacing third.

MARCEL, the boy who grows up in the course of the novel and who does not know at any given point what the future holds for him, says *I*. Though the given name, Marcel (with no family name to complete it), is mentioned only twice in three thousand pages—and even then skittishly and not for direct attribution—I feel that no other designation will serve for the "hero" or protagonist as he develops in the narrative. Second, the NARRATOR says *I;* he is Marcel grown old and become a writer who, as he tells his own story in roughly chronological order, both reflects on it and refers to events that violate the chronology. Third, on the rare occasions when he materializes beside the two others, the AUTHOR says *I* (see pages 17–18 and 157). He is not the biographical Proust but his literary persona, commenting on his novel and its relation to truth and reality. Within and around the essentially double *I* of the story sparks a constant arc of irony, sympathy, and regret. Marcel and the Narrator move slowly toward one another across the long reaches of the book, constantly signaling, sometimes lost, until they finally meet in the closing pages. That reunited *I*, like Plato's lovers, produces a whole, which is represented symbolically by the book we are reading.

Along the way, this linguistically single yet ontologically double *I* produces several curious effects. In spite of his constant efforts to do so, Marcel never adequately beholds himself and cannot really believe in his identity or his role, a condition I diagnose in Chapter IV as "Proust's complaint." As a result, it is as if a segment of negative space occupies the center of the action, a hole in the fabric. Marcel eludes himself and eludes us. We never learn what he really looks like. He seems as much of an absence as a presence. Understandably, the reader has difficulty identifying with this inchoate creature and sifts the evidence in order to find appearances and character traits to square with the reported events. The Narrator collaborates by presenting Marcel as piteous, weak-willed, egotistical, and sometimes downright deceitful. Yet somehow Marcel makes his way in the world and seems to have more friends than enemies. This wayward and uncertain nature of the principal character gives the reader an active part to play. He cannot coast through the incidents by stepping into the shoes of the hero. Identification does not function. The reader must seek out the Marcel almost crouching behind the events and reluctant to be brought forward as a person with a name and a recognizable character.

These fluctuations in the first person of Proust's novel also mean that (except in "Swann in Love") the question of omniscience is never settled. There are only conflicting claims. Marcel observes everything yet cannot trust his perceptions. What he learns from experience is that appearances deceive us. The Narrator commands wide knowledge and often speaks with a wisdom that seems to rise above the transitory. For he has learned that general laws and character types inlay our experience with many striking regularities. The shadowy figure of the Author lurks behind them both, barely whispering that knowledge comes of having truly lived one's life and belongs therefore to death. These approaches to wisdom vie with one another throughout the *Search*. The simplest aspect of the novel, the presence of an *I* speaking, leads into unforeseen complexities and subtleties held together primarily by that speaking *I*. In the pages that follow I shall try to distinguish carefully between "Marcel" and "the Narrator," but that terminology will not do full justice to their counterpoint in the text.

In the course of his life Marcel moves among several recognizable groups of characters. The members of his family form the most compact group. In fact his MOTHER and GRANDMOTHER virtually fuse into a single maternal presence that hovers over Marcel until close to the end. AUNT LEONIE is an eccentric imaginary-invalid, who keeps track of every living thing in Combray from her top-floor observation post. As he ages, Marcel comes to resemble her in many respects. The FATHER's undefined professional eminence and official connections inspire awe and respect. UNCLE ADOLPHE, the black sheep of the family who keeps mistresses and lives high, leaves an indelible impression on Marcel.

Second, there are the various people Marcel knows from his childhood in Combray and who for that reason alone form a class apart. FRANÇOISE, the eternal and ever-present servant, embodies the durability of the peasantry and the stern demands of a muse. SWANN, a wealthy Jewish neighbor with unassuming manners and an entrée to the most elegant Parisian society, is the first person to trouble Marcel's secure world. Swann's earlier love affair and eventual marriage with the cocotte ODETTE sets the motifs of Marcel's own troubled life. Their daughter, GILBERTE, is his first love. LEGRANDIN, the local snob, and BLOCH, a precocious ill-mannered comrade, also enter the story in Combray. The Swann family preoccupies Marcel until he becomes obsessed by the noble family of Guermantes.

Long after the apparition of the DUCHESSE DE GUERMANTES in the Combray church, Marcel meets the members of this group in loose order of ascending social rank: the MARQUISE DE VILLEPARISIS, a school friend of Marcel's grandmother; her nephew, the MARQUIS DE SAINT-LOUP; his uncle the BARON DE CHARLUS, the most haughty and the most debased personage of the entire clan; the DUC and DUCHESSE DE GUERMANTES, neighbors both in Combray and in Paris; and the PRINCE and PRINCESSE DE GUERMANTES, who occupy the pinnacle of Paris aristocracy and whose "world" Marcel finally enters. MLLE DE SAINT-LOUP, daughter of Robert de Saint-Loup and Gilberte Swann, appears briefly at the end of the novel. Swann's way and the Guermantes way unite in her youthful form.

Beyond these clearly defined groupings are several looser sets of characters. The three major artists—BERGOTTE, a writer; VINTEUIL, a composer; and ELSTIR, a painter—exert a profound intellectual influence on the action and, through their works, on three of the principal love affairs. They do not know each other, and they stand apart from the three performing artists: MOREL, a violinist; and LA BERMA and RACHEL, both actresses. Morel becomes deeply entangled in the story through sexual intrigue. FRANÇOISE, the family servant, excels in the essential arts of cuisine and couture.

The remaining personages do not really form a category. MONSIEUR and MADAME VERDURIN belong to the wealthy bourgeoise, play at being bohemian, and have immense (and successful) social am-

bitions. DR. COTTARD lends his medical renown and preposterous
conversation to their little group of friends. ALBERTINE, captured
and kept but never fully possessed, occupies more of Marcel's attention
than any other single character. The MARQUIS DE NORPOIS is the
perfect ambassador; JUPIEN, his counterpart at the other end of the
spectrum, is the ultimate functionary of vice.

Approximately eight great love affairs establish powerful and lasting
links between certain of these characters (see Diagram III). Five in-
volve Marcel, and three introduce other couples. The two sets alternate
so that the first-person account of one of Marcel's loves is usually followed by the third-person account of another couple. The passionate,
enduring, and never sullied love between Marcel and his mother and

III. COUPLES

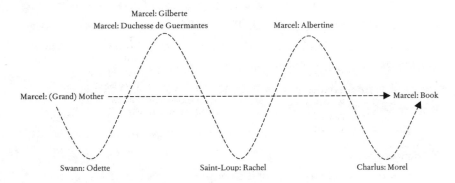

grandmother is fully introduced before the long arabesque-like curve of
the affair between Swann and Odette. Then, like a juvenile echo of
"Swann in Love," we are immersed in Marcel's adolescent love for
Gilberte. Later he shyly and fruitlessly follows the Duchesse de Guermantes through the streets. (For the sake of simplicity I omit Marcel's
general infatuation with the band of young girls on the beach at Balbec.
A season later his sentiments converge on one of them: Albertine.) The
next love to appear is Saint-Loup's prodigal passion for the actress
Rachel, whose talent is almost equal to her ambition. Marcel's jealous attachment to Albertine, the girl who came up out of the sands of Balbec,
lasts through four volumes. Meanwhile, Charlus has pawned what re-

mains of his reputation for the handsome, philandering violinist Morel. To these six one must add a seventh complex and overarching case: narcissism, both Marcel's and the Narrator's. For long stretches they cannot remove themselves from the focus of their own fascinated gaze at the world. I shall try to show that the final commitment of that pair to writing a book about their milieu and their double life redeems them, and their book, from the slough of narcissism. For they have formed a true love—the love of literature.

The society scenes (see Diagram IV) with their ritualized pomp and gossip complement the exasperated intensity of the love affairs. These dinners and receptions and parties make up about a third of the book and lie along a gradually ascending social curve that finally turns back

IV. SOCIETY SCENES

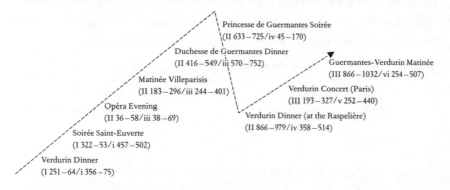

Princesse de Guermantes Soirée
(II 633–725/iv 45–170)

Duchesse de Guermantes Dinner
(II 416–549/iii 570–752)

Guermantes-Verdurin Matinée
(III 866–1032/vi 254–507)

Matinée Villeparisis
(II 183–296/iii 244–401)

Verdurin Concert (Paris)
(III 193–327/v 252–440)

Opéra Evening
(II 36–58/iii 38–69)

Verdurin Dinner (at the Raspelière)
(II 866–979/iv 358–514)

Soirée Saint-Euverte
(I 322–53/i 457–502)

Verdurin Dinner
(I 251–64/i 356–75)

on itself. In the first volume Swann attends both a pretentious bourgeois dinner party at the Verdurins', at which the hostess directs her guests like performing animals, and an elegant musical soirée given by the Marquise de Saint-Euverte. Marcel's social progress begins humbly on the evening ex-Ambassador Norpois dines with his parents. Later, sitting in the orchestra during a charity evening at the Opéra, he watches the godlike Guermantes assembled in their box. Two receptions given by the Marquise de Villeparisis, a dinner with the Duc and Duchesse de Guermantes, and finally a soirée given by the Prince and Princesse de Guermantes, carry him to the pinnacle of aristocratic society in Paris and of his social ambitions. After this, social elevation becomes blurred by the intermingling of characters and castes. Twice Marcel attends major events at the Verdurins'. As time goes on, their social chic and their wealth rival the status of the Guermantes. The most rewarding musical performance in the entire book takes place in their salon. Ultimately the astounding remarriage between the Prince de Guermantes and Mme Verdurin *veuve* transforms the social terrain to prepare for the last great reception, the novel's finale where all opposites meet.

Another third of the *Search* consists of passages of solitary meditation on perennial themes: childhood and sleep; love, death, and time; art and morality. These psychological and philosophical thoughts cannot be described as detachable or extraneous. They enter the action as subtly and vitally as dreams shadow our waking life. It is essential to the mood and movement of the novel that it should open and close as it does with a sustained reflective passage by the undivided *I*. Marcel's thoughts on sleep, for example, are acts of mind that affect his development as much as any acts of love or social behavior.

The Plot

Proust's story does not emerge steadily from his prose like news on a ticker tape. The narrative current is highly intermittent. Incidents collect in a series of great pools, like the social scenes just discussed. These pools engulf the landscape and give the impression of near motionlessness while we plumb the depths. Then, usually with little transition, we are carried to another wide basin of incident. Each of these pools has a geographical setting and, with the exception of "Swann in Love," covers a surprisingly short time interval. Usually it is a single season represented by a few crucial days. They are really pools of imperceptibly flowing time. The Narrator means more than mere topography when he refers to "the Combray basin" (III 968/vi 409), for that quiet body of time turns out to be an expanding universe that encroaches on all others.

Three significant sections stand outside these pools. The seven pages that open the book and the fifteen that close it frame the story by presenting it first as dream and last as art. Spanning the center of the novel is a third sequence split into two parts that form an internal frame: the grandmother's death and (many months and four hundred pages later) Marcel's delayed realization of his loss (II 314–15, 755–63/iii 427–28, iv 210–20). He experiences the full force of "the heart's intermittence." The maturity Marcel attains after this rite of passage is incomplete and transitory, for it occurs in the midst of powerful distractions. Yet it reintroduces the almost forgotten forces of death and memory. This double incident holds the action in place from within, a recall to mortality in the middle of a story that is turning strongly toward frivolity.

In summarizing the plot now, I shall try above all to sketch the large movement of the action as it flows from pool to pool. It seems practical not to follow all Proust's divisions, which are makeshift or misleading at a few points, but to deal with large-scale, coherent bodies of event. Parts 2 and 8 in the scheme followed below serve as intervals or intermissions. Though essential for spacing and timing, they fall outside the main action.

1. COMBRAY (I 3–187/i 265–543). An unnamed Narrator of uncertain age is writing about himself in the first person. Yet he seems to be cut off from himself and from his past, out of which he can genuinely remember as his own only one vivid scene. One night during the Narrator's childhood (we shall call the boy Marcel), Monsieur Swann's company at dinner led Marcel's mother to withhold her customary evening ritual: to come upstairs to kiss him good night. In protest, he kept himself awake until Swann had gone. She then relented, read to him, and spent the night in his room. Surprised, Marcel almost regretted her decision, which the Narrator calls "a first abdication" (I 38/i 51). But this is all the Narrator can recall of his early childhood until, suddenly and unexpectedly, stimulated one day by the savor of a madeleine cake dipped in tea, he recovers the whole panorama of his childhood summers in the village of Combray. There Marcel lived surrounded by

older members of his family, according to the established routines of village and domestic life, discovering the pleasures of walking and eating and reading. Gradually his idyllic security is undermined by experiences that lead beyond "the drama of going to bed." People show unexpected and even contradictory sides. He sees they have no adequate way to express their feelings. Meanwhile, Marcel becomes deeply aware of "the two ways," or paths, that divide the village: one goes to the distant estate of the aristocratic Guermantes family, the other to Swann's house. Both ways whisper alluringly to the boy, drawing him away from his own lowly path. He feels the first stirrings of a literary vocation, along with an even stronger despair of ever becoming a writer.

2. SWANN IN LOVE (I 188–382/i 265–543). Dropping back almost a generation, the Narrator relates in the third person the love affair between the Jewish man of the world, Swann, and the cocotte, Odette. She is really not his type of woman at all, yet his aesthetic imagination propels him slowly through a powerful cycle of attraction toward this ordinary and enigmatic woman. Though he usually travels in the highest society, Swann begins to frequent the bourgeois Verdurin circle, where Odette is welcome and where he is finally humiliated in punishment for his lofty connections. His jealousy of Odette grows to pathological proportions before he begins a slow recovery. One assumes they will drift apart. Yet when they reappear in the narrative, they have married and had a daughter.

3. PARIS: GILBERTE SWANN (I 383–641/i 545–ii 298). As a boy playing in the Champs-Elysées gardens, Marcel falls in love with Gilberte, the daughter of Swann and Odette. He also feels a strong fascination for the society of the father and mother. His love goes through an evolution similar to that of Swann's love for Odette and finally fades. Meanwhile, he is introduced to the charm of the theater, to sexual satisfaction, to the restraints imposed by his own poor health, and to literary eminence as embodied in the successful author, Bergotte. Marcel becomes increasingly aware of the difficulty of attaining happiness and of the unpredictable nature of human character.

4. BALBEC AND THE YOUNG GIRLS (I 642–955/ii 299–730).
Now in his teens, Marcel goes with his grandmother for the summer to
Balbec, a fashionable resort on the English Channel. The Marquise de
Villeparisis is staying in the same hotel. This former schoolmate of the
grandmother's is a lady of high birth and scandalous past. Through her
Marcel now meets the Baron de Charlus, as changeable as he is haughty,
and her nephew, Robert de Saint-Loup. This elegant and intelligent
young man is about Marcel's age; against all expectations they become
the best of friends. Both Charlus and Saint-Loup belong to the Guermantes family. Yet for Marcel these summer days beside the beach focus
increasingly on a somewhat rowdy band of young girls with bicycles,
and then on one of them in particular, Albertine, apparently their leader.
Her free behavior carries a hint of license and even of vice. After observing her for weeks, Marcel meets her in the studio of the painter Elstir, whose work he begins to understand and admire. When, at the end
of his stay, Marcel tries to kiss Albertine in her hotel room, he fails ig-
nominiously. Her true nature seems impenetrable, and he cannot even as-
certain his own feelings toward her.

5. ENTERING THE GUERMANTES WORLD (II 9–750/iii 1–iv
203). Back in Paris, Marcel and his family move into an apartment that
belongs to the Duc and Duchesse de Guermantes and overlooks their
town house. He saw the Duchess once in Combray during a church service. She struck him at first as ugly. Yet, as he watched her across the
church, she seemed to assume the symbolic beauty of her name. He now
falls awkwardly in love and schemes shamelessly to meet her. For this
purpose he goes to visit her nephew, Saint-Loup, who is doing his military service in Doncières. Robert is very friendly, yet remains guarded
about his Guermantes relatives. He takes Marcel to lunch in Paris with
his mistress, Rachel, and to one of her rehearsals. They go on to a reception at Mme de Villeparisis's, where Marcel finally does meet the
Duchess. He also again sees the Baron de Charlus, who takes a curiously personal interest in him.

After this first glimpse of the Guermantes world, Marcel's grandmother dies at the end of an exhausting ten-day agony.

Marcel's initiation into society continues, but along two complementary paths he had not foreseen: elegance and vice. Attending a dinner
given by the Duke and Duchess, Marcel is first dazzled by the artisto-
cratic guests, including the Princesse de Parme, then disappointed by the
mediocrity of their conversation and behavior, and finally reenchanted
by the historical and genealogical patina of their mere names. Late that
night Marcel visits Charlus, as invited, and is received in an ambiguous,
almost violent manner. He cannot fathom the reasons. We have reached
the center point of the novel; Marcel's naïveté has been stretched to the
limit. A few months later he watches from a window while Charlus accosts another man in the courtyard of their house. Marcel finally realizes
that the Baron is homosexual.

Marcel's ultimate advance into the Guermantes society associates elegance and vice even more dramatically. At a huge evening reception
given by the Prince and Princesse de Guermantes, the eminences of
Parisian aristocracy are laid out for Marcel's inspection in a crowded
ceremonial portrait. Beneath the resounding titles, the magnificent surroundings, and the polite conversation, Marcel soon detects not only
snobbery and political depravity (the Dreyfus case is at its height) but
also ubiquitous homosexuality that destroys some of the most honorable
names. After this hollow realization of his social ambitions, Marcel decides that what he really wants more than anything is to have Albertine
to himself.

6. BALBEC: ALBERTINE AND THE VERDURIN CLAN (II
751–1131/iv 204–724). The first night of his second visit to Balbec,
Marcel is overwhelmed by the recollection of his grandmother and the
meaning of her death. He sees Albertine regularly, and at the same time
begins to suspect her of being a lesbian. His jealousy makes increasing
demands on her. The young couple attends the weekly dinner parties
given by the Verdurins at the country place they rent for the summer.
Their circle of bourgeois friends has its own quaint customs and its own
snobbery. The presence among them of the Baron de Charlus and of his
protégé, the violinist Morel, adds a now familiar note of elegance and
corruption to these dinners. But as the summer goes on, Marcel finds that

both Balbec and Albertine have lost their charm. Just at this point, he is appalled to discover that his companion is a close friend of a well-known lesbian. He decides that he wants to marry Albertine.

7. ALBERTINE IN PARIS: CAPTIVITY AND ESCAPE (III 9–677/v 1–921). There is no marriage. That winter Albertine comes to live with Marcel in his apartment. Françoise and his mother hover disapprovingly in the background. He establishes a tyrannical routine in which he barely lets Albertine out of his sight without careful supervision. Spying and lying become their way of life, from which neither can escape. In order to pursue his suspicions about Albertine, Marcel goes to a reception at the Verdurins' Paris apartment. Charlus has arranged for Morel to give a concert that evening and has invited a small number of his aristocratic friends and relatives to attend this bourgeois affair. For Marcel the evening brings a great and lasting revelation of the pleasures of music. For most of the others, the evening devolves into a shameful public struggle over the dubious loyalty and real talent of Morel. Both the Guermantes and the Verdurins behave like boors. Unable to control either his sexual overtures or his snobbery, Charlus is finally humiliated by his own protégé.

More than ever obsessed by jealousy and driven to deceit by a feeling of being himself a caged bird, Marcel hypocritically suggests separation to Albertine. He hopes that the prospect will strengthen her attachment to him. Instead, he wakes up one morning to find she has packed up and gone.

Marcel cannot bribe her to come back, nor can he resolve his own contradictory feelings. A telegram informs him that Albertine has been killed in a fall from a horse. Immediately afterward two confusingly dated letters from her arrive. In one of them, she asks—apparently sincerely—to come back to him. In Marcel's mind all sentiments and motives seem to crumble at this touch. Yet a jealous curiosity to know the "truth" about Albertine's private life continues to absorb him for some time. Slowly he gains a little distance, helped by the publication of one of his articles in the *Figaro* and by seeing Gilberte again. She has a new name and a new social being. Marcel also visits Venice with his mother.

Certain earlier portions of the action now begin to drift back toward the surface of the story.

8. INTERMISSION (III 677–854/v 921–vi 237). Robert de Saint-Loup and Gilberte marry and are unhappy. Robert turns out to be homosexual and neglects his wife. Marcel goes to visit Gilberte at Tansonville, the estate where Swann lived near Combray. The village and its surroundings have lost their magic. One night he reads a passage in the Goncourt brothers' journal about the Verdurin salon in days past. The aura of their prose convinces him once again that he will never become a writer. While at Tansonville, Marcel discovers that the two "ways," which seem to lie in totally opposed directions, do finally join farther out in the countryside, just as the marriage of Gilberte and Robert has united two alien elements of society.

World War I now interrupts the story. Marcel makes several long stays in a rest home outside Paris. During his rare visits to the city he learns how wartime conditions are transforming everyday life and the social hierarchy. Saint-Loup dies a hero at the front. Charlus descends further than ever into vice and self-degradation. Only Françoise survives, barely changed by age, the eternal attendant.

9. TIME REGAINED (III 854–1048/vi 238–532). Many years later, Marcel returns to Paris resigned to a life of boredom and indifference. An engraved invitation to a reception given by the Prince and Princesse de Guermantes reawakens a little of the original spell of that name. Marcel finds no reason to deprive himself of the frivolous pleasure of seeing all those people again. First in the street outside the Guermantes house and later while he waits in the study for a musical interlude to finish, five successive *moments bienheureux* wash over him. These felicitous sensations, resembling the madeleine incident of the opening pages, set off a great sunburst of memory reaching all the way back to his earliest childhood and his mother reading to him in Combray. Alone in the study, he meditates on the nature of art and literature and reencounters what he has believed utterly lost: the vocation to write. His subject will be this very loss of his calling—and the rediscovery of it. Having found the shape of his book in his own erring life, he feels ready to begin work.

However, when he enters the salon and meets his acquaintances, his new optimism crumbles into dust. For he cannot recognize any of these people who are, in effect, the substance of his past and the subject of his book. Age has transformed them all into grotesque puppets of their former selves. At the same time the very poles of society have reversed themselves through marriage, money, and natural evolution. The title of Princesse de Guermantes now belongs to no one else but—in her third marriage—Mme Verdurin. Stunned, Marcel recovers himself only when he meets Mlle de Saint-Loup, Gilberte's daughter, who fuses in her flesh the two ways of his childhood and renders visible the intervening years. Reconciled to time and to his own place both in it and outside it, Marcel at last resolves to write the book he has carried within him, and avoided, for so long. It will embody his response to time. He sets to work, troubled only by the realization that he has little time left in which to complete his task.

Verisimilitude and Homosexuality

After a long life of false starts and distractions, a man finally discovers that he can after all reach a goal he gave up while still a boy: to write a novel. For that purpose, he renounces the vanities of life and society, but only after having experienced them and learned from them. On the threshold of death he chooses art—an art directed toward life and mortality.

It is not a complicated plot in spite of its length. Marcel attains true mortality by assuming both its greatness and its puniness and by becoming his own Narrator. The story does not arrange the world into opposed forces vying for victory. For Marcel, all creatures, including those he loves most, are at the same time antagonists and accomplices. He struggles to see and to be—himself. When he holds his mother or Albertine captive, he has won no victory. There is only the long search, whose reward is the discovery that it all makes a story worth telling.

Do we believe such a story enough to respond to it? Though much

modern criticism dismisses such considerations as entirely alien to literature, we can appropriately raise the question of verisimilitude.
Proust's "rule" of writing to the point of exhaustion led to obvious extravagance. Some operatic or analytic passages overwhelm us. And
how could any reader accept the coincidences on which the plot often
turns? At the perfect moment Marcel moves into an apartment right in
the Guermantes back yard. Is it a fairy story? Charlus's great passion
turns out to be for Morel, the son of Uncle Adolphe's valet and an acquaintance of Marcel's. Marcel is even on the scene and watching
through the train window when Charlus picks up Morel on the platform. Yet Proust's universe, including Paris, is so small, so provincial
even, that such events seem to belong. They were bound to happen.
There is a similar inevitability about the characters as well. Like Goya
and Daumier, Proust created devastating caricatures without sacrificing the complexity and humanity of his personages. Few of us have
known people so distinguished and so debauched as Charlus, or so alluringly evasive as Albertine. Psychologically one of the most extravagant situations is Marcel's obsessive fascination with the name and
nature of the Guermantes. He has a veritable love affair with a noble
family. In context, these portrayals achieve the unforgettable truth of
fiction.

The theme of homosexuality creates far more ambiguities and conflicts for Proust. The reader encounters it in Charlus, Saint-Loup, Mlle
Vinteuil, Albertine (probably), Gilberte (possibly), the Prince de Guermantes, Morel (who is bisexual), and a large number of people in all
strata of society. Proust is working with a set of characters who are, in
varying degrees, so homosexually active that the novel, especially in the
latter books, appears at times to lose sight of the story itself. Not all of
Charlus' harangues on the subject deserve the space they occupy. But it
is worth noting that Proust, unlike Gide, never treated homosexuality as
a higher form of love. He portrays it either as a condition determined by
natural biological forces or as a taint, an unfortunate flaw in the distribution of human traits. And he sometimes acknowledges his obsession by
releasing it in a scene of Rabelaisian exaggeration, like the first reception
given by the Prince and Princesse de Guermantes.

Proust places a thirty-page section on homosexuality at the center of the novel to open the volume called *Sodom and Gomorrah*. These deliberately scandalous pages contain some of his most impassioned writing as well as his most judicious. After the celebrated fifteen-page scene of sexual encounter between the Baron de Charlus and Jupien, a tailor, Proust continues with fifteen further pages of reflection and lament about the behavior. They contain, like a steep mountain range blocking the way, the longest sentence in Proust's novel—close to two and a half pages (II 615–18/iv 21–24). It enumerates nine nearly disabling burdens under which this "accursed race" must live and compares its predicament to that of the Jews. Having established and surmounted the barrier of that mammoth sentence, Proust interjects the story of a solitary homosexual, abandoned by his only lover "like a sterile jellyfish stranded on the beach." The last page of this intense section offers us a succinct summary of the narrator's and, I believe, Proust's attitude toward homosexuals.

> In all countries surely they form a colony of exotic, cultivated, musical, sharp-tongued members, who have charming qualities and unbearable faults. They will appear in higher relief in later pages of this book. But here it is appropriate to warn provisionally against the fatal error of creating, as people have encouraged the creation of a Zionist movement, a sodomite movement and the rebuilding of Sodom. (II 632/iv 43–44)

Proust has been accused recently of not having had the courage "to come out of the closet"—openly to admit to his own homosexuality. But Proust wished to reject the false solidarity of labels and banners and special causes. He concerned himself with all humanity, not with one segment of it. His vision was shaped by his desire not to allow his sexual identity to define the scope of his novel.

Despite its extravagances, the *Search* remains a convincing portrait of an era. Certain details are priceless. When he begins going to exclusive parties, Marcel is utterly confused by the fad among the chic men of leaving their hats on the floor instead of consigning them to a footman.

The descriptions of the telephone, automobile, and airplane in their early days have astonishing freshness, both documentary and poetic. More important is the fact that Proust inherited from Stendhal and Balzac a sensitivity to the process of social change. One gets the feeling that he takes time to paint the mores of Combray and of the Guermantes and Verdurin clans—three contrasting spheres of life—in order to be able to display the revolving motion that will gradually shift everyone's relative position. Yet the change does not obliterate all continuity. Though an era may be closing, the generations come and go in a cyclic movement that re-creates as much as it destroys. The wheel of fortune remains.

In living through the incidents I have summarized, Marcel reacts to more than society at large. He enacts a three-way conflict. We see him first shaped and defined by his family, whose members surround him with love yet never fully understand him. We see him reaching out yearningly toward society—society both in the form of an aristocratic caste that for a time he admires and envies, and in the form of men and women he seeks to know as individuals and possibly to love and possess. But one comes to wonder whether either Marcel or Albertine is capable of the loyalty and trust needed to anchor their drifting liaison. And we see him retreating increasingly within himself to find a quiet domain from which to observe others covertly yet understandingly. A great steady eye, he watches, trying never to condemn family or society, but letting us behold all the ways in which they fail him. In the end he does not fail us, or himself. For he tells his story in full.

III

THE COMIC VISION

Four Scenes

BY ONE OF THE ESSENTIAL CONVENTIONS IN THE *SEARCH*, Marcel remains innocent for a long time. "Innocent" is of course a relative term. This tender young boy catches on very early to what makes the world go round. Not unlike his invalid aunt Léonie, he learns to bend his mother and his grandmother to his will. Françoise, the family cook and retainer, shows him that even a stern code of conduct compromises with reality. And Marcel contrives to spy on some juicy goings-on in Combray and to pick up all available scandal and gossip about the guests at the Grand Hôtel in Balbec. Yet the way the story is told implies that all worldly wisdom belongs to the Narrator and that Marcel drifts wide-eyed through the wicked world as a kind of cultivated cherub. Even though Marcel's age is not made clear, the scenes where he supposedly fails to comprehend the Baron de Charlus's sexual signaling in Balbec are disingenuous. But innocence has its limits. With a dramatic sense of timing not easily discernible behind the slow-moving narrative, Proust finally stages the great reversal. Approximately halfway through the novel he places four pivotal scenes in which Marcel loses his youth, his innocence, and his illusions.*

The first of these four scenes, probably the most moving one in the entire book, is the weeklong agony and death of the grandmother. The kindest, truest person in the story metamorphoses into a series of human and bestial figures before death lays her to sleep, restored to herself as a little girl. The event has a strong though delayed effect on Marcel. Henceforward, in spite of his mother's continuing solicitude, Marcel senses that he is alone and unprotected. Immediately following this death sequence, and almost without transition, Albertine visits him in his apartment and yields to his desire, thus confirming his earliest sexual experience. A long society scene intervenes before the third climactic sequence: Marcel happens to observe the startling encounter between the Baron de Charlus and Jupien and comprehends at last that they are homosexuals. This recognition scene reveals a whole new world to Marcel; the Narrator compares him to Ulysses, who at first did not recognize Pallas Athena. That same evening, Marcel achieves the ultimate social honor of being received at one of the elegant evening receptions given by the Prince and Princesse de Guermantes. The account of that event—a 150-page novella in itself—describes Marcel's loss of any last shred of belief that these "aristocrats" have something special or godlike about their persons and their lives. Despite their prestigious names, they are as stupid, as self-centered, and as unhappy as the rest of the world. Furthermore, they are even more racked than others by the vice of snobbery, from which one might think they could free themselves.

Thus Marcel's eyes are finally opened. This succession of scenes turns Marcel away from his social climbing and back toward his highly unsatisfactory yet absorbing relationship with Albertine. The respective themes of these four passages—death, love, vice, and social behavior—

---

*His virginity slipped away earlier, first in a clumsy encounter with an anonymous cousin, then in a *maison de passe* with Bloch (I 575–78/ii 205–9). Though these incidents "opened a new era" in his life (I 711/ii 396), the narrative does not fully register them until later.

give them a distinctness that is reinforced by the settings and the characters. Yet they share a common attitude toward experience, an understanding of which I consider crucial to a responsive reading of the novel. In order to bring out this aspect of Proust's work, I shall examine all four scenes, beginning with the shortest, Albertine's visit.

Scene 1

Late one afternoon in Paris, as Marcel lies moping on his bed, Albertine walks in unannounced. He finds her changed since the preceding summer, more sophisticated. She responds to his advances, letting him kiss her. The copious yet discreet narrative implies that their caresses lead to further satisfactions, though apparently not coitus. After a long, banal conversation about mutual acquaintances and a fond good-bye, Albertine leaves. Summarized in this bare form, the incident promises very little more than the commonplaces of sex. Let's see what Proust has done with it.

When Albertine walks in on him, Marcel is thinking quite lascivious thoughts, not about Albertine but about another attractive girl from Balbec from whom he expects a message that evening. Two hours later when Albertine leaves, Marcel will not commit himself to a time to see her again. The other girl is still very much on his mind, and he wants to keep his time open. Thus the scene is framed in carnal desire, but carefully deflected so that Albertine's entrance comes both as a total surprise and as perfectly appropriate to the mood.

We are reminded, however, that when Marcel first tried to make a pass at Albertine the preceding summer in what looked like a perfect setup in his hotel room, she literally pulled the cord on him and rang for help. Will she respond now? The real question, the old refrain of every unexpected or long-delayed encounter with her is, Who is Albertine? Marcel stumbles about among sensual memories of Albertine in Balbec and present realities. "I don't know whether what took possession of me at that moment was a desire for Balbec or for her" (II 351/iii 480). He decides in any case that he is not in love with Albertine and wants no more than a simple, peaceful satisfaction from her presence.

But now he notices her language, the expressions she calmly produces from the new "social treasure" she has accumulated since the preceding summer. Marcel makes a number of "philological discoveries" about her vocabulary. They provide the "evidence of certain upheavals, the nature of which was unknown to me, but sufficient to justify me in all my hopes" (II 356/iii 486). Marcel is indeed reading Albertine like a book.

> *To my mind* [Albertine said], that's the best thing that could possibly happen. I regard it as the perfect solution, the stylish way out."
>
> All this was so novel, so manifestly an alluvial deposit leading one to suspect such capricious wanderings over terrain hitherto unknown to her, that, on hearing the words "to my mind," I drew her down on the bed beside me. (II 356/iii 486)

Marcel has interpreted the signs correctly. If one is familiar with the way Proust moves calmly away from such moments and continues as if from another planet, the next sentences will come naturally. "No doubt it does happen that women of moderate culture, on marrying well-read men, receive such expressions as part of their dowry. And shortly after the metamorphosis which follows the wedding night, when they start paying calls. . . ." The sentence goes on for twenty lines. Having succeeded in maneuvering Albertine onto the bed, Marcel has wits enough about him only to try the "I'm not ticklish" approach. Albertine cooperates and, as they shift into position, asks considerately if she isn't too heavy. Then it happens. "As she uttered these words, the door opened and Françoise, carrying a lamp, walked in." Albertine scrambles back to a chair. It is not clear whether Françoise has been following every move from outside the door or is simply bringing in the lamp at the usual hour. In the two-page examination of this interruption, we learn that Françoise's smallest actions constitute a moral language inflicting her code of values on everyone around her. She emerges convincingly from the analysis as the mythological figure of "Justice Shedding Light on Crime." Caught practically in flagrante delicto, Marcel tries to carry it off.

"What the lamp already? Heavens, how bright it is." My object, as may be imagined, was by the second of these exclamations to account for my confusion, and by the first to excuse my slow reactions. Françoise replied with cruel ambiguity, "Do you want me to sniff it out?"

". . . snuff?" Albertine murmured in my ear, leaving me charmed by the lively familiarity with which, taking me at once for master and accomplice, she insinuated this psychological affirmation in the form of a grammatical question. (II 360/iii 492–93)*

When Françoise leaves, Albertine is ready for action again. But not so Marcel. There is a precedent. Swann, about to kiss Odette, tries to delay things in order to take full cognizance of what is happening. He senses something momentous and final in the act they are about to perform. Marcel holds off for similar reasons, about which we learn in some detail. Unhurriedly he rehearses the successive stages of their acquaintance and tries to reconstruct "this little girl's novel"—that is, her life beyond his ken. Knowing that it is now possible to kiss Albertine means more to Marcel than acting on the opportunity; his principal concern seems to be to breathe back into her person all the "mystery" she once carried so that, in kissing her cheeks, he will be kissing "the whole Balbec beach" (II 363/iii 496). Next comes a short disquisition on kissing and the dubious prospect of knowing anything by lip contact. We are now fifteen pages and probably an hour's reading time into the scene, and there would seem to be no way of spinning things out much longer. Marcel has her where he wants her, except that the old refrain never ceases: Who is Albertine? I quote with only a few cuts.

To begin with, as my mouth began gradually to approach the cheeks which my eyes had tempted it to kiss, my eyes, in changing position saw a different pair of cheeks; the throat, studied at closer range and

*Moncrieff translated Françoise's faulty subjunctive, *"Faut-il que j'éteinde?"* as "Do you want me to extinguish it?" Albertine supplies, "-guish!"

as though through a magnifying glass, showed a coarser grain and a robustness which modified the character of the face.

Apart from the most recent applications of the art of photography—which can set crouching at the foot of a cathedral all the houses, which time and time again, when we stood near them, appeared to reach almost the height of towers. . . . [ten more lines on photography] I can think of nothing that can so effectively as a kiss evoke out of what we believed to be a thing with one definite appearance, the hundred other things which it may equally well be, since each is related to a no less legitimate view of it. In short, just as at Balbec Albertine had often appeared different to me, so now . . . [here seven lines to say that such slow motion really serves to pass very rapidly in review all the different impressions one has had of a person] during this brief passage of my lips toward her cheek, it was ten Albertines that I saw; she was like a goddess with several heads, and whenever I sought to approach one of them, it was replaced by another. At least so long as I had not touched her head, I could still see it, and a faint perfume reached me from it. But alas—for in this business of kissing our nostrils and eyes are as ill-placed as our lips are ill-shaped—suddenly my eyes ceased to see; next, my nose, crushed by the collision, no longer perceived any fragrance, and, without thereby gaining any clearer idea of the taste of the rose of my desire, I learned from these unpleasant signs, that at last I was in the act of kissing Albertine's cheek. (II 364–65/iii 498–99)

Notice, among other things, that it is never directly recorded in the testimony given here that Marcel kisses Albertine. At the crucial moment he literally loses his senses. She vanishes. Consciousness cannot track experience to its lair. It must wait outside while another being, blind but active, performs a deed that the consciousness then reconstructs ex post facto from flimsy evidence. The question "Who is Albertine?" pales to triviality beside its counterpart: "Who am I?" But here Proust has done two things simultaneously. He has shown how sheer awareness, self-reflexiveness, erodes the reality of any action, even, or rather particularly, when we attach great significance to it; and he has written a superb pastiche of his own style, a savage-sympathetic blowup of all the gestures with which he usually introduces us to reality and its bitter disappointments. The relaxed reader can be amused both by Marcel's resounding defeat of his own purposes *as he achieves them* and by the Narrator's detachment from his own involuted narrative.

This "Kissing Albertine" sequence will bear sustained scrutiny. Most obviously, it dramatizes the dissociation of love, an idealized sentiment created by the imagination, from desire, focused on a material object. The passage also hints at Marcel's great yearning, in the midst of jealousies and disappointments, for the peaceable kingdom. He hopes Albertine will calm his life as his mother and grandmother were able to do. But few moments of serenity will come from this budding affair. The action here echoes several other themes: the power of language to influence thought, the intermittent quality of character and identity, and the ironic timing of important events in our lives. But more important than this disparate content is the fact that all of it fuses not into a romantic or erotic scene but into a primarily comic incident. There is no element in the scene that fails to contribute to the mood of self-mockery leading to open laughter.

This is the shortest of the four sequences that turn Marcel's life toward the long plateau of maturity. It will be revealing to look at the other three in reverse order.

Scene 2

At the evening reception that the Prince and Princesse de Guermantes gave at their sumptuous *hôtel particulier,* Marcel attains his social ambitions and, through 150 pages, observes the inflated emptiness and corruption of that society. The description of the characters recalls Daumier and even George Grosz. The Duc de Guermantes' crinkly hair, when he is angry, "seems to come out of a crater" (II 683/iv 112). The Marquise de Citry is "still beautiful, but barely suppressing a death rattle" *("encore belle, mais presque l'écume aux dents")* (II 687/iv 117). The comic element here is no mere matter of applied detail. From the start Marcel suspects that the invitation he has received to this chic affair is a hoax, and that he will be turned away at the door. His attempts to track down the origin of his invitation lead nowhere. Yet he cannot stay away. It gradually builds up to one of the great drolleries in Proust. The scene begins with an elaborate preparatory sequence about the head footman having been picked up the night before by an anonymous and generous gentleman who was in fact the Duc de Châtellerault. As it happens the Duke is just ahead of Marcel in line as they wait to have their names belted out to the guests by this same, now imposing footman. The Duke is terrified at the thought of being recognized by his lover. When the footman learns, from the man's own lips, his anonymous lover's exalted identity, he "shouts [it] out with truly professional gusto tinged with intimate tenderness." Marcel now totters forward. His fears about the spuriousness of his invitation to this prestigious event have been building up for pages. I can only quote.

> But now it was my turn to be announced. Absorbed in contemplation of my hostess, who had not yet seen me, I had not thought of the function—terrible to me, although not in the same sense as to M. de Châtellerault—of this footman garbed in black like an executioner, surrounded by a group of lackeys in the most cheerful livery, stout fellows ready to seize hold of an intruder and cast him out. The footman asked me my name, I told it to him as mechanically as the condemned man allows himself to be strapped to the block. Straightening up he lifted his majestic head and, before I could beg him to announce me in a lowered tone so as to spare my own feelings if I were not invited and those of the Princesse de Guermantes if I were, shouted the disturbing syllables with a force capable of shaking the very vaulting in the ceiling.

The famous Huxley (whose grandson occupies an unassailable position in the English literary world of today) relates that one of his patients stopped going out socially because often, on the actual chair that was pointed out to her with a courteous gesture, she saw an old gentleman already seated. She could be quite certain that either the gesture of invitation or the old gentleman's presence was a hallucination, for her hostess would not have offered her a chair that was already occupied. And when Huxley, to cure her, forced her to reappear in society, she felt a moment of painful hesitation when she asked herself if the friendly sign that was being made to her was the real thing, or if, in obedience to an imagined gesture, she was about to sit down in public upon the knees of a flesh-and-blood gentleman. Her brief uncertainty was agonizing. Less so perhaps than mine. After the sound of my name, like the rumble that warns us of a possible cataclysm, I was bound, at least in order to plead my own good faith, and as though I were not tormented by any doubts, to advance toward the Princess with a resolute air.

She caught sight of me when I was still a few feet away and (in an action that left no further doubt about my being the victim of a conspiracy) instead of remaining seated, as she had done for her other guests, rose and came toward me. A moment later I was able to heave the sigh of relief of Huxley's patient, who, having made up her mind to sit down in the chair, found it vacant and realized that it was the old gentleman who was the hallucination. The Princess had just held out her hand to me with a smile. (II 637–38/iv 50–51)

Proust narrates the incident with a precision of timing and flourish worthy of an acrobat balanced on top of a thirty-foot stack of tables. Twice he lets us think he is going to fall, first when he allows the Duke's subplot to take over, and later when he interrupts the story at the climax with the tantalizing Huxley digression. But he never loses control, and the story inches on. Basically Proust draws his effects here out of the double *I*. The enigmatic appearance of all unfamiliar things fills Marcel with anxiety and the Narrator with amusement. The resultant text shows us hallucination playing tag with perception, danger with detachment. We smile or chuckle each time the acrobat comes close to falling, though we remain apprehensive. After this opening, it is hard not to look for comedy in the rest of the scene.

We are not disappointed. Another comic motif helps to bind together these 150 pages. After this reception at their brother's house, the Duc and Duchesse de Guermantes plan to go on to a costume ball where the Duke, an incorrigible ladies' man, will see his latest mistress. One of his cousins, we learn, is at death's door. The rules of decorum would normally keep them home, but they find an excuse to go to the Prince's reception anyway. When they return home between parties to change into their costumes, they learn that the cousin has finally died. All is lost. They can no longer ignore the proprieties. But the Duke, intent on his rendezvous, will not accept defeat. He girds himself to brush aside this obstacle with barely a nod toward decorum. "You're exaggerating!" he says resolutely to the two ancient ladies who have brought the news. He and the Duchess sally forth. The little motif of whether or not they will finally attend the costume ball winds through the entire episode. It is the same narrative device as the uncertainty in "Combray" over whether Mme Goupil arrives at mass before the elevation, a kind of refrain to lead the reader through a prolonged development. Yet this induced suspense over a triviality and its mechanical repetition has a comic effect that Proust exploits to the hilt.

SCENE 3

It is natural enough that such society scenes should be decked out in comic accouterments. But there's something more disturbing and complex in the third of the four scenes I am examining. In it we learn, beyond a doubt, that Charlus has been promiscuously active with other men. Proust warned his prospective editors that the scene was shocking—as indeed it was over seventy-five years ago. Out of sight in the stairway, Marcel watches Charlus and Jupien identify and approach each other in the courtyard and finally retire for half an hour to an inside room. Comic details and lines keep cropping up, though they remain a quiet obbligato. (At one point Jupien, suspecting Charlus may be a bishop, is himself scandalized.) Proust asks us to see the scene in three perspectives: as the demonstration of a set of scientific laws of attraction, here presented in precise botanical terminology; as a scene having a special kind of aesthetic tone, comparable to the music of Beethoven; and as a comedy of shifting identities. The weave is very tight, and he maintains a careful balance among the three. The Narrator is more explicit than usual. "This scene, moreover, was not positively comic, it was overlaid with a strangeness or, if you will, with a naturalness, whose beauty kept growing" (II 605/iv 6).

Now, Proust's book has no villain; his psychology is too subtle for so static a classification of character. Charlus increasingly grows into an evil genius. He abandons health, reputation, and fortune for his vices. Nevertheless, even in the humiliating scene near the end of the book, where he is being flagellated by a young man in Jupien's male bordello, a curious innocence hangs over the events. We are told that Charlus really has a good heart. None of the hired hands is vicious enough to get any kick out of whipping the old man; they do it reluctantly, only for money. And in the penultimate moment when Marcel meets Charlus on the Champs-Elysées after the latter has had a ravaging heart attack, Proust paints the semiparalyzed Baron both as an indomitable Lear and as a senile puppet bowing to old enemies at Jupien's prodding. The most pathetic vice is not excluded from the comic vision.

SCENE 4

We can now move back to the first of the four crucial scenes. Proust brings to bear on the grandmother's death in her family's Paris apartment his broad medical knowledge and a devastating insight into what happens to people in the presence of death. These forty pages contain one of the most unsparing descriptions of a death agony in all literature. Her loss confronts Marcel with the full burden of selfhood. And the weeklong sequence displays the heroism of the grandmother as she faces death and tries to sustain her disintegrating humanity, and the courage of Marcel's mother. Her grief surpasses words and gestures, and at the same time she must try to control a household gone mad. Everything is brought to bear on this test of mortality. Yet, against all odds, even this is a strong comic scene, drawing on deep-seated traditions of danse macabre and gallows humor. Without comedy, the heroism would be strained and

unconvincing. As things stand, the courage and dignity of the two afflicted women shine out through multiple layers of burlesque.

Most obviously there is Françoise, whose devotion and feeling cannot
be distinguished from peasant insensitivity. She keeps acting as if the
whole affair were a special holiday, a *jour de gala* for which her most important mission is to have her mourning clothes properly fitted. Over
everyone's objections, especially the victim's, Françoise wants to set the
grandmother's hair. "By dint of repeatedly asking her whether she
wouldn't like her hair done, Françoise managed to persuade herself that
the request had come from my grandmother" (II 333/iii 454). The faithful servant never stops massacring the French language. Having no adequate way to express deep feelings in words, she comes out with this
urgent signal of moral distress: "This really bothers me" (II 340/ii 464).

Meanwhile, Proust keeps wheeling in unlikely visitors. When the still
articulate grandmother refuses to see the specialist, he insists on examining everyone else in the household instead—and infects them all with
head colds. Françoise is then distracted by an electrician, whom she cannot bear to send away. She talks to him for a quarter of an hour at the
back door just when she is needed in the sick room. The Duc de Guermantes arrives, insists on speaking to Marcel's stricken mother, and is unable to get over his own graciousness in visiting this bourgeois family. A
mysterious and distantly related priest comes to read and meditate by the
bedside; Marcel catches him peeking between the fingers he holds folded
over his face. Finally, when the celebrated consultant, Dr. Dieulafoy,
makes his ceremonial entrance *in extremis,* the text blurts it right out: "We
thought we were in a Molière play" (II 342/iii 466). Indeed they are—
in a Molière play written by Proust. Right up to the time one reaches the
sudden surge of stage movements and missed cues that surrounds the actual death, laughter is one among the strong conflicting responses.

A Matter of Temperament: The Opening Stumble

Proust is conventionally portrayed as a brooding figure, bedridden and
secretive, given to devious sentiments and suspicious medications. Be-

cause his psychological analyses never move briskly but swing slowly back and forth like the long-stemmed neurasthenic water lilies he describes near Combray, we tend to find him solemn. Brevity is said to be the soul of wit; a work as long as the *Search* must be directed toward high seriousness or gloom. Even sympathetic and intelligent critics have been blinded.

Proust had many vices, and at times his behavior seems a little spooky. But no reliable account of his life could picture him as an old sobersides. Many of his most revealing letters, once past the ingratiating phrases and the self-deprecation, take on a bantering tone. He seemed to nourish his restless intelligence on a diet of gossip about everyone he knew, including those closest to him; yet his curiosity was not so much malicious as finely sensitive to all human foibles. In a letter to Antoine Bibesco he reports this telephone conversation with the Marquis Louis d'Albufera, an unbookish young rake who fascinated Proust:

"Well, Louis, have you read my book?"

"Read your book? Did you do a book?"

"Of course, Louis, I even sent it to you."

"Ah . . . Well, if you sent it to me, my dear Marcel, I've surely read it. Only I'm not sure I received it."

Proust apparently had a special propensity for *le fou rire*—uncontrollable laughter. Lucien Daudet, a close friend from Proust's early twenties, makes much of the fact that even in later years he and Proust sometimes could not contain themselves. It happened not only when they were tweaked by a specific comic incident or expression, but often because, in a mental set created by an unexpected shift in their sensibility, *everything* suddenly became hugely funny. It is a precious state of mind—an ontological high.

Careful attention to biographical accounts reveals a gay, often mischievous Proust, endowed with tremendous verbal spontaneity. He carried his friends along with him in perpetrating elaborate verbal pomposities, like saying "Albion" for England and "our loyal troops" for the French army.

The waggishness that runs through Proust's conversations and correspondence entered his literary works slowly. His first book, *Pleasures and Days,* attempts only the gentlest of comic effects. In the heaped-up materials of the projected novel *Jean Santeuil,* the comic touches are much more frequent, yet still tentative. The most amusing sequence comes at the very start, where the young narrator describes and implicitly ridicules his own excitement on discovering that a famous author is living in the same rustic hotel on the Brittany coast. The whole section mocks the literary convention, to which it belongs, of the manuscript found in a bottle. Fully matured, the same attitude guides the masterly *Pastiches,* which Proust wrote for practice and for publication. These pieces are so fully controlled that it is impossible to do them justice by fragmentary quotation. Proust's sly mimicry of an author belongs to his text as a whole; its individual parts seem perfectly normal. The pastiches demonstrate that style as a self-conscious personal mode tends fatally toward the ridiculous. The greater the stylist, the more vulnerable he is to pastiche. Yet far from inhibiting Proust, that discovery apparently liberated him to write according to his own bent and face the consequences. He acknowledges the perils of a personal style by incorporating into the *Search* passages that function in part as self-parody. As I have tried to show, the "Kissing Albertine" sequence is one such passage. Proust referred to his published pastiches as "a matter of hygiene" (*CSB* 690), which purges him of other writers' influence. Self-mockery helped him navigate among his own excesses.

The brooding and even grim image of Proust's work is inappropriate. Released from it, one soon discovers a novel overlaid with amusing scenes and details. The benevolent Princesse de Luxembourg has difficulties adjusting to the social distance that separates her from Marcel. When he is presented to her, she almost pets him, like an animal at the zoo, out of sheer kindness. The celebrated wit of the Duchesse de Guermantes jeers at the world, and is itself jeered at in turn as self-centered and artificial. Verbal comedy permeates every scene and every character, major and minor. Dr. Cottard is an unstoppable machine for producing the most cobwebbed cliché for any situation. Françoise's endless howlers prevent Marcel from ever taking his own language for granted. And she is helped by a small cast of characters whose principal role seems to be exclusively that of fracturing French. To the elevator boy in Balbec, Mme de Cambremer will never be anything but Mme de Camember—Mrs. Cheese. To process everything novel back into familiar terms is a form of intellectual deafness most prominently displayed in language. The elevator boy's director, a Romanian émigré out of his depth in his adopted tongue, produces solid paragraphs of untranslatable barbarisms: *"fixure"* for "fixture," *"granulations"* for "gradations." Proust sometimes allows the director to carry on his word scrambling for too long. Yet one cannot help laughing aloud.

There is a scene in which Mme Cottard falls asleep in her chair after a big dinner at the Verdurins' summer place. Proust rides the crest for three pages, obviously enjoying himself. Spoofing all his own earlier scenes about sleep, he runs through a learned medical discussion on the subject and has Dr. Cottard cruelly keep waking his wife to tell her it's time to leave, only to let her relapse again. When she finally comes up blinking out of the depths, she is still talking in her dream. The guests enjoy the performance.

> "My bath is just right," she murmured. "But the feathers on the dictionary . . . ," she cried, straightening up. "Oh, Good Lord, how foolish I am. I was thinking about my hat, and I must have said something ridiculous. Another minute and I would have dozed off. It's the heat from that fire that does it." Everybody began to laugh, for there was no fire. (II 962/iv 491)

Mme Cottard looks ridiculous because she has confused waking and dreaming and produces the anomaly of "dictionary feathers" as a souvenir of her trip. But this little scene tucked away in the middle of the novel reveals unexpected links with the opening of the book. Both moments are located in the precarious zone between sleep and waking, and Mme Cottard's very human behavior sets the novel's first three sentences in a new light. Listen to them again. These are the first words Proust offers us, a subtle gambit, the flash of mental and physical movement that will influence every moment to follow.

For a long time I used to go to bed early. Sometimes, when I had barely put out the candle, my eyes would close so quickly that I did not even have time to say to myself, "I'm going to sleep." And half an hour later the thought that it was time to go to sleep would awaken me.

When we first see him, Marcel is as confused as Mme Cottard by the disorienting overlap between sleep and waking. His attention, his grasp of what he is and what he is doing, collapses under him. I interpret this incident as an epistemological stutter or stumble, deliberately placed ahead of all other incidents. It functions like a standard vaudeville routine: the curtain opens; an actor walks out onstage; he commences a gracious gesture; before he can open his mouth, he trips hugely and barely saves himself from falling. Laughter.

Proust's *I* does something very similar. He stumbles over himself before the book is under way. According to one scale of events, he regains his balance forty pages later as the child, Marcel, in the "Combray" section. According to another, more basic scale, the equilibrium of self-recognition does not occur until three thousand pages later. And even then Marcel, metamorphosed into the Narrator of his own life, is perched on grotesque stilts, which reach back into his past and on which he can barely stand. Montaigne uses the same carnival metaphor in the closing lines of his last essay, "On Experience," and tells us to keep our feet on the ground. Proust does not shrink from portraying the elevations and pratfalls out of which our deepest insights may emerge.

The Uses of the Comic

Beyond its natural existence as playful exuberance and celebration, the comic has earned a place in "serious" literature through three potential roles: as social corrective, as relief from the tensions of plot or implacable fate, and as a vehicle for forbidden content. These categories will shed some light on Proust's practice.

What is excessively individual or conformist in us usually comes out as rigid, mechanical behavior. By temperament following Bergson, the French philosopher who wrote a brilliant study on comedy, *Laughter* (1900), Proust brought his characters onstage both masked and revealed by their tics. Mme Verdurin has a sobbing ritualized laugh that betrays the artificiality of her feelings. Saint-Loup, though favored with elegance and savoir faire, slips sideways through all doorways, as if he has something to hide. (He does.) Proust excels in depicting exaggerated, socially compromising conduct, but the corrective edge of the comic in the *Search* is constantly blunted by uncertainty about what represents appropriate behavior in a society coming apart before our eyes. The grandmother's death suggests a Molière play in that large portions of the action veer toward satire and even burlesque. But in Proust there is no assumed universe of harmonious manners to appeal to, no *juste milieu*.* Awkwardness is simply part of our lot. Corrective action will not avail. Nevertheless, laughter usually sides with mental health and social well-being.

Many of the comic elements I cited earlier are undeniably diverting and may provide "relief" from a highly extended story. A superb two-page caricature of monocle styles in the middle of a social scene (I 326–27/i 463–65) seems to serve such a purpose. Yet a monocle described by Proust reveals social manners as well as individual character. And from what could we be relieved by comic elements merely inserted or pasted on? For Proust has jettisoned many conventions of linear plot and character development. We are rarely sure of motivation and intention, or of where events are headed. When the Narrator proposes three or four possible explanations for what happens, and an equal number of possible results, a sense of dislocation and anomaly becomes the

---

*In a passage not incorporated into the novel, Proust gave a notion of how far the comic sense of life, free of moral overtones, invaded his sensibility. He described Bergotte as leading an unrepentantly dissolute life, yet writing books that set very demanding moral standards. The morality of such people, the Narrator states, "makes the good consist in a sort of painful consciousness of evil . . . rather than in abstention from it" (Maurois, 146–47). The revealing yet disturbing thing about this fragment is that Bergotte's friends find his inconsistent behavior, not in bad faith or hypocritical, but "comic."

very ground out of which the action springs. This sense does not just raise its head at long intervals as "comic relief." As I have tried to show, it weaves tightly through scenes one would usually consider serious or emotional.

The third role conventionally assigned to comedy figures more importantly in the *Search* than the first two, and Proust explicitly recognized this function. By depicting a libertine character like Charlus as comic, ultimately as a mock-heroic figure, Proust seems to pass sentence on him as a departure from the norm and simultaneously to grant him pardon for that departure. Charlus's vices look like a grotesque caricature, and thus Proust sought dispensation for the forbidden content he felt compelled to deal with. He wrote to the publisher Fasquelle to say that nothing was really shocking in his novel, and then corrected himself in a parenthesis: "(or rather it is saved by the comic, as when the concierge calls the white-haired Duke [*sic*, for "Baron"] a 'big kid' . . .)." As Freud insisted, in writing about wit, the comic furnishes protective coloring for themes that cannot be introduced without it. Social corrective and comic relief do not help much in understanding the *Search*, but the novel does rely sometimes on the camouflage effect of the comic.

From the start of the *Search*, we are given the record of a sensitive consciousness eager to discover and enter the outside world of appearances, and apparently unable to do so in any satisfactory way. Marcel remains confined inside a pliable but impenetrable membrane of self-consciousness. Yet he cannot turn away from the universe of attractive enigmatic beings that present themselves outside his consciousness and his identity. The comic element in the novel follows this division into outward and inward.

In the external world the comedy arises from many sources. The French critic Gilles Deleuze has emphasized the way in which Proust presents people inhabiting a world of signs and clues needing astute interpretation. One result of this constant decoding, a result Deleuze fails to bring out, is a parade of *gaffes*, a comedy of errors. Marcel is forever getting his signals switched and confusing identities. He even mistakes the color of Gilberte's eyes and falls in love particularly with her "azure" eyes, when in fact they are black (I 140–41/i 198). Yet there is no surer path to the truth than through such foolish blunders. "An error dispelled gives us a new sense" (II 613/iv 18).

Most tellingly, however, the comic tone in outward events results from botched timing. Few things happen when expected, or as desired, or as might be appropriate. Usually things come too late; by the time their charms become available to him, Marcel has half lost interest in the haughty Guermantes family as in the person of Albertine. At other moments the timing is too perfect; the unlikely coincidences and windfalls that favor Marcel usually paralyze him. Both kinds of timing make him look ridiculous. Combined and reinforced, they persist into the novel's closing sequence, which relates Marcel's encounter with death.

After long absence from Paris, now aging more than he realizes, Marcel attends the last great Guermantes reception. With difficulty he recognizes his old friends and, through them, the tortuous track of his own life. He resolves once and for all to sit down and write the book he has been carrying inside him all these years. Françoise, the only surviving witness, recognizes the change in him and at last "respected" his work (III 1034/vi 509). Immediately, however, Marcel finds himself blocked. The discovery of the essential truths about time that give him the confidence to begin his novel also makes him aware of his vulnerability to contingent time. For time can inflict death on him at any moment, wipe out "the precious deposits within him," and prevent him from completing his work. At the start of the book, Marcel fumbles his timing in falling asleep. At the close, he picks the wrong time to settle down to producing a work of art. Yet this worst of all threats is given detached, almost amused treatment. "Now, by a bizarre coincidence, this carefully considered fear [of death] came alive in me at the moment when the idea of death had just recently become indifferent" (III 1037/vi 515). Marcel appears always out of step, always the victim as he confronts the external world.

Yet inwardly he remains undiscouraged in spite of all. Resignation and lucidity give him strength. Self-deprecation is his form of courage. In later years he finds it incredible that he should ever have bestowed special status on the Guermantes clan. And it is even more ludicrous that anyone, particularly a Guermantes, should see merit *in him*. "Later, I learned that the Guermantes believed that I belonged to a race apart, but a race that aroused their envy because I had merits unknown to me and that they prized above all others" (II 439/iii 601). Marcel cannot believe in his own accomplishments. When he happens upon an article he wrote, finally published in the *Figaro*, he fails for a time to register the fact. "I opened the *Figaro*. How annoying! The lead article had exactly the same title as the article I had sent them and that they hadn't printed yet" (III 567/v 766). Self-deprecation turns into slapstick when the Narrator describes Marcel's first entrance into a very chic café. ". . . I had to go in alone. Now, to begin with, once I had ventured into the revolving door, a device I wasn't accustomed to at all, I thought I'd never get out again" (II 401/iii 549). Such incidents have a theatrical flavor. Proust carries the effect even further in the carefully planned double incident of Mme Swann promenading at noon in the Bois de Boulogne surrounded by her reputation and her admirers. In the first incident (I 419–21/i 594–98), Marcel is "an unknown young man whom no one noticed." Palpitating yet resolute as he sees her approaching, acting on the dubious basis of his acquaintance with Mme Swann's daughter and his parents' acquaintance with her husband, "I raised my hat to her in so exaggerated a gesture that she could not help smiling. People laughed." Though merely an "extra" on the fringes of her performance, Marcel feels more pleasure than humiliation in accomplishing this exploit.

A few years later, when Marcel has come to know Mme Swann quite well, the scene is restaged with Marcel placed inside the magic circle, under Mme Swann's parasol, talking confidentially with her, holding her jacket. Looking out at the public, he sees one or two unknown young men summoning up the courage to greet her. Then, in fascination, he watches the ceremonial entrance of the most elegant aristocrat of the era, historically the genuine article, the Prince de Sagan. "The Prince, turning his horse's head toward us as if for an apotheosis on stage, or in the circus, or in an old painting, addressed to Odette a grand, theatrical, almost allegorical salutation" (I 640/ii 297). It is all *performed*—both vivid and unreal, thus held far enough away for a subtle destructive element to seep in around the edges. When Marcel first greeted Mme Swann, people laughed. Now that he stands among the mighty, there is no open laughter. But having reached the apparent center of the universe in this scene of apotheosis, Marcel still seems vaguely out of place—and this time the others along with him.

At least this is how the Narrator paints things. And it may be evident how the double *I* of Proust's narrative helps create the novel's gently mocking tone. Marcel and the Narrator form a contrasting pair like comic and straight man—*clown et auguste*. Either one without the other would not hold our attention for long. Together they combine innocence and wisdom. The jokes are on Marcel, told by his alter ego, the Narrator, looking back on his former self. The syntax of the story carries inside it this enlarged and ultimately comic perspective of reflection and memory. That perspective cannot be peeled off the body of the narrative as incidental entertainment or social commentary. It constitutes one of the most human and organic aspects of Proust's vision. This is a far cry from the gloomiest book ever written.

IV

PROUST'S COMPLAINT

I N THE DISCUSSION OF PROUST S LITERARY WORK, I HAVE
placed his comic vision first because it is essential and because, like
Poe's purloined letter, its very obviousness escapes some readers' observation. I now move to a second pervasive mood in the *Search*, a frame
of mind that appears to come from the opposite side of human nature.
Yet the comic vision and what I shall call "soul error" are not unrelated.

False Scents

Like the youngest son in a fairy tale, Marcel is given three chances to succeed. He tries three solutions to the puzzle of life, and one after the other
they fail. Of course, it turns out in the end that he has won without
knowing it, as if he had walked backward into paradise. The three magic
stones, the three wishes he was allowed, come to naught. But since error
recognized is a source of personal knowledge, the years of quest have
not been wasted.

The first false scent leads to the faubourg Saint-Germain, the quarter of Paris inhabited by the oldest families of the nobility. Marcel smells

from far off the legendary amalgam of birth, title, and landed property
that forms aristocratic society. It showed its last spark of life in France
during the prewar years in which the *Search* is set. Marcel supposes that
there is a fourth ingredient as well: nobility of character. Instead, he
finds totally human lineaments exaggerated and distorted by the setting.
The *prestige* (a key word in Proust) of the rich and titled turns to tinsel
when approached close-up. After preliminary trials and rehearsals, Marcel enters the select domain on the evening he is invited to dine with the
Duc and Duchesse de Guermantes. The Duke himself, displaying his
most considerate politeness, meets him at the door. After visiting the
collection of Elstir paintings, Marcel is presented to the Princesse de
Parme. She seems to radiate a Stendhalian aura and a gentility all her
own. Then, before Marcel can begin to identify the other guests, dinner
is announced, the machinery starts, the Duchess circles the salon like a
protective huntress to take his arm, and they enter the dining room "in
a rhythm of exact and noble movements" (II 434/iii 595). At this point
the action freezes, and the Narrator opens an unsparing fifty-page digression on the wit and politics of the Guermantes. Marcel tries to find
some ground on which to resist his initial negative reaction to his hosts.
"But just as in the case of Balbec or Florence, the Guermantes, after
having first disappointed the imagination because they resembled their
fellow men more than their name, could afterward, though to a lesser degree, hold out to one's intelligence certain distinguishing particularities" (II 438/iii 600).

By the end of the dinner a hundred pages later, it is the remarkable ge-
nealogy of their names and the history of their titles that reendows these
vulgar citizens with fascination, with "their lost poetry" (II 532/iii 730).

Thus the prestige of the Guermantes and their kind survives essentially as an established form of *snobbery*. For Proust, snobbery is the
great cohesive force that holds society together. He studies it tirelessly
at every social level. The word itself covers two major attitudes or classes
of snobbery. Proust contrasts them in a semimathematical formula while
describing the Duchesse de Guermantes when she still had the title of
Princesse des Laumes. "She belongs to that half of humanity in whom

the curiosity the other half feels toward the people they don't know is replaced by an interest in the people they do know" (I 335/i 476). The sentence bears expansion. Persons securely favored with high rank and
wealth are prone to a snobbery of self-satisfaction, expressed in their exclusive attention to their own class and milieu. Those not so favored, and
who aspire to social position, are prone to the snobbery of social envy,
a desire to spurn their own class and milieu. Of course, the snob rarely
occurs in the pure state, without a tincture of the other category. Charlus "combined in himself the snobbery of queens and that of servants"
(III 598/v 809). Proust is using the word in the second sense when he
refers to a woman as "snobbish even though a duchess" (III 266/v 354).
The varieties of *mondanité* gradually give Marcel an understanding of
the springs and wheels that turn the social machine.

One of Proust's early titles for the first volume of his novel was "The
Age of Names." He means *proper* names, of places and of people. Only
such names seem to stand for "something individual and unique" (I
387/i 551). The false scent of social success corresponds closely in the
novel to the age of names. For years what ignites Marcel's imagination
is always in a name. A train timetable listing luscious place-names reads
like poetry, just as a noble title has the magic power of "a fairy" (II
533/iii 731). As time goes on, these names, the most eminent and effective vehicles for prestige, wither and almost die. The "semantic illusion"
of social prestige, despite its poetic origins, hardens into the dry husk of
snobbery.*

The second false scent is love, both as sentimental attachment and as
physical desire. (I omit from this discussion Marcel's passionate affection
for the compound figure of his mother and grandmother. That powerful emotion permeates the first half of the *Search*.) The two can be distinguished, but neither leads to true gratification. Swann's famous last
words on the death of his love for Odette catch the mood of disappointment. "To think that I wasted years of my life, that I hoped to die,

---

*The best description and analysis of this "semantic illusion" can be found in
"Proust et le langage indirecte," by Gérard Genette, collected in *Figures* II (1969).

that I had my greatest love affair with a woman who didn't appeal to me, who wasn't even my type" (I 382/i 543). Proust extends to the verge of solipsism what Stendhal and Nerval knew about the imaginary subjective nature of love. In his liaison with Albertine, Marcel makes his own special variation on Swann's pattern. In both cases a transformation takes place not unlike that which we have seen modifying the dynamics of the social sphere and turning respect for rank and honor into snobbery. By a kind of psychological fate, love decays into the very different yet equally powerful force of *jealousy*. It happens to Swann and to Marcel (and to Saint-Loup and to Charlus) before love has achieved fulfillment or equilibrium. Why must it be so? It is as if the capacity of physical actions and ordinary words to reach behind appearances and touch another person fails us when we most need it. Communication falls short—whereupon love and desire yield to a kind of emotional envy that feeds on the possibility that the loved one is communicating better with someone else. Given its head, the imagination then runs away with everything. ". . . the mind goes to work; instead of a need one finds a novel" (III 1022/vi 491).

What disturbs many Proust readers more than his uncompromising criticism of love is the fact that he does not spare friendship. Gradually we are forced to perceive that egotism, distraction from boredom, and insecurity reign over the only friendship Marcel allows himself, that with Saint-Loup. And the Narrator leaves no room for doubt. Friendship tends to make us "sacrifice the only real and incommunicable part of ourselves . . . to a superficial self which does not, like the other one, find any joy in its own being, but is consoled to find itself held up by external props, taken in and sheltered by an individual foreign to itself" (II 394/iii 540–41).

Proust's correspondence and biography demonstrate the importance that friendship held for him and the steadiness with which he honored its rituals and its sentiments. Thus it is perplexing to read a letter he wrote in 1901 to Antoine Bibesco (who became one of his closest friends), upbraiding him for abusing the code of friendship and in the same breath affirming that friendship is "something without reality." We will simply have to live with the fact that profound skepticism about generally recognized sets of human feelings can coexist with a yearning for those feelings. In the *Search*, the Narrator's description of Marcel's long detour through the false promises of love and friendship is virtually congruent with the story itself.

The third false scent in the novel will be harder to deal with than the social ambition and love because it carries us into the domain of the intellectual and the aesthetic. Furthermore, not only did Proust's own thinking in this area shift and evolve over a long period; he also represented and dramatized in the novel views opposed to those in which the Narrator and Proust ultimately place their faith. This complex third false scent is the domain of art.

From an early age, Marcel appears to sense, and to have learned from his extensive and spellbinding readings, that he is called upon to create something, to respond adequately and in written words to the vividness of his impressions. The first time it happens, all he can utter is "Gosh" (see below, pages 108–10). The second time, whirled across the landscape on top of a carriage, he manages to jot down a fairly convincing account of the experience. But he mocks his own accomplishment by referring to himself as a hen clucking and carrying on over having laid an egg (I 182/i 257).

The attractions and rewards of art remain close to the central narrative yet always in doubt, always threatened. Swann, a devoted amateur of art, can never begin work on his book about Vermeer. The eminent Marquis de Norpois both belittles Marcel's talents as a writer and persuades his father to allow him to follow a literary career (a development that amounts to a second "abdication" after the good-night kiss scene). But, once established, the refrain of Marcel's literary vocation gradually diminishes in the face of an opposing obbligato: Marcel's poor health and weak will. He avoids and postpones the moment of beginning work in order to follow his many pleasures. "Well, what's happening? No more talk about this great work of yours?" (I 580/ii 211). Even his grandmother's gentle goading merely irritates him.

At times the Narrator goes out of his way to explain and almost to excuse Marcel's fecklessness. Marcel has just spent an evening of warm friendship with Saint-Loup recalling earlier memories.

> In remembering them I experienced an enthusiasm which could have been fertile if I had remained alone, and that way I would have avoided this long detour of misspent years through which I still had to travel before the revelation of the invisible vocation of which this book is the story. (II 397/iii 544).

The ideal of art serves as a contrast that, for long periods, convinces Marcel of the emptiness of his life. A performance of Vinteuil's septet inspires in Marcel a meditation on the transcendent rewards of musical art (III 248–65/v 330–53). Twice he refers to the effect of the music on him as a "call" *(appel)*—a call to "superterrestrial joy he would never forget." Then the crucial and haunting question, the obbligato that persists: "But would [such joy] ever be realisable for me?" (III 261/v 347). Many years of obsession with Albertine stand in his way. His utter lack of confidence in himself stands in his way. After reading the Goncourts' journal about the very same people he might write about, Marcel loses faith all over again in his literary gifts (III 723/vi 46). Years later, this conviction that he has no literary vocation is reinforced by his failure to respond to a certain optical effect of the setting sun lighting up just the upper half of a line of trees outside the window of his train. His heart has sometimes leaped in his breast on beholding such a scene. But now he knows better: "The years when I might have been capable of celebrating [this effect of nature] will never return" (III 855/vi 238). The long action of the *Search* holds out to Marcel the vocation of art as his only salvation. His weak, pleasure-loving temperament and poor health, plus many false aesthetic leads in the story, withdraw that goal from him. He cannot win, it seems, yet the tension remains.

I have not told the whole story concerning the role of art and literature in Proust. But it is essential to insist at this point that through more than 99 percent of the *Search*, art beckons to Marcel without drawing him, without his yielding. And, as I shall show when I come back to this topic in Chapter VI, art harbors its own temptations and dangers.

Everything seems to go wrong for Marcel. Social success is empty. Love and friendship carry him not to the discovery of another person but into closer quarters with himself. Art escapes him. The passage about Marcel reading himself to sleep over the Goncourts' journal is particularly revealing.

This scene near the end, which includes Proust's masterly nine-page parody of the Goncourts' arty journalism, suddenly turns the action of the story back on itself, as when a passenger is startled to see the other end of his train while going around a curve. In the Goncourt "extract," Marcel finds himself reading about a dinner at the Verdurins'. The apartment, the people, the stories are all familiar. Yet, as now described, they appear bathed in a miraculous glow of literary and historic importance. The Goncourts have observed everything, right down to the elegant plates the meal is served on. Every detail of that life seems exciting and significant. In consequence, as he reads, Marcel feels everything tumbling down around his ears. He knew all these people. How could he have gone so far astray as to consider the Verdurins a couple of mediocre bourgeois social climbers and bores if they can inspire these ornate pages? The people he had classified as mere bit players *(figurants)* turn out, in the Goncourts' authenticating account, to be the leads *(figures)*.

When he closes the book, Marcel's first exclamation to himself is "The Prestige of Literature!" (III 717/vi 38). There is something about a literary work—its vision, its transparence, its metaphoric quality—that makes it very strong magic. Even against our will it can enter our mental system and exert a lasting influence. Prestige in this sense begins to look little different from snobbery in the social domain. If the patina of heightened existence that hangs over certain lives can be attributed to the secret power of literature, then we can accept the need for a certain portion of artifice to save reality from triviality and platitude. But the converse case that Proust puts forward and that troubles Marcel seems far more devastating. Is there a quality in some people that makes them highly susceptible to the prestige of literature and yet incapable of finding its counterpart in their own existence?

The closing sentences of the scene describe Marcel's quandary as belonging both to life and to literature.

. . . it amounted to wondering if all those people whom one regrets not having known (because Balzac described them in his books or dedicated his works to them in admiring homage, about whom Sainte-Beuve or Baudelaire wrote their loveliest verses) or even more if all the Récamiers and the Pompadours would not have struck me as insignificant people, either because of some infirmity in my nature . . . or because they owed their prestige to an illusory magic belonging to literature. (III 723; cf. II 30/vi 46; cf. iii 30)

Everything is now in jeopardy. Either Marcel has misjudged all the apparently tiresome and fraudulent people of fashion he knew and has been blind to their real importance; or else they are indeed as ordinary as they appeared and it is the magnifying, transforming power of literature that has raised them to an imaginary and fraudulent prestige.* He is unable to reject either alternative. Both ways, he loses. Marcel perceives that the Goncourts write as snobs, and that at the same time their mannered style affects his sensibility more forcefully than he would like. This lucid grasp of a contradictory dilemma affords him no comfort. It is precisely at this point in the story that Marcel takes refuge "for long years" in a *maison de santé* outside Paris.

The crucial phrase in the last passage quoted, a phrase that opens in Marcel's line of thought a crevasse falling away to unknown depths beneath, is *"some infirmity in my nature."* What precisely is this infirmity that makes Marcel incapable of taking full account of and giving full value to the very scenes he has lived through? The answer will tell us what has made Marcel so prone to the false scents of society, love, and art.

---

*Confronted by a similar problem in social relativity theory, Marcel's great-aunt has no trouble finding a solution. She discovers that their nice but slightly disreputable neighbor in Combray, Monsieur Swann, is a close friend of the nephews of the Marquise de Villeparisis, her most aristocratic schoolmate. "Now, this information about Swann had the effect, not of raising him in my great-aunt's estimation, but of lowering Mme de Villeparisis" (I 20/i 25).

From Places to People: The "Infirmity in My Nature"

During the extended nocturnal musings at the start of the *Search*, the voice of Proust's Narrator first gathers strength and identity in a kaleidoscopic description of bedrooms. He is trying to orient himself, to establish where he is. Wallace Stevens in his "Adagia" could have been speaking for Proust: "Life is an affair of people not of places. But for me life is an affair of places and that is the trouble." Proust's universe hangs together at the start more substantially by places than by people, who are forever disappearing behind new incarnations of themselves. Each important place takes shape as a vividly experienced and basically stable association of light effects, smells, tastes, sounds, history, habitual behavior patterns, and predictable deviations. Combray forms a "closed society" (I 110/i 153) with its own laws and legends. Marcel as a boy comes to rely on a similar ritual of familiar place when he plays in the Champs-Elysées gardens in Paris. Balbec also stands for a reassuring stability of life. When Marcel returns for his second visit to this alluring seaside resort, only his outlook on things has changed. Balbec with its familiar landmarks and leisurely life seems motionless in time. The early volumes of the *Search* depict in convincing detail what Proust states bluntly in *Jean Santeuil*. "Places are people, but people who do not change and whom we often see again after a long time in wonderment that we have not remained the same" (*JS* 534). One can rely on places, above all on landscapes like Combray and Balbec where human handiwork blends with nature.

But as time goes on, Marcel loses this security. Paris apartments and fashionable salons replace countryside and landscape. These city interiors frame not the durable objects of nature but the inscrutable metamorphoses of people. Even the attractions of Balbec fall victim to this movement. After a summer full of visits to sites in the area, Marcel realizes that the exotic local place-names have slowly been "humanized" (II 1098/iv 678). He decides to leave this "much too social valley" (II

1112/iv 697). When his special sensibility to landscape has withered away, only Venice, still unvisited and unknown, seems to hold out the power to move him.

The last exterior in the *Search* comes only a few pages before the last Guermantes reception. Marcel's train stops in the countryside next to a line of obliquely lit trees. A sensitized reader will at this point see several hovering images—the half-lit tower of the Combray church, the trees the Narrator reflects on in the Bois, the three trees from which Marcel receives mysterious signals in Hudimesnil near Balbec (I 64, 423, 717/i 87, 600–601, ii 404–5). But not Marcel. His light has gone out.

> "Trees," I thought, "there's nothing more you can say to me, my chilly heart can no longer hear you. Yet here I am in the very lap of nature. Well, I feel only indifference and boredom when my eyes follow the line that separates your illuminated forehead from your shadowy trunk. If I could never before fully *believe* myself a poet, I now *know* that I am *not* one." (III 855/vi 238)

Landscape serves no longer, even in retrospect. Marcel's collection of vivid scenes has been subordinated to the characters and absorbed by them. Albertine, an unknowable mixture of innocence and vice, takes shape out of the exotic topography of Balbec and then displaces it. The richly colored landscapes of Combray and Balbec fade into the background as the cast of characters moves forward. People have taken over from places.

This large-scale shift from place to person as the focus of the narrative provides the background for Marcel's long dedication to society, love, and art. Though these pursuits may not bring him the rewards he hopes for, they do seem to lead him out of childhood and toward maturity. Haltingly, he begins to make his way in the world outside the family unit. Yet Marcel has the desperate feeling that life is escaping him precisely when he can for the first time find friends and protectors and lovers. What has gone wrong? We are dealing again, I believe, with a quirk of mind that begins very early in the story as a kind of contrariness, of perverseness in a spoiled boy.

As a child in Combray, Marcel goes to Machiavellian lengths to lure his mother up to his bedroom to say good night when she should be downstairs attending to her guests. The scene is justly celebrated, for it sets the novel in motion and anticipates many themes to be developed later. The close of the incident brings its most revealing moment. When finally his mother does come, Marcel's father indulgently persuades her to spend the night in Marcel's room and read him to sleep—thus compromising her principles and her authority. Marcel cannot cope with so great a success and inwardly reverses himself. "If I had dared to now, I would have said to maman: 'No, I don't really want you to, don't sleep here with me' " (I 38/i 51). Her capitulation unmans him.

From this seed will grow a vine of constrictive experience, a veritable tree of forbidden knowledge. In a letter to the Princesse Bibesco, Proust generalized the same reaction. "A sensation, no matter how disinterested it may be, a perfume, or an insight, if they are present, are still too much in my power to make me happy." Steadily and disturbingly, the novel develops this mental set: it is the same "infirmity in my nature" that troubles Marcel when he reads the Goncourts' journal. Toward the end of the evening when he dines for the first time with the Duc and Duchesse de Guermantes, Marcel tries to take stock of his disappointment. I have described how his entry into this most elegant and inaccessible layer of society fails to meet expectations. He finds the explanation not in the other people but *in himself*.

> Several times already I had wanted to leave, and, more than for any other reason, because of the insignificance which my presence imposed on the party. . . . At least my departure would allow the guests, once rid of the interloper, to form a closed group. They would be able to begin the celebration of the mysteries. (II 543/iii 744–45)

Because this is still a young dilettante among the dowagers, we might easily laugh off such a moment as something like a failure in social depth perception. It should all straighten out as Marcel gains experience and confidence. Yet he and we remain apprehensive. Even Swann fell victim to this vision of his own presence blighting reality. The part of Odette that he longs above all to know is her "real life as it was when he wasn't there" (I 299/i 424). Marcel feels the same way toward Albertine, and could barely bring himself to kiss her when available.

It is this clouding of the mind at the moment of achieving what it most desires, this "infirmity in my nature," that I call Proust's complaint. He was not the first to discover it, of course. He did not even give it a consistent name. But more than any other writer, Proust explored this distressing perverseness that dogs the most enterprising activities of the human mind and seems to deprive it of satisfaction. One finds, knit tightly into the comedy of the *Search,* a long lament of self-deprecation.

Soul Error

Throughout the seventeenth and eighteenth centuries, in England and on the Continent, the psychological investigations of human motives concentrated on the theme of pride and the search for fame. The French rolled the two together into the term *la gloire.* It haunts the work of La Rochefoucauld and La Bruyère, of Corneille and Racine. Milton knew that "Fame is the spur . . ." *(Lycidas)* yet proceeded to condemn it in all its forms except the divine. When Voltaire, Hume, and Kant picked up the theme in an age less concerned with a Christian God, they treated the desire for esteem in the eyes of others as a socially beneficial infirmity. This powerful doctrine accepts human vanity or pride as the necessary engine of culture and as the source of the fair edifices of civilization. The current still runs strong in the nineteenth-century novels of Stendhal and Balzac, who were absorbed by the myth of the young adventurer out to make his mark in the world.

Against this background of *gloire,* Marcel's "infirmity in my nature" looks ludicrous. He hopes for success and fame; what holds him back? Why is he such a miserable hero? Considering his accomplishments, why does he feel this way? The answer is confounding. Marcel cannot win—not because he lacks talent or looks, but *simply because he is Marcel.* His very presence discredits, in his own eyes, whatever he does. After the most elaborate efforts, he attains goals that turn out to be valueless—precisely because *he* has reached them. When he kisses Albertine, he confronts ten Albertines, no one of whom he desires. The Guermantes don't live up to expectation. By a fatality that lodges in his bones or his name or his being, Marcel carries a pall wherever he goes. His passage turns the world to ashes.

The pattern is endlessly repeated. Having heard from Swann about the beauties of the Balbec church, Marcel visits it before going on to the hotel and the beach. When he finds the church surrounded by ugly buildings and "reduced to its own stone countenance," he is bitterly disappointed. The precious work of art is overwhelmed by the proximity of a pastry shop and the branch office of a bank. The promise of its name crumbles under "the tyranny of the Particular" (I 660/ii 323–24). Later, near Balbec, Marcel accosts a pretty fishergirl in such a boasting manner that he knows she will remember him. For a moment he desires her and forces himself on her attention. "And that capturing of her mind, that immaterial possession, was enough to strip her of mystery as fully as physical possession" (I 717/ii 404). From his success springs his failure.

Does the flaw that causes this condition lodge entirely in Marcel's sensibility, as is implied by the phrase "infirmity in my nature"? Before accepting this verdict, we would do well to look again at the pattern of events that surrounds Marcel. One persuasive answer to the question would be that the real flaw is not simply a character trait but arises out of the relation between subject and object. We already have the terms available. When the intermittence of our natures meets the perverse timing of events, the result is a puzzling disarray. "Our desires interfere constantly with one another, and, in the confusion of our existence, it is rare that happiness coincides with the desire that clamored for it" (I 489/ii 83). The two series will not mesh. Odette falls passionately in love with Swann when she first meets him, yet those feelings fade before his infatuation begins. This explanation of Proust's complaint by intermittence and timing appeals to an unexamined fatalism. It posits that we must simply accept the fact that his (our) condition springs from a near-inevitable semicomic discrepancy between subjective desire and objective reality.

I believe we can go further in seeking the origins of Marcel's habit of self-doubt. It seems fully appropriate that one of the keenest descriptions of this temper was written four centuries ago by Montaigne. In the first version of the essay "On Presumption," he is speaking of the outward signs of vainglory. That vice arises, he says, either out of too high an opinion of oneself or out of too low an opinion of others. Then suddenly—at least it feels sudden when you come upon the passage Montaigne inserted many years later into the original text—he shifts his ground. Now it is a sixty-year-old man speaking a deeper truth than he knew at forty.

> I feel oppressed by *an error of mind* which offends me both as unjust and even more as annoying. I try to correct it, but I cannot root it out. It is *that I attach too little value to things I possess, just because I possess them; and overvalue anything strange, absent, and not mine.* This frame of mind extends very far. As the prerogative of authority leads men to regard their wives with monstrous disdain, and sometimes their children, so too am I afflicted. Whatever I am responsible for can never, as I see things, meet the competition. To an even greater degree, any desire for advancement and improvement clouds my judgment and closes off the path to satisfaction, just as mastery in itself breeds scorn of whatever one holds in one's power. Exotic societies, customs, and languages attract me, and I realize that the dignity of Latin impresses me more than it should, just as it does children and common folk. My neighbor's house, the way he runs his affairs, his horse, though no better than my own, are all worth more than mine precisely because they are not mine. [italics added]

In this passage Montaigne is right on pitch, perfectly in tune with himself and with that human condition we share with him. Here is the subtlest and most far-reaching fault of all. It strikes at our very sense of reality. *Soul error** is the incapacity to give full value or status to one's

---

*Montaigne's phrase is *une erreur d'âme.* Florio and J. M. Cohen translate it as "an error of the mind." Donald Frame tries "an error of my soul." Montaigne does not use the genitive, which would be *erreur de l'âme.* The French syntax implies substance, essential composition, as in the forms *crise de nerfs, état d'esprit,* or even *chemin de fer.* My own translation proposes "an error of mind." However, English and American usage of both sixteenth and twentieth centuries offers a tighter version than any of the above: *soul error.*

own life and experience. This quiet southern gentleman, former mayor of Bordeaux and companion of kings, retired to a tower and devoted his life to writing about himself. One would expect to find the most self-satisfied, the least self-deprecating of men. Yet it is he who tells us in the same essay, ". . . it would be difficult for any man to have a poorer opinion of himself."

Here, then, is the "tyranny of the Particular"—but directed by Montaigne back at ourselves. For we are our own principal particular. We find ourselves and all that belongs to us very hard to live with. Soul error: Proust, the Narrator, and Marcel wrestle with it. The only escape Proust suggests is to seek an impossible perfection (II 46/iii 52) or the inaccessible (III 384/v 517). That way one keeps one's face averted from the real. But in his writing, soul error is never far away. In one of the early stories published in *Pleasures and Days*, Proust writes of a ten-year-old boy who tries to kill himself out of love for an older girl. Has she scorned him? No. "He felt disappointment every time he saw the sovereign of his dreams; but as soon as she had gone, his fertile imagination gave back to the absent girl all her charms and he wanted to see her again" (*JS* 111). At the restaurant in Rivebelle, the elegant customers act as compulsively as Marcel. ". . . at each table the diners had eyes only for the tables at which they were not seated . . ." (I 810/ii 532). When Mme de Stermaria accepts Marcel's invitation to an intimate dinner in the Bois, he finds he would prefer to have the evening free to try to see other women (II 391/iii 535). Whatever bends to our desire *disqualifies* itself by becoming a part of ourselves. Whence the flat statement from the Narrator during Marcel's agonizing separation from Albertine: "Man is the being who cannot get out of himself, who knows others only in himself, and, if he denies it, lies" (III 450/v 607).

Once it has attacked, there is no escape from the worm of self-contempt. For Marcel, only one set of experiences remains immune: the closed world of Combray, where place, family, and nature congeal into a vision barely shadowed by advance warnings of dangers to come. For a precious moment Marcel was content to be himself. Childhood provides the standard of things as they were before the worm attacked them.

Still, it is too imprecise simply to say that soul error arises from a loss of the unified world of childhood. For just how does it come about that reality and appearance part company? Combray exists retroactively for Marcel as a benevolent but inflexible routine, a *train-train,* within which he discovers for himself the catastrophic factor of time. His good-night kiss is withheld when he needs it and granted when he wants it no longer. That incident breaks the spell of Combray and infects his experience with the decay of time. Marcel has to face what Proust had already expressed in *Pleasures and Days.* "No sooner has an anticipated future become the present than it loses its charms." Temporality introduces "an incurable imperfection into the very essence of the present" (*JS* 139). When Marcel gets high on wine while dining with Saint-Loup at Rivebelle, the euphoria or "pure phenomenalism" (I 816/ii 540) he feels approximates a return to total immersion in the present. Exalted tipsiness annuls the discovery of time. While tingling with wine, he could forget everything but the intensity of the moment. However, this state represents not a conquest of temporality but a surrender to it.

The "imperfection" in reality imposed by time is accompanied, Proust shows us, by an increased (but far from compensating) power of the imagination. It is the principal internal organ of desire. When Proust describes the young boy in love with a girl who disappoints him every time he sees her, he attributes the boy's malady to his precocious imagination (*JS* 111). Albertine's "mystery, which she had for me on the beach before I knew her" (II 363/iii 497), is a pure product of the imagination. And its functioning observes a precise relation to presence and absence. "Man of imagination, you can find enjoyment only through regret or expectation, that is, in the past or in the future" (*JS* 54). Twenty years later, Proust was even more categorical. He sees "an inevitable law which arranges things so that one can imagine only what is absent" (III 872/vi 263). We may have learned why. Thwarted by intermittence and the warped timing of experience, the imagination falls victim to soul error and seeks its object forever elsewhere.

The Paradox of Consciousness

All literature may aspire to the condition of the proverb. Proverbs and maxims appear to record a state of things so compact and definitive that we can tuck them away and forget them until their turn comes around again—as it always does. Because of their brevity, proverbs lack the dramatic dimension of suspense. At the opposite end of the scale, the manner in which Proust (like Montaigne) devoted the last fifteen years of his life to a single monumental work, and with such intensity as to signify that the work *took* his life, created several strands of suspense, which tighten and tune the novel like a musical instrument. (See Chapter VII.) Nevertheless, roman-fleuve and proverb are by no means irreconcilable modes. Raymond Radiguet, a sage at seventeen when he wrote *The Devil in the Flesh*, spoke cannily of literature as a means to *"déniaiser les lieux communs."** There is much to be learned from the wisdom worn into the folds of language itself. It is not surprising to find a pair of matched proverbs in English to elucidate Proust's complaint. A comparable pair exists in many languages.

The romantic version has a strong ironic counterthrust, and its pastoral metaphor makes it suitable for hymns and popular songs: *the grass is greener on the other side of the fence—or hill*. The realist version is terser and has an edge of cynicism: *familiarity breeds contempt*. Once heard, they remain. Of all the major characters in the *Search*, Françoise has the most humble origins, yet she outlasts all the others, including the Narrator himself. Similarly, Proust finally leads us to maxims, some traditional, many more his own, sturdy little shrines in the landscape of human experience. They cannot replace his novel, but they may well outlast it. And they also caution us not to dismiss or underrate the state of mind I have been describing. Through Marcel, Proust places soul

---

*Here lies a translator's nemesis—or fortune. "To give meaning to the commonplace." "To teach clichés the facts of life." "To make a man of a maxim."

error at the crossroads of his novel and develops it as a powerful meta-morphosis of the flaw we knew first as Greek hubris and Christian pride. The *Search* makes a man of its maxims by gradually laying bare several closely joined aspects of Proust's complaint. I shall distinguish here be-tween three: the pathos of thought, the pathos of self, and the paradox of individual consciousness.

If, as I wrote earlier, Proust shows temporality and the imagination working together to infect the present with unreality, then we confront an essential character of thought: our incapacity to conceive and assim-ilate what immediately confronts us. The pathos of thought begins with the realization that thinking always operates at a distance, at one remove. The subjective mind cannot fuse with objective reality. All the examples I have been giving outline an attitude very close to the one Rousseau has Julie express in *La Nouvelle Héloïse:* "In this world the realm of fantasy or of fiction *[chimères]* is the only one worth living in, and the emptiness of human things is so great that, except for Being itself, nothing is beau-tiful but what does not exist." This is an extreme form of our yearning for elsewhere, of our squirming against being where we are. The mood creates around it an aura of anxiety, emanating from the knowledge that our very presence anywhere is a form of intrusion. An added con-sciousness interferes with the goings-on. Whence Marcel's eternal desire to spy on people, to be simultaneously present and absent.

As is often the case when he wants to give particular emphasis to his point, Proust finds a scientific comparison for the pathos of thought. Marcel is reading, hidden in a little shelter or recess in the depths of the garden.

> And didn't my thinking resemble yet another recess in the depths of which I felt caught, even if I wanted to look out at things around me? When I saw an external object, my consciousness that I was seeing it remained between me and it, outlining it with a narrow mental bor-der *[liséré]* that prevented me from ever touching its substance di-rectly; in some way the object volatilized before I could make contact, just as an incandescent body approaching something moist never

reaches moisture because of the zone of evaporation that always pre-
cedes such a body. (I 84/i 115)

Mere awareness volatilizes what it seeks and hampers its own functioning. The most reflective of us are endowed with this antithesis of the
Midas touch; it turns the things we want, or want to know, into dross. In
the sphere of love, Stendhal gave a name to the common and distressing
weakness that renders a man sexually incapable of doing precisely what
he most desires to do. *Fiasco,* in any language, can no longer mean just
a jug of wine. But Proust felt fiasco writ very large. He comprehended
a greater disaster: not only that familiarity breeds contempt but also that
merely to think something diminishes the dimensions of its reality. Imag-
ining impedes realization. It is impossible to be present at the coronation
of one's own happiness: recall Marcel kissing Albertine. No wonder
Proust spent his years writing his way out from under the burden of
being alive, and of being aware of being alive. For our culture, Faust represents this first pathos of thought. There is no happiness or repose for
his overactive mind. He strives always for something other and elsewhere and better.

In this perspective of restlessness, Faust's lot looks very similar to
that of Don Juan, who embodies the pathos of self. Both their stories
arise from a perception of life as flawed. We are born into dissatisfaction
with our estate. Society constrains us to limit our behavior to patterns assigned not only by our public role but also by expectations of consistent
character. We are usually barred from acting out all our conflicting feelings and responses. But even without social conventions, our behavior
displays the features of what I have referred to as intermittence. It is beyond our power as humans to be all of ourselves at once. Our finite capacity for existence makes our character successive, dependent on time
to reveal itself in any depth. Impatient with this inability to assume ourselves entire at any point in time, we react by yearning to enter into or
become someone else, to escape the limits of our own body and being.
What Marcel shares with Don Juan is a gnawing dissatisfaction with
himself, compounded by the feeling that he cannot fully possess the per-

sons he desires. The urge for self-transcendence burns a hole in our being without ever attaining its goal: true otherness.

Proust's Narrator comes back many times to the dynamics of this process. He describes it as a consequence of the pathos of thought. The "narrow mental border" that isolates us from the world around us has an effect on our sense of self.

> For even if we have the sensation of being always enveloped in, and surrounded by, our own soul, still it does not seem a fixed and immovable prison; rather do we seem to be borne away with it, and perpetually struggling to break out of it into the world, with constant discouragement when we hear endlessly, all around us, that unvarying sound which is not an echo from without but the resonance of a vibration from within. (I 86/i 119)

We are stuck inside ourselves. Two thousand pages later the narrator has still not found his way out. He says that even a pair of wings and a new respiratory system that would allow us to survive on Mars would not take us out of ourselves so long as we had to use the same senses and our own consciousness. The conclusion has a desperate ring. "The only true voyage, the only Fountain of Youth, would be found not in traveling to strange lands but in having different eyes, in seeing the universe with the eyes of another person, of a hundred others, and seeing the hundred universes each of them sees, which each of them is" (III 258/v 343). The desire of the imagination to outstrip the self is as urgent as it is hopeless. Marcel moves through the world in a kind of tightly enclosed, yet partially transparent, gondola. This confinement, and the intense spiritual and even physical activity it provokes, is what I mean by pathos of self.

My third gloss on the proverb version of Proust's complaint departs only slightly from the other two. Yet it introduces a now familiar concept that may illuminate a key segment of Proust's thinking. It also displays the way our universe seems to fold back on itself when one reaches one of its remotest corners.

When modern physicists began to explore elementary particles of matter, they realized that certain things were happening that ran counter to accepted laws or regularities of determinism. In order to explain these events, Werner Heisenberg formulated the indeterminacy principle. Fully developed, that principle combines two very different sets of phenomena, on an atomic order of magnitude. First, submicroscopic events like the radiation of a specific particle of radium cannot be predicted. Even statistical probabilities can be calculated only for significant quantities of particles. Single particles appear independent of traditional determinism. Second, the impress of energy required for accurate observation (i.e., some equivalent of light on the subject) is in itself sufficient to modify the event under observation. Thus, at the level of atomic magnitudes, we can neither predict nor observe with accuracy.

I would suggest that probers of the human consciousness like Proust reveal a comparable indeterminacy principle that describes processes on the level of individual thought. The disruptions and irregularities of one man's thinking cannot be predicted. General statements about a statistically significant sample of individuals are another matter. Furthermore, observation (including self-observation) close enough to penetrate inside a person's consciousness provokes a disturbance sufficient to vitiate the observation. (See Proust's second answer to the question "Your ideal of earthly happiness?" cited above, page 11.) Mere witnessing modifies the course of human actions. Many authors, from Rousseau to Dostoevski, lead us toward an awareness of this double bind. Proust's exploration of the psyche makes it almost impossible to deny the validity of something like an indeterminacy principle at the level of individual thought. This paradox of consciousness fetters us to a modicum of ignorance about what we might otherwise expect to know best: our kind and ourselves. Proust is describing the condition in the passage quoted on page 88, particularly with the word *liséré*—border, or outline, or margin. He uses it one other time, near the end of the novel, unforgetful of the earlier passage, and now making perfectly clear the double thrust he means to give the word. Uncertainty inheres both in things (contingencies) and in consciousness (perception).

For there exists between us and all beings a border *[liséré]* of contingencies, just as I had understood while reading in Combray that there
is a border of perception which prevents perfect contact between reality and the mind. (III 975/vi 420)

The origins of Proust's complaint reach back to this dark region of
mind where, alone, we face the problems of reality and communication.

The all-pervading self-deprecation and self-doubt that I am calling
Proust's complaint reached an extreme point in Marcel. His paralysis
before his most desired experiences appears ludicrous to the point of
neurosis. He yearns to witness life without intruding his own denatur-
ing presence on it. But Marcel is not alone in his neurosis. And here
hangs a tale, an episode in the history of psychology, which deserves to
be told in full. It highlights, among several eminent nineteenth-century
authors, an interplay of opposed attitudes that finally converges on
Proust. To my knowledge, this sequence has not been brought out before.

In 1904, when he was thirty-three, Proust published in an obscure
journal a laudatory review of a two-volume book in German on John
Ruskin. At the time Proust was occupied with translating Ruskin into
French and struggling to distance himself from Ruskin's powerful mind.
In the review, Proust passionately identifies and describes a "great debate . . . which will eternally divide all sects and schools" (*CSB* 480). He
traces the debate back more than a century to a passage in Goethe's 600-
page, loosely constructed narrative *Wilhelm Meister's Apprenticeship*
(1795). In it, a capable, forthright, well-born woman called Theresa be-
friends Wilhelm and expresses a wish that they confide completely in
each other. She speaks urgently to him about herself and others like her
who seek true companions.

The world is so waste and empty, when we figure only towns and
hills and rivers in it; but to know of someone here and there whom we
accord with, who is living on with us, even in silence—this makes
our globe of earth into a peopled garden. (bk. 7, chap. 5)

This passage about the rewards of genuine friendship and sympathy between two people was translated in 1824 along with the rest of the novel by Thomas Carlyle, barely thirty and still floundering in Scotland, where Emerson visited him in 1833. Emerson's first letter after the visit reached Carlyle in London, where he had just moved. The letter so touched him that he opened his response to Emerson by quoting from memory from the above passage out of his own translation of Goethe. Thus Carlyle acknowledged that Emerson's new friendship now brought a remote part of the world to life for him. Carlyle used quotation marks without mentioning Goethe or *Wilhelm Meister*. Presumably Emerson recognized the source.

The Emerson-Carlyle correspondence was published in 1883 and came into the hands of John Ruskin, a member of Carlyle's circle. Out of the lofty pages by Emerson and Carlyle touching on philosophy and society and literary topics, Ruskin lit upon the above quotation to cite in his autobiographical *Praeterita* (1885). It comes at the end of a lyric chapter, "Le Col de la Faucille" ("Sickle Pass"), which describes in detail an 1835 carriage journey from Dijon to Geneva. One of its last stages brought the sixteen-year-old Ruskin and his parents to the ridge line of the Jura Mountains. From that high pass, he could suddenly see opening out before him "the whole lake of Geneva and the chain of the Alps along a hundred miles of horizon." Ruskin makes it sound like Moses coming upon the Promised Land. And he explains that the happiness and delight provoked in him by mountainous landscapes are "impersonal" compared with the feelings of others.

Just here, without transition, the sixty-five-year-old Ruskin, remembering his youth, quotes the above passage from the Emerson-Carlyle correspondence and attributes the words, not to Goethe, but to "my master"—namely, Carlyle. One can hear Ruskin's growl. Ruskin now squares off for a full-page encounter with his master's gregariousness. The passage reveals the springs of Ruskin's temperament.

My training, as perhaps the reader has enough perceived, produced in me the precisely opposite sentiment. *My* times of happiness had al-

ways been when *nobody* was thinking of me. . . . [T]hat the rest of the
world was waste to [Carlyle] unless he had admirers in it, is a sorry
state of sentiment enough; and I am somewhat tempted, for once, to
admire the exactly opposite temper of my own solitude. My entire delight was in observing without myself being noticed—if I could have
been invisible, all the better. I was absolutely interested in men and
their ways, as I was interested in marmots and chamois, in tomtits
and trout. If only they would stay still and let me look at them, and
not get into their holes and up their heights. This was the essential love
of Nature in me, this the root of all that I have usefully become, and
the light of all that I have rightly learned. *(Praeterita, 1:9)*

Ruskin makes a startling association between disinterested, near-
scientific observation, aesthetic voyeurism, and social benefit. The in-
tersubjective communication yearned for by Goethe's Theresa and by
Carlyle, if it were truly possible, would impede Ruskin's objective pursuit of natural phenomena. Ruskin's combination in this chapter of travel
account, nature description, and moral argument makes it a major declaration of his aesthetic philosophy. He did not go unheard.

The German book on Ruskin by Charlotte Broicher juxtaposes the
two opposed passages by Goethe and Ruskin in a chapter entitled
"Personal-Impersonal," and then passes on to the question of the influence of landscape on authors. But in reviewing the Broicher book,
Proust seized on the two quotations as the center of his discussion. Not
only do they lay out the terms of a "great debate"; they distinguish "the
only two great families of mind *[esprit]*" *(CSB* 481). Some temperaments seek human friendship to bring the world to life, to personalize
and familiarize distant places. Other temperaments value precisely the
distance and impersonality of foreign places and experiences.

Proust's response to the debate does not palter. He writes that Goethe
in *Wilhelm Meister,* Emerson in *Representative Men,* and Carlyle in *Heroes, Hero Worship and the Heroic in History* have limited themselves to
human greatness, whereas nature has larger dimensions than the human.
Then Proust's verdict.

In comparison with the all too human eighteenth century, which de-poeticizes the world by filling it with people and deprives it of mys-tery by anthropomorphizing it, it seems to us that Ruskin is right. And, by not having everywhere a friend "whom we accord with," he has discovered the inspiration afforded only by solitude. (*CSB* 480)

Anyone who has read into the second of Proust's volumes knows how stern he is in portraying all social exchange and friendship as a dis-traction from our true self found in solitary meditation. Proust rein-forces this attitude in other pages he wrote about Ruskin during the same period. Here he welcomes as true "conversation" only the exchange we carry on with the great minds of the past by reading their books (*CSB* 173–78). Does Proust capitulate completely to Ruskin's reclusiveness and voyeurism as antidotes to his own soul error and self-deprecation?*

Before I answer that question, let me point out that this great debate identified by Proust at the opening of the twentieth century between per-sonal sociability and impersonal solitude parallels a major division of minds that has taken shape a century later. The new division concerns our attitude toward the environment, toward the nature of nature. An-thropocentrists present nature as containing human beings and serving our interests; ecocentrists present human beings as destructive of na-ture and needing restraints on our cultural behavior. Thoreau's *Walden* describes and enacts (without resolving it) the struggle between socia-bility and solitude, between culture and nature. The "hard bottom" of reality Thoreau seeks with his Realometer lies in both domains; yet he

---

*Ruskin's most extreme expression of aesthetic distance casts a chill: "Does a man die at your feet—your business is not to help him, but to note the color of his lips" (Library Edition, 6:388). Proust probably knew this passage, as well as its equivalent in Zola's naturalistic fiction. In Chapter 10 of *The Masterpiece* (1885), the obsessive painter Claude Lantier witnesses the death of his nine-year-old son and briefly shares his wife's sobbing grief. Then he "gave way, fetched out a small canvas, and set to work on a study of the dead child . . . work soon dried his eyes and steadied his hand." In five hours of uninterrupted painting, Lantier created a true masterpiece. Total observation excludes human feelings.

appears to favor solitariness in nature and living lightly on the land. A strong Thoreauvian strain runs through Proust, even though he turned only rarely to nature for communion and consolation. And the division of minds he discerned between Goethe-Carlyle and Ruskin has survived transformed in our year-2000 debates over the manipulation of our physical, biological, and genetic environment.

Proust was barely thirty when he joined Ruskin in declaring the antisocial, voyeuristic, solitary doctrine I have just described. It never disappears from Proust's writing, though it takes a distinctly comic turn at some points (e.g., Marcel's introduction to Albertine, I 870–76/ii 613–22). But Marcel's spontaneous fascination with other people and with other social worlds rounds the sharp edges of his philosophical and moral misanthropy. He describes a means of indirect communication with other people through art (see Chapter VI). The final pages explicitly return to the opposition between solitude and society (III 918/vi 332–33) and imply that "in a new life" they may become compatible. Though that possibility is severely undermined by the following costume ball scene, the reconciliation has been held out as an ideal. The near-fanaticism with which Proust seconds Ruskin's antisocialism subsides in later years and in later portions of his novel into a greater tolerance for other people. His aloofness struggled with his warm heart. The *Search* records the slow trajectory of that shift.

Marcel's efforts to break out of the confinements of self have already been described in terms of social climbing, love, and art. Those three false leads throw him back even more desperately on himself. He is left with few resources, one of which we hear about very early in the *Search*. "Habit! that skillful arranger" (I 8/i 8). As the novel opens, and repeatedly thereafter, Marcel imagines his life as a series of bedrooms to which he becomes accustomed. Their familiarity as places sustains his identity as a person. The accomplishment of life's major tasks, the Narrator tells us, relies more on habit than on "momentary transports" (I 93/i 128). It also provides our security, for habit "drapes over things the guise of familiarity rather than showing their true being, which would frighten us" (II 764/iv 221). Marcel's psychic survival under the curse of soul error depends on the defense of habit, which "regulates the economy of our nervous system" (III 918/vi 333); but it is survival on a low level of being and happiness. Marcel clings to routine and blesses the comforts of the familiar even while another part of his mind knows that he is missing the truths and satisfactions he seeks from life.

The Narrator's presiding presence in the novel embodies a different response to the paradoxes of consciousness and self. (Marcel gradually approaches this attitude, which is more flexible and rewarding than his reliance on habit.) It is the opposite of intolerance and defiance of those inward failings in an effort to overcome them. In seeking to transcend their humanity, Faust and Don Juan aimed at glory and immortality as ambitiously as any pharaoh or world conqueror. Yet their aspirations to divinity by means of surpassing the human condition contain the seeds of a tragic fall.

What Proust portrays in the Narrator is a more direct and modest attitude toward mortality. The descriptions of consciousness as rarely whole and beset by impossible desires for otherness show how deeply flawed life is. The *Search* as a whole seeks not to transcend that condition but to encompass it. *Intermittence* is the guiding principle. The action transpires by lingering seasons and stages. The book becomes oceanic in scale in order to contain the changing weathers and tides and crosscurrents of a long voyage. There is no synthesis, no higher calculus to which these manifold cycles can be reduced. Intermittence describes a sequence of variations without prescribing their course or regularity. Correspondingly, since we cannot assume all parts of our character at a particular moment or grasp the full significance of our experience as it occurs, it is wise to recognize and tolerate this temporal aspect of our humanity. To oppose it is folly. As a basic insight into the pulse of life, intermittence means that Marcel gradually learns to bear and reflect upon fluctuations of self and experience through periods of long duration. He speaks occasionally and misleadingly of general laws, but he lives with, and through, vividly alternating particulars. The same applies to the reader following the narrative. In letters to two prospective editors in 1912, Proust proposed a general title for his unpublished novel: "The Heart's Intermittences." He would have done well to keep it.

Without shuffling off the tribulations of soul error, we have reached a universe of sympathy and understanding far removed from the fanaticism that propels tragedy. In Proust's universe, where everything connects, the next observation should seem natural. "The infirmity in my nature" that convinces Marcel he is always a wet blanket and "the narrow mental border" that intervenes between his subjective perceptions and the objective world he longs to reach are extensions of the comic vision. Consciousness itself partakes of the comic. Marcel, watched patiently by the Narrator, stumbles over his mortality both when he ventures out into society, or tries to kiss a girl, and in the innermost workings of his thought. "Intermittence," an important life principle for Proust, links the conflicting segments of his life and allows him, in their disappearances, a foretaste of death. Fully understood as part of our lot, Proust's complaint leads not to despair but to a gentle smile at the vagaries of human persons and at the time it takes us to recognize ourselves for what we are.

V

PROUST'S BINOCULARS

Memory and Recognition

Optics and Vision

O UT OF THE VASTNESS OF HIS LITERARY WISDOM AND THE
extensiveness of his literary work, Proust himself made most of
the relevant comments on his own writings. Like the Bible, *A la recherche
du temps perdu* embodies its own sources, myths, and criticism. Like an
archaeological site, the novel has come to stand for a state of civilization.
Yet Proust's excavation of his particular world through the artistic
process became so rich in detail that we often fail to discern what he was
digging for and what he found. Furthermore, what he writes impinges
upon our consciousness of ourselves as human beings faced with the
appalling responsibility of living our lives. Challenged both to understand and to act accordingly, we tend to neglect his true meaning for pe-
ripheral and exotic parts of his work.

After the comic vision and the perverseness of his personal "complaint," the surest entry into Proust's country is suggested by one of his
most celebrated passages on style. It concludes, ". . . truth will begin only
when the writer . . . comparing similar qualities in two sensations, makes
their essential nature stand out clearly by joining them, in order to re-

move them from the contingencies of time, in a metaphor" (III 889/vi 289–90). Metaphor here means all types of imagery. The variety and power and significance of Proust's images have been widely studied. The portions of the world he invoked most frequently to yield comparisons are the realm of art and the realm of science. The two great illusory values in the book, the sentiment of love and the prestige of aristocracy, crystallize and dissolve in a solution of images based on music and painting; the great transformations of social upheaval and old age at the end are set before us in terms of zoology. And like Homer, Proust is full of images of eating and culinary enjoyment, as if the surest way of knowing a thing is to eat it, or at least to pick it up and smell it. Some of the novel's most quoted passages celebrate sounds, often isolated from sight—street noises heard from bed, the hidden insinuations of the human voice. Yet there is a further class of images, partaking of both art and science, which gradually reveals itself as significant in a particular manner. I refer to optical images.

The first objects distinct from the conscious *I* in the *Search* appear in the second sentence: Marcel's candle and his eyes. On the following page his reveries on the verge of sleep are condensed into the image of "the kaleidoscope of darkness"; six pages later the first familiar object identified and described out of his childhood world of Combray turns out to be a magic lantern or slide projector; it entertains Marcel by transforming his bedroom into a series of legendary and historical scenes. This strand of imagery, linking not so much things seen as particular transformations or modes of vision, never slackens through three thousand pages of text. Thus we should reach the final figure in the book prepared to understand its composite meaning. The "stilts" on which a man sways dizzily in old age represent not only the precariousness of his life and the awkwardness of his movements but also the perspective of his mind, the lofty vantage point from which he views the world. The point is worth belaboring. Proust drew on an incredibly rich repertory of metaphors. But it is principally through the science and the art of *optics* that he beholds and depicts the world. Truth—and Proust believed in it—is a miracle of vision.

I shall now devote several pages to surveying Proust's visual or optic figures. I do so because they illuminate the complexities and refinements of "seeing" and also because they assemble evidence for a hypothesis about Proust's mental grasp of the world around him—his epistemology.

The simplest optical imagery results from the particular attention Proust pays to visual and light effects, most of them in nature, a few of them associated with art. The description in the early pages of the novel of the setting sun lighting only the upper portion of the steeple of Saint-Hilaire (I 64/i 87) prepares the way for a similar view of obliquely illuminated trees in the last volume. The stained-glass windows of the same church seem to come to life in the play of sunlight—or perhaps it is only the movement of Marcel's glance (I 59–60/i 80). At the sea resort of Balbec, the beauty and fascination of the ocean consists in the "diversity of its lighting" (I 673/ii 342). Marcel speaks of the room of his friend Saint-Loup in Doncières as an "optical center" (II 81/iii 101) because of its excellent view of a hillside. The range of sensations afforded by the sight of Venice suggests the idea of an "optical pedal" (II 146/iii 191). In his imagination Marcel sees the row of holy days at Easter as if touched by a special light (II 143/iii 187–88). Less through lengthy description than through vivid highlighting, Marcel's world is rendered visually.

The further one advances into the work, the richer the optical imagery becomes. To refine and intensify the visual effects in nature, Proust unlimbers a whole set of optical instruments to accompany the kaleidoscope and magic-lantern figures of the opening pages, often reused. The magic aura of Balbec lingers in Marcel's mind as if he could see it "in the magnifying lens of one of those fountain pens for sale at beach resorts" (I 389/i 554). The monocle, described at length in all its comic varieties, becomes one of the principal attributes of a whole set of characters among the nobility (I 326–27, 729, III 953, 984/i 463–65, ii 421, vi 384–85, 434). At the crucial moment of the scene in which Marcel kisses Albertine, Proust abruptly veers off into what appears to be a digression on "the latest applications of photography" that reveal the face of the earth in new perspective. Yet he is really closing in on his subject: only photography "can, to so great a degree as a kiss, summon forth out of what we may believe to be the definite aspect of a thing the hundred other things which it also is, for each one is related to a perspective no less legitimate" (II 365/iii 499). The same photographic imagery and vocabulary give an intensely visual cast to the scene of Marcel's walking in on his grandmother when she does not expect him and suddenly beholding her as an old woman, a stranger whom he does not recognize (II 140–41/iii 183–84). And it is for his grandmother that the act of being photographed by Saint-Loup assumes momentous proportions (I 786–87, II 776–77/ii 500–502, iv 238–39). In the last volume, the comparison of a writer seeking psychological laws to a surgeon seeking the seat of a disease condenses into an optical image of the artist who "X-rays" what he sees (III 719/vi 40).

A further set of optical images also effects changes in perspective or point of view, but without the use of an optical instrument other than our own consciousness—the most sensitive of all. Marcel speaks of "the general laws which govern perspective in the imagination" (II 235 /iii 317). In the opening volume the key incident associated with the steeples of Martinville rests on the visual experience of Marcel's seeing from a moving carriage three church steeples in rapidly shifting perspective. The painter Elstir exploits the same effect of disturbed or confused vision: "The attempt to show things not as he knew they were but according to these optical illusions out of which our primary vision is made, led him . . . to illuminate certain of these laws of perspective" (I 838, cf. II 419 /ii 570, cf. iii 574). One of the best passages to illustrate the optical illusion of our perception of the world comes at the very end of Swann's protracted and agonizing love affair with Odette. He sees her for the last time in a dream that ends with the tolling of a bell and the spectacle of a city in flames. Swann's servant wakes him, saying it is eight o'clock and the barber has arrived. "But these words, penetrating into the depths of sleep where Swann was plunged, had reached his consciousness only after undergoing that deviation which makes a ray of light appear under water as a sun, just as a moment before the sound of the bell, in taking on in the depths the sonority of a curfew, had given birth to the incident of the fire" (I 380/i 541). This passage, coming just as Swann begins to recover from his love in the closing pages of the section, presents itself as a figure not only for his dream but for the entire love affair in which he was submerged as in a new medium. Every sensation penetrated his consciousness on a bias. More even than the dream, his love has been an optical illusion to which he has devoted several years of his life.

It is not merely the number and vividness of these optical images that indicate their importance in Proust's work. They occur at the most strategic places and illuminate values central to the development of the action. The social ordering of the novel will bring this out most readily. At first the social classes appear to Marcel and to the reader as clearly defined layers; and, of necessity, perception from one level to the next, or to a level several times removed, entails severe refraction and distortion. Marcel, looking up toward the higher circles, misjudges everyone in the beginning. This distortion in social depth perception is described occurring in the opposite direction in the scene where the Princesse de Luxembourg, from the altitude of her nobility, miscalculates the distance between herself and Marcel and his grandmother. (See page 62.) "And, even, in her desire not to appear to hold forth from a sphere superior to ours, she had miscalculated the distance, for, by an error in adjustment, her looks were filled with so great a kindness that I foresaw the moment when she would pet us like two lovable animals who had stretched out our necks toward her through the grillwork at the Jardin d'Acclimatation" (I 699/ii 379).

This miscalculation of station is brief and trivial compared with the complex stages of Marcel's attitude toward the Guermantes. Out of his youthful admiration for the Duchesse de Guermantes—a sentiment projected in him like a "magic-lantern slide and a stained-glass window" (II 11/iii 3)—grows the "artificial enlargement" (II 568/iii 780) of his image of that whole clan. It engulfs him. Gradually these simple images of distorted perception yield to figures that contain an expression of social mobility—above all, the famous "social kaleidoscope" (II 190, III

893/iii 252, vi 296). The social levels lose their hierarchy, and by the end we lose sight even of the two *côtés* whose originally opposed perspectives are fragmented and crossed in both social and subjective upheaval.

The individual order of love suffers, or benefits, from comparable distortions, as has already been brought out in the passage on Swann's dream. Having spoken in his preface to Ruskin's *Le Sésame et les Iys* of "the optics of minds" (*CSB* 177), which prevents us from absorbing knowledge from others, Proust goes on to write of the "infra-red" by which Marcel perceives Gilberte's secret qualities (I 416/i 591) and of "those two equally distorting optics" (I 587/ii 221) of his love for her that he could not reconcile. Finally comes this description of the women we love: "Those women are a product of our temperament, an image, a reversed projection, a 'negative' of our sensibility" (I 894/ii 647). Even more than love, jealousy is victimized by twisted perspective, and Marcel wonders "by what optical illusion" (III 190/v 248) he missed seeing some minor detail about Albertine, "for the world of stars is less difficult to know than the real actions of people." And just as we witness two different versions of Rachel, as seen by her lover Saint-Loup and by the indifferent Marcel, we are finally offered two different versions of Albertine, as seen by the same two men with their roles reversed. Saint-Loup cannot believe that the photograph Marcel shows him is of the girl he has been talking about. The whole passage turns on the faculty of sight. After an inevitable astronomical reference to the illusory location of the sun, we read, "So difference in optic extends not only to people's physical appearance but to their character, and to their individual importance" (III 439/v 591).

There was a time when Proust, like the Romantics, believed that the eyes of lovers could pierce material obstacles. In his earliest writings, characters look deep into one another's eyes in order to see the soul within. The mysterious attraction of the Duchesse de Guermantes resides ultimately in her *regard*, carefully described both in the church at Combray and in her *baignoire* at the Opéra. But the eye loses its powers of revelation for Marcel, and neither Albertine nor Charlus is capable of looking at anyone directly. Before the shiftiness of their look, Marcel is thrown back upon an inner optics, an investigation of subjective states.

Sleep, memory, social status, love, personal identity—these are basic areas of refraction and illusion, and Proust allows his optical imagery to crystallize around these crucial mental operations. Rather than accumulating further examples of how Proust proceeds in these cases, I shall quote one extended passage to indicate the central role of optical imagery as he used it, and the extent to which he adapts it to both social and subjective spheres. Even before attending his first important social gathering, the *matinée chez* Mme de Villeparisis, Marcel has been amazed by the unreliability of our relations with people and by the "mobility" of their opinion of us. He learns now that the Marquis de Norpois, a distinguished ex-embassador and friend of his father's, who has always appeared to have a benevolent attitude toward Marcel, has called him in public a "semi-hysterical flatterer." I quote the following paragraph in its entirety:

> I have recorded a long way back my stupefaction at the discovery that a friend of my father, such as M. de Norpois was, could have expressed himself thus in speaking of me. I was even more astonished to learn that my emotion on that evening long ago when I had asked him about Mme Swann and Gilberte was known to the Princesse de Guermantes, whom I imagined never to have heard of my existence. Each of our actions, our words, our attitudes is cut off from the "world," from the people who have not directly perceived it, by a medium the permeability of which is of infinite variation and remains unknown to ourselves; having learned by experience that some important utterance which we eagerly hoped would be disseminated (such as those enthusiastic speeches which I used at one time to make to all comers and on every occasion on the subject of Mme Swann) has found itself, often simply on account of our anxiety, immediately hidden under a bushel, how immeasurably less do we suppose that some tiny word, which we ourselves have forgotten, or else a word never uttered by us but formed along the way by the imperfect refraction of a

different word, can be transported unimpeded by any obstacle to infinite distances—in the present instance to the Princesse de Guermantes—and succeed in entertaining at our expense the banquet of the gods. What we actually recall of our conduct remains unknown to our nearest neighbour; what we have forgotten that we ever said, or indeed what we never did say, flies off to provoke hilarity even in another planet, and the image that other people form of our actions and behaviour is no more like our image of ourselves than a spoiled copy, in which, at one point, for a black line, we find an empty gap, and for a blank space an unaccountable contour, is like an original drawing. It may be, however, that what has not been drawn is some non-existent feature which we behold merely out of self-esteem, and that what seems to us added is indeed a part of ourselves, but so essential a part as to have escaped our notice. So that this strange print which seems to us to have so little resemblance to ourselves bears sometimes the same stamp of truth, scarcely flattering, indeed, but profound and useful, as a photograph taken by X-rays. Not that this is any reason why we should recognise ourselves in it. A man who is in the habit of smiling in the glass at his handsome face and stalwart figure, if you show him their x-ray photograph, will have, face to face with that rosary of bones labelled as the image of himself, the same suspicion of error as the visitor to an art gallery who, on coming to the portrait of a girl, reads in his catalogue: "Dromedary Resting." Later on, I became aware of this discrepancy between our portraits, according to whether it was our own hand or another that drew them, as it applies to others than myself, people living placidly in the midst of a collection of photographs which they had taken of themselves, while all around them grinned another set of frightful portraits, invisible to them as a rule, but plunging them into stupor if anyone pointed to the portraits with the words: "This is you." (II 271–72/iii 367–69)

This is vintage Proust, blending the profound and the grotesque, the personal and the social. The progression from general optical laws in a permeable medium to x-ray photography corresponds to the shift in theme from the confounding in society of acts, words, and attitudes

(summed up in an astronomical image), to our inability to confront ourselves (expressed by the flimsy likeness of snapshots). The transition is
made perfectly nakedly in the sentence beginning, "It may be . . . ,"
which says that we can be mistaken as much about ourselves as about
others.

Reserving other aspects of this paragraph for later consideration, I
shall emphasize here that its underlying theme of the inaccuracy of perception furnishes us with the first clue to the significance of all this optical imagery. The science of optics forever shows the *errors* of our
vision, the distortions from accuracy, deviations from the straight line,
reductions in point of view and perspective. Error establishes itself as
one persistent principle of Proust's universe, error in both social and
subjective domains. (See Appendix I, page 251.)

Within this skewed world Marcel erects and clings to three structures
that offer temporary habitation to the questing mind. There is the refuge
of habit, which allows us to adjust to new surroundings and new people
by becoming blind to all but the parts we can put to our own personal use;
the refuge of laws, which define and explain the mystery of human behavior without penetrating it; and the refuge of the comic, which perceives the ridiculousness of both the above procedures and enjoys that
absurdity without surpassing it. All three afford us limited security in
pursuing our daily lives. It is the role of optics and its accompanying errors and distortions to project uncertainty into these three domains.
There is no sure refuge.

Proust's optical imagery reveals considerable scientific knowledge
and represents a unifying element in his style. It will also afford us an approach to a basic question about how Proust portrayed Marcel's frame
of mind and his experience of the world around him.

Happiness and Memory

Does Marcel have a happy childhood? Many readers tend to keep in
mind the anguish he feels when deprived of his mother's good-night
kiss, the neurasthenic excitability that prevents him from visiting Italy,

and the frustration he encounters during his periods of love for Gilberte. Nevertheless, Proust portrays the prevailing mood of Marcel's early years as one of happiness and pleasure. Most of the time, Marcel's mother lavishes attention on him, and he develops a deeply sensuous response to the world around him—to objects and landscapes and buildings, to ritual family activities such as eating and walking, to people like the servant Françoise and Aunt Léonie whose familiarity never deprives them of mystery, and to the magical rewards of reading. It is important for the reader to acknowledge Marcel's capacity for *pleasure,* a word Proust uses often. Up to the middle of the novel, when disillusionment about aristocracy and love and his own vocation overtakes him, and when he loses faith in the reality of appearances, Marcel has a happy childhood and youth. Through his wonderfully responsive sensibility, as alert to comedy as to treachery, the world comes vividly alive. The first fifteen hundred pages of the *Search* rarely slacken their flow toward the promises of lived experience.

That flow toward life follows a rough sequence of two steps, which the optical figures will help us to perceive.

At the start, the most vivid segment of Marcel's world is made up of *impressions.* These isolated perceptions of the natural world discover an indefinable yet almost palpable aura of significance in the ordinary objects and places that provoke them. Such moments bring Marcel a feeling of happiness and a heightened sense of reality; they seem to ask for some kind of response. Yet the response usually languishes, and the moment passes. It is worth looking at a specific instance of these impressions.

Marcel, not yet in his teens, is taking one of his customary autumn walks "out Swann's way" after a morning's reading. Both the landscape and the windy weather seem to answer his need for animated motion after a sedentary morning. Every feeling in him seeks immediate release. The whole tradition of the promenade, from Petrarch to Rousseau to Rimbaud, hovers over this carefully constructed page. Proust frames the sensuous description of the scene between accounts of two human discrepancies: the inadequacy of our actions and words to express our feelings, and the contrast between the feelings of different people reacting to the same situation. Those discrepancies cause frustration in Marcel without diminishing his pleasure in the incident. For he perceives a delicate pattern of elements that gives the scene, for his sensibility and possibly for no one else's, a wondrous beauty. In the first two sentences the Narrator is speaking; then he dissolves into Marcel in a clear instance of the double *I*. I quote the scene in full:

When we attempt to translate our feelings into expression, we usually do no more than relieve ourselves of them by letting them escape in an indistinct form which tells us nothing about them. When I try to reckon up all that I owe to the "Méséglise way," all the humble discoveries of which it was either the accidental setting or the direct inspiration and cause, I am reminded that it was that same autumn, on one of those walks near the bushy slope that overlooks Montjouvain, that I was struck for the first time by this lack of harmony between our impressions and the way we usually express them. After an hour of rain and wind, against which I had put up a brisk fight, as I came to the edge of the Montjouvain pond and reached a little hut, roofed with tiles, in which M. Vinteuil's gardener kept his tools, the sun shone out again, and its golden rays, washed clean by the shower, gleamed once more in the sky, on the trees, on the wall of the hut, and on the still wet tiles of the roof, where a hen was walking along the ridge. The wind pulled out sideways the wild grass that grew in the wall as well as the chicken's downy feathers, both of which floated out to their full length in the wind's breath with the unresisting submissiveness of flimsy lifeless things. The tiled roof showed up in the pond, whose reflections were now clear again in the sunlight, as a pink marbled area such as I had never noticed before. And, when I saw both on the water and on the surface of the wall a pale smile answering the smile in the sky, I cried aloud in my enthusiasm and excitement while brandishing my furled umbrella, "Gosh, gosh, gosh, gosh."

And it was at that moment too—thanks to a peasant who happened by, apparently in a bad enough humor already, but who became even

more so when he nearly got a poke in the face from my umbrella, and
who barely replied to my "What a fine day! Good to be out walking!"—that I learned that identical emotions do not arise in the hearts
of all men simultaneously according to a pre-established order. (I
155/i 218–19)

Movement, light, and texture compose a landscape as unified as a
Corot painting. Marcel recognizes it as something exceptional, yet ineffable. The Narrator describes it in an accelerating paragraph that seeks
to follow the rapid motion of Marcel's glance. The dynamics of light and
wind are forceful enough to connect all elements of roof, pond, and sky
within Marcel's sensibility as a set of Baudelairean correspondences. For
a moment the "border" of consciousness is lifted. Then come the umbrella flourishing and the childish exclamations to a passing peasant. Inevitably, the Narrator brings out the comic side of Marcel's frustration
before such great beauty. All he can say is "Zut!"

After all this, Marcel soon turns away from the scene as if it were an
unattached detail, a fortuitous moment of delight, transitory because it
fits into no established sequence and leads nowhere. Not long after, the
Narrator explains.

It was certainly not impressions of this kind that could restore the
hope I had lost of succeeding one day in becoming an author and a
poet, for each of them was associated with some material object devoid of any intellectual value, and suggesting no abstract truth. (I
179/i 252)

Though such occasional impressions provoke great happiness in him,
Marcel turns his back on them. He is grievously mistaken. Only years
later does he realize that they are the very stuff of reality and have prepared him for a later stage of perception, designated in the novel by four
interchangeable terms: involuntary memory, the *moments bienheureux*,
reminiscences (with Platonic overtones), and resurrections (with Christian overtones).

This heightened stage of perception builds on earlier impressions. When one reencounters some part of the sensation that provoked the original impression, the new sensation may (if there has elapsed an adequate interval for forgetting) trigger a *moment bienheureux*, a reminiscence, a twinge of pleasure. One may or may not identify the original impression. When one does, the pleasure is enhanced. We are talking about a close relative of déjà vu, an unexpected short circuit between past and present in our apparatus of perception. In the madeleine episode near the opening of the *Search,* a specific taste-odor summons up out of the distant past a corresponding sensation that sparks across the interval and brings back with it the Narrator's past in Combray in all its "form and solidity" (I 48/i 64). This resurrection starts the forward movement of the narrative.

At the end of the novel, resurrections are assigned the even greater power of affording us a glimpse of "the essences of things" (III 871/vi 262). Without being explicit, Proust implies that the mental functions that permit reminiscences to occur exist at least potentially in all human beings, and that we have probably experienced them without paying much attention. They represent a rudimentary form of true spiritual experience, without reliance on a divine being or on the miraculous. They signify the existence of a realm of awareness beyond the ordinary. Marcel's resurrections are usually accompanied by his exhortations to himself to "go beyond the moment," to "get to the bottom of" *[approfondir]* the experience. From his friends' accounts we know that Proust's own reminiscences were so acute as to constitute a form of hyperaesthesia. By attributing this condition to Marcel, he made it crucial to the novel.

The most condensed explanation of involuntary memory can be found in a scene where the process fails to occur. Late in life Marcel revisits Combray, where he might expect a torrent of reminiscences. He is disappointed.

I found the Vivonne narrow and ugly along the towpath. Not that I noticed particularly great inaccuracies in what I remembered. But, separated by a whole lifetime from places I now happened to pass through again, there did not exist between them and me that contiguity out of which is born, before one even notices it, the immediate, delicious, and total flaming up *[déflagration]* of memory. (III 692/vi 2)*

Though he switches terms disconcertingly, Proust here does not depart from the principles by which Hume and, after him, Bergson deal with the association of sensation and perception. Hume recognized the relations of *contiguity* (in the temporal aspects of simultaneity or close succession and in the spatial aspect of proximity) and *similarity,* and devoted much of his career to an attempt to reduce a third principle, causation, to a special case of succession. In his second book, *Matter and Memory* (1896), Bergson picks up Hume's terms. He even puts forward a capsule version of Gestalt theory by insisting that our first perceptions come in "an aggregate of contiguous parts" and that the primary mental process is one of dissociation from "the undivided unity of perception." Usually our psychological life oscillates between similarity and contiguity. Yet in one key passage Bergson suggests that the two processes may work together. ". . . once the memory trace has been connected [by similarity] to the present perception, a multitude of events contiguous to the memory trace immediately attach themselves to the perception."

In passages of phenomenological description whose ideas and introspective tone anticipate Proust's writing, Bergson argues that pure or spontaneous memory is "independent of our will." Both men describe how a tiny link of similarity between present and past can provoke a sudden spreading of recollection to all contiguous elements—Proust's

---

*As we know from several other passages on successful resurrections, what Proust refers to in the above passage as "contiguity" really means *similarity* between a material object in the present and one in a past impression. The Vivonne today does not resemble his childhood impression of it. He probably says contiguity here because similarity is felt subjectively as a form of closeness, a near relation.

"deflagration." The power of involuntary memory lies in combining two associative principles.*

Similarity triggers contiguity, and the explosion blasts a whole segment of contiguous past events into the present. The force of this explosion stops Marcel in his tracks and elevates him to a state approaching felicity. He comes back to contingent reality only with great difficulty and reluctance.

The impressions, and the reminiscences that resurrect them years later, resemble privileged shrines in the narrative landscape. Both the psychological intensity they produce and the poetic style in which they are written attest to their special status. The drafts of the novel reveal that Proust conceived most of these passages very early, revised and perfected them through many versions, and placed them carefully in the story. As he states explicitly many times, he found precedent and confirmation for his experiences of memory in a number of his favorite authors: Nerval, Chateaubriand, Baudelaire, George Eliot, Ruskin. Each of them depicts a particular mode and mood by which the present comes into phase with the past.† But the nature of memory in Proust will be

---

*Gérard Genette has written a penetrating article on this subject: "Métonymie chez Proust," *Poétique*, no. 2 (1970). He borrows his terms from the linguist Roman Jakobson, who, in an article on aphasia, equates metaphor with similarity and metonomy with contiguity. By using the rhetorical terms, Genette makes a good case for the hybrid state of Proust's work as both realism and poetry. In order to comprehend the phenomenon of reminiscence in Proust, I find it wise to stay with the philosophical terms.

†The eminent Russian neurologist and psychologist A. R. Luria has written an absorbing study of the vaudeville mnemonist S., who could memorize almost anything and never forget it. Certain aspects of his case seem to relate to Proust's, or at least to the experience of memory Proust projects in the *Search*. S.'s memory was basically nonverbal and highly synaesthetic. Out of professional necessity, S. had developed a technique for remembering items, including words, by distributing them along a kind of mental walk or improvised story. Thus linked, these images "reconstructed themselves whenever he revived the original situation in which something had been registered in his memory." *The Mind of a Mnemonist*, trans. Lynn Solotaroff (New York, 1968), 63. It might almost be a systematized reminiscence. The differences may be even more re-

best illuminated by referring to two philosophers, one ancient and one modern.

Beginning in the *Meno* Plato developed a theory of knowledge based on reminiscence. Its greatest importance was to deny the empirical origin of knowledge from sense experience. True knowledge is understood to mean true beliefs dialectically rooted in the logical reasons for their truth. And those reasons, as the *Meno* demonstrates, are found within us by *remembering*. We may remember from an earlier existence; Plato's first affirmation of the doctrine of the transmigration of souls comes in this dialogue. The theory of Ideas, developed later, is his response to the question of how the soul attains knowledge in the first place. The significant element here is that Plato discredits empirical knowledge or sense observation in favor of the recognition or recollection of logical relationships. Truly to know something means reconciling past and present experience; the soul's bumpy journey through previous lives greatly extends the reservoir of past experience available to our present lives. Proust had studied Plato and was familiar with this nexus of ideas.

I have already mentioned Bergson. *Matter and Memory* appeared with great éclat in 1896, when Proust was twenty-five. Its blend of phenomenological description, scientific attitude, philosophical intent, and lucid style must have been irresistible to a young author who was already absorbed in closely related problems of subjective experience. In his second chapter Bergson spends fifteen pages distinguishing two forms of memory. "The memory of habit" enables us to develop a series of motor responses to present reality and to learn how to cope with our environment. "Pure or spontaneous memory" occurs when a chance event disturbs the

---

vealing. S. developed his memory by long training and careful attention to items given to him to remember. Proust insisted on the primacy of *involuntary* memory and implied that attention upsets the mechanism. Nevertheless, in the course of the novel Marcel develops a kind of negative technique in which successful forgetting serves as the prelude to later retrieval. Marcel has to forget and later remember his grandmother's death in order to feel its reality. He even has to forget his vocation in order to find it. Proust was a mnemonist looking the other way.

equilibrium established by habit and brings back the complete image of a past moment still stamped with "a date and a place." In the third chapter Bergson examines the various ways in which these two forms of memory interpenetrate and tend to fuse in ordinary experience. Despite Proust's statements to the contrary,* the distinction between voluntary and involuntary memories is basic to Bergson's argument. "This spontaneous memory, which no doubt lurks behind acquired or habitual memory, can reveal itself in sudden flashes: but it withdraws at the tiniest movement of voluntary memory" (98). Bergson's patient probing of memory provides an essential complement to the commonly cited "classic" on the subject, F. C. Bartlett's experimentally based *Remembering.*

Furthermore, Bergson makes memory the central principle of his psychology, very nearly the equivalent of Freud's unconscious. Everything seems to depend on the way we deploy the two kinds of memory. The basic processes of adaptation grow out of it, as well as our mental health, our character, and our oscillation between contrasting mental states. Bergson constantly uses ideas and turns of phrase that Proust also favored, even the term "resurrection." What strikes one particularly in *Matter and Memory* is Bergson's strong interest in pure or spontaneous memory. Toward the end he argues that withdrawing attention from life and abandoning oneself to spontaneous memory amounts to the state of dreaming, and "dream in every respect imitates insanity." Bergson keeps a firm hold on the *juste milieu*. But earlier passages do not hide a deep fascination with "the storehouse of memories" and the circumstances that bring them into play.† Proust's denials of Bergson's influence can only be termed disingenuous.

---

*For example, in his 1913 interview with Elie-Joseph Bois (*CSB* 558).

†Bergson occasionally even sounds like Proust. This sentence recalls one of Proust's near the opening of the novel and glows with the same sympathy for certain privileged subjective states. Bergson: "A human being who *dreamed* his life instead of living it would probably thus keep constantly in sight the infinite multitude of details of his past history" (172). Proust: "A sleeping man keeps arrayed in a circle around him the stream of hours, the ordering of years and worlds" (I 5/i 4).

Plato, Bergson, and Proust assemble in the vicinity of the philosophical conviction that a single direct sense perception does not suffice to
furnish right knowledge. Though they describe contrasting ways in
which sense perceptions combine into pairs and patterns, none of them
describes association taking place without the individual's interests and
volition playing a crucial role. Recognition, recollection, binocular vision, stereo reception in time—all these modes characterize our mental
processes. A wholly unique sensation remains incomplete and alien until
associated with another or others. Consciousness in full command of its
powers is double or even multiple—divided between waking and sleep
(as in the opening of the *Search*), between habit and disruption by the unfamiliar (as in many of the middle sections), between past and present
(toward the end). The crucial moments in the *Search* belong to composite states.*

This compound nature of consciousness applies particularly to the
resurrections of involuntary memory, and they, more than other experiences, afford Marcel the rewards of "pleasure" (I 45/i 60) and of "felicity" (III 867/vi 255). What links memory to felicity? Why is Proust

---

*Medical research into brain functioning corroborates these theories. Proust schol-
ars will be fascinated by Dr. Wilder Penfield's report "Some Mechanisms of Consciousness Discovered during Electrical Stimulation of the Brain" (*Proceedings of the
National Academy of Sciences*, January 1958). This eminent neurosurgeon demon-
strated the existence of "a permanent record of the stream of consciousness" in an unmapped area of the brain, which he names the "interpretive cortex."

> No man can recall by voluntary effort such a wealth of detail. . . . Many a patient has
> told me that the experience brought back by the electrode is much more real than re-
> membering. . . .

> In addition to the experiential flash-backs, there is one other type of response. . . .
> When the electrode is applied, the patient has a sudden "feeling" about the present
> situation. . . . It is a signal, for example, that the present situation is familiar, that it
> has been experienced before. Or it is strange, perhaps.

> Dr. Penfield suggests that this interpretive cortex functions in situations like the
> recognition of a friend after long absence. It is all there.

universally identified as the novelist of memory when he writes about so much else as well? Once again, optical imagery will guide us toward the answer.

On leaving a dinner party of the Duchesse de Guermantes in a carriage, Marcel reflects on the boring conversations he has just had at the party. Yet in looking back at them, he experiences a fleeting "exaltation." The sentence that explains his state of mind is crucial. He is speaking of the fresh images in his mind of the evening's events. "I had just slid them into the interior stereoscope by means of which, as soon as we are no longer ourselves, as soon as, endowed with a worldly attitude, we wish to receive our life only from others, we give high relief to what they have said, to what they have done" (II 548/iii 751). At this early stage of his aesthetic education, Marcel has deceived himself about the evening he has just spent and exaggerates its value. The metaphor of the stereoscope to represent the transformations of subjective process takes on meaning far beyond this context. It is increasingly in such optical terms that Proust gave figurative expression to his sense of memory and reality. When Marcel cannot recognize the three trees near Balbec that seem to have particular significance, he wonders if it all could be due to "visual fatigue which made me see them double in time as one sometimes sees double in space" (I 719/ii 407)—an optical illusion of memory. Later, in Balbec, he is attracted by the odor of hawthorn blooms: "I went nearer but my eyes did not know at what adjustment *[cran]* to set their optical mechanism in order to see the flowers at the same time along the hedge and in myself" (II 786n/iv 251n).

Depth, or what is in optics called penetration effect, cannot be found in a single image. The visible world reaches us through a continuous double take based on the stereoscopic principle. Two slightly different versions of the same "object" from our two eyes are combined subjectively with the effect of relief. The binocular nature of human vision is achieved through some of the most delicate adjustments of which our organism is capable.

To perceive depth properly, our eyes are set apart in our heads by a distance that is proportional to our size and our need to judge the distance

of objects in our environment. Two eyes separated by several yards or
several miles would not serve us effectively, for our minds would not be
able to assimilate and collate two views of the world so different from
each other. The interval between our human eyes permits us to register
depths in space on our scale and instantaneously.

Normally, we confine this stereoscopic effect, which gives an impress
of reality in depth to the world around us, to perception in space. Proust
undertakes a transposition of spatial vision into a new dimension. The
accumulation of optical figures in the *Search* gradually transposes our
depth perception from space into time. When we finally reach *Time Regained*,
the last volume, the transplanting has been completed and there
can be no doubt about the privileged nature of involuntary memory. It
allows us not just to see across time but to see time itself.

Proust wrote out of an inner vision increasingly trained on time. As
boldly as Minkowskian geometry, his enormous novel revolutionizes
our sense of "here" and "now." The allusion to Minkowsky, who succeeded in graphing the space-time principle of Einstein's special relativity, has more than casual pertinence. Relativity tells us that no object
by itself has either definable location or measurable velocity. *Two* objects
are required to yield a relative reading, and there is no universal grid like
the ether to give an absolute figure. An object can be described as located
somewhere and as having a certain motion only in reference to what is
around it. And so it is also with memories or experiences. One alone
will disappear under our scrutiny, like a star or a dial stared at too long.
Physiologically and psychologically and metaphysically, "to see" means
to see *with* or *against* or *beside* something. The school of Gestalt psychology has long since developed this simple truth of the relativity of
perception: we grasp things juxtaposed in clusters, framed by one another. It is all too easy to make irresponsible comparisons between Proust
and Einstein. In his letters to the mathematician Camille Vettard, Proust
himself was party to those comparisons. But here we can see the particular respect in which Proust's treatment of memory, as always multiple,
implies a relativity principle in consciousness itself based on an optics of
time.

The equidistance from our eyes of non-identical stereoptican views*
creating the illusion of depth perception provides an analogy for an unexpected realignment of present and past into equidistance in stereologic time—the experience Proust calls a *moment bienheureux* or
resurrection. A second factor governing stereoscopic optics now reveals
its pertinence to Proust's composition. The interval between our mental eyepieces in time, the interval between juxtaposed impressions, must
be in scale to human life so that we can register and collate the temporal
gap. Scale and timing became all-important to Proust.

The chronology of the *Search* is not so intricate as it first appears. (See
the synopsis above, pages 39–45.) After fifty-odd opening pages, which
carefully avoid any relapse into calendar or clock time and take place in
a kind of temporal limbo, the subsequent portions of the novel observe
a reasonably clear chronological sequence. Temporal gaps are specified
and allusions are made to past and future developments with a feeling of
temporal and logical continuity. But as early as the middle of *Within a
Budding Grove*, we run across this parenthesis, like a clue to the wary:
"(our life being to so small a degree chronological, and interjecting so
many anachronisms into the sequence of days)" (I 642/ii 299). As we advance into the central and later portions of the novel, the chronology of
the action, like the ages of the characters, becomes increasingly undefined and ambiguous—in part the result of Proust's perpetual inflation
of the original text, but also the result of a sense of structure that carries

---

*"Stereopticon views" are sturdy eight-inch cards bearing two near-identical pho-
tographic images and designed to fit into a handheld "stereoscope." That device confines the vision of each eye to one image, whose difference from the other corresponds
to the difference in normal binocular vision. Looked at through a stereoscope, and compared with the flatness of an ordinary photograph, a stereoptician view is endowed with
almost magical three-dimensional depth and verisimilitude. One encounters an equally
stunning contrast between looking through a telescope and looking through binoculars.

After Dr. Oliver Wendell Holmes improved the English model, the stereoscope
with its accompanying collection of stereoptician views became, in the latter half of the
nineteenth century, the standard piece of optical equipment for home entertainment.
Only moving pictures would displace it.

all that bulk. Not until the opening pages of *Time Regained* is the chronology finally specified again—by Marcel's three sojourns for "long years" in two mental hospitals and by the advent of war in 1914 (III 723, 751, 755, 854/vi 46, 88, 93, 238). And appropriately it is here that a marginal comment on change of personality in several characters comes to a different conclusion from what we have been told earlier. "Everything is a matter of chronology" (III 737n /vi 68). But "chronology" means something far different now after the several decades covered by the narrative. At the crucial moment of change in perspective at the end, the chronology at stake is a temporal interval rather than a linear progression.

"The new *maison de santé* to which I returned did not cure me any more than the first, and many years passed before I left it. During the train trip I made to return at last to Paris . . ." (III 854/vi 238). With so gentle and imperceptible a movement as this the tide begins to turn. One sentence of transition and, hidden away in it, two words we could easily miss: "many years." But Marcel's career and the approaching resolution of the novel depend on that barely stated temporal span; it corresponds to the spatial gap between our eyes. In order to perceive relief in time, our consciousness must behold, simultaneously, impressions removed from one another by "many years." Proust goes on to define that interval with increasing exactness as the duration of a complete social cycle.

In referring to the unpredictable reception given writers by critics and the public, he states, "Their logomachy renews itself every ten years" (III 893/vi 296). For some observers Proust specifies the same cycle of ten years for an adequate perception of the turnover of society (III 964 /vi 403). Others, whose historical depth perception is weaker, need thirty years (III 965/vi 404). In settling on a median figure, Proust identifies the interval of significant social change with the interval of significant individual change. In both cases a cycle is completed. "For if, in these twenty-year periods, the conglomerates of little coteries fall apart and reform according to the attraction of new stars, themselves destined moreover to move away and return, then also there take place in people's

minds crystallizations and then crumblings followed by new crystallizations" (III 992/vi 446).

Twenty years, one now realizes, is the inner span of Proust's novel—
not from one end to the other (Swann's story reaches back two decades
earlier than Marcel's), but from the midpoint of Marcel's growing up (the
Dreyfus affair, the turn of the century) to the last sequence (approximately 1920). The wider range of thirty years embraces most other portions of action pertaining to Marcel.

This does not mean that if we merely look back twenty years, we
shall automatically have a new perspective on everything, a new vision
of reality. If an image or sensation out of the past is to be truly registered
in the Proustian sense and not merely recollected, it must be summoned
back by a related experience in the present *after a period of absence*. For,
if an image remains constantly present, it becomes familiar, freezes into
habit, and loses its potential effect. The original experience or image
must have been forgotten, completely forgotten, a circumstance that
turns the elapsed years into a true gap. This is Proust's "general law of
memory." True memory or reminiscence surges into being out of its
opposite: *oubli*.

> . . . what a person recalls to us most vividly is precisely what we had
> forgotten, because it was of no importance, and had therefore left in
> full possession of its strength. That is why the better part of our mem-
> ory exists outside ourselves. . . . Outside ourselves, I say; rather within
> ourselves, but hidden from our eyes in an oblivion more or less pro-
> longed. It is thanks to this oblivion alone that we can from time to time
> recover the creature that we were, range ourselves face to face with
> past events as that creature had to face them, suffer afresh because we
> are no longer ourselves but he, and because he loved what leaves us
> now indifferent. (I 643, cf. III 531/ii 300, cf. v 715)

And Proust is again explicit, at the beginning of the final sequence of
recognitions. "Yes, if the remembered image, thanks to forgetting, has
been unable to contract any link, to forge any connection between itself

and the passing moment, if it has remained in place, in its time, if it has
kept its distance, its isolation in the hollow of a valley or at the summit
of a mountain, then it suddenly makes us breathe a fresh air, precisely because it is an air which one has breathed long ago . . . for true paradises
are those which one has lost" (III 870/vi 261). Thanks to forgetting,
then, the image can keep its purity, the singular quality it displays when
set alongside the later image that evokes it. The twenty-year gap must be
one of *oubli*—a blank, a hole in time, represented in Proust's novel by
the undescribed time Marcel spent during three successive sojourns in
mental hospitals. How else could Proust have created such a gap? In
other eras, a hole in time took the form of retirement to a monastery, lan-
guishing in prison, banishment, or a long voyage. Proust chose not so
much physical as mental and psychological separation. Marcel simply
withdraws into an unspecified condition of suspended life. Since he
states explicitly that he never was cured, it is as if he returns to life after
a purely ritual period of waiting in the wings. The *maison de santé* represents the *néant mental* of forgetfulness (I 821/ii 547) in terms of a familiar institution.

We are perfectly justified, then, in saying that Proust-Marcel's phe-
nomenal memory consisted in his capacity to forget in the intervals. "A
man with a good memory," writes Samuel Beckett, "does not remember
anything because he does not forget anything" (*Proust*, 17). Beckett, like
Proust, was alert to the advantages of having a bad memory. Proust admitted to the Princesse Bibesco that "he had staked his life in a game of
qui-perd-gagne [loser takes all]" (*Au bal avec Marcel Proust*, 121), and
the paradox of memory-by-forgetting resembles just such a game.

Once we have become aware of the enormous role of *oubli* in determining the action of Proust's novel, we hold the key to other parts of his
work that show *oubli* in different forms. The most important passages on
sleep in the *Search* (I 821, II 84–91, 981–84/ii 547, iii 104–15, 517–21) describe sleep as a forgetting, a foreshortening of time. It permits the
reawakening of a purified individual who has lost himself and found
himself again. And we are in effect perpetually asleep to most of ourselves until recognition or remembering brings a fragment of us back

from *oubli*. Sleep reproduces daily and in miniature the whole rhythm of life: forgetting and self-recognition, death and resurrection. For *oubli* in the form of sleep places death beside us each night. The *maison de santé* represents an institutionalized, all-devouring form of sleep. And in the special universe of love, *oubli* works in a particularly paradoxical fashion, for to forget a loved one leads both to indifference and to the possibility of renewed desire. Proust marked the following passage "capital" in the unfinished manuscript. "In this particular form *oubli*, though it worked to accustom me to separation from her, still, because it also showed me a kinder and more beautiful Albertine, made me desire her return all the more" (III 461n / v 622).

We have been tracking involuntary memory and the *moments bien-heureux* for a dozen pages. In that perspective, the climax of the novel occurs just as Marcel, now an aging man after a twenty-year interval, returns to the Guermantes mansion for a concert-reception. Three successive resurrections—the uneven cobblestones under his feet, the clink of a spoon on a plate, and the stiffness of a starched napkin on his lips—restore his appetite for life and work by reviving genuine moments from his past. Is this the link between memory and pleasure? But Marcel, now metamorphosing into the Narrator of his own story, insists on seeking further explanation for his exalted state of mind. He is inspired to produce what I would call the most important passage in the novel on memory. Enfolding a real psycho-physiological experience into a poetic-rational elucidation, the passage connects past and present, absence and presence, the functioning of the imagination, and the sensation of existence. Everything I have been saying about stereoscopes and the interplay of two images and the optics of time should now find its place.

Three times in close succession, Marcel says to himself, a past moment has been vividly reborn to him. Then he seeks further.

Merely a moment from the past? Much more than that, perhaps; something which, common to both past and present, is far more essential than either. How many times in the course of my life had reality disappointed me because at the time I was observing it, my imagination,

the only organ with which I could enjoy beauty, was unable to function, by virtue of the inexorable law which decrees that only what is
absent can be imagined. And now suddenly the operation of this harsh
law was neutralized, suspended, by a miraculous expedient of nature
by which a sensation—the sound of the spoon and the hammer, a
similar unevenness of two paving stones—flashes back and forth
[*miroiter*] between the past (which made it possible for imagination to
take pleasure in it) and the present (where the physical stimulus of the
sound and the contact with the stones contributed to the dreams of the
imagination something they usually lack, the idea of existence), and
this subterfuge made it possible for my being to grasp, to isolate, to immobilize for the duration of a lightning flash what it normally never
apprehends, namely, a fragment of time in its pure state. (III 872/vi
263–64)

It's almost a trick, a "subterfuge," that allows Marcel here—and presumably all of us on our own schedule—to have it both ways, to see past
and present together, and to see time in its pure state. At these moments
of reminiscence, we have two probes in time the way we have two feet
on the ground and two eyes watching space. What would otherwise be
a meticulously analytic explanation is suddenly set in motion and
brought to life by the verb *miroiter*—to glisten, to flash back and forth,
to shimmer. The sensation of time becomes iridescent, like a soap bub-
ble, like the plumage of certain birds, like an oil film on water. This enlarged double vision of the world projected in time embodies a parallax
view: it provides a sense of depth resulting from a displacement of the
observer. Marcel's and the Narrator's pleasure and happiness caused by
these resurrections arise from the heightened reality of a world that glis-
tens in time.

Recognitions

We have now presumably reached the ultimate recompense for Marcel's
long wandering in the wilderness of his own life. These resurrections,

these doublings of past and present, lift him to a renewed sense of the vocation that awaits him, of the work of art he has postponed for so long. The great procrastinator has exhausted his excuses. In the glistening of time, he has glimpsed his "true self" (III 873/vi 264).

But let us pause for a moment. We must not completely overlook a number of weaknesses and drawbacks lurking in the *moments bienheureux*. One such moment, the madeleine episode, essentially sets the novel in motion. After that, however, the occurrence of such episodes in Marcel's life falls off in a steep curve. (See Appendix II, page 257.) Only at the very end do they recur in a rush so intense that the aging Marcel is transported into a lengthy meditation and stocktaking. Through two thousand pages, however, involuntary memory has virtually deserted him. Furthermore, these moments occur completely by chance, cannot therefore be chosen or willed, and leave Marcel the mere passive beneficiary of so significant a phenomenon.

Above all, the resurrections are fleeting. In the passage just quoted, a phrase in the next-to-last line—"for the duration of a lightning flash"— serves as counterweight to all the positive words that precede it. On the following page the narrator adds, "This *trompe l'oeil* did not last" (III 873/vi 265). The intense reward of the resurrections is now associated with illusion and deceit. Furthermore, toward the end of the fifty-page meditation on reminiscences, the fugitive pleasure and happiness they offer have been challenged by a deeply opposed experience. *Suffering*, the Narrator implies, may lead to a healthier and more lasting moral condition than pleasure can provide (III 897, 905–10/vi 300, 308–20).

Nevertheless, in spite of these drawbacks and warnings, Marcel arrives at the moment of entering the Guermantes salon all pumped up with confidence inspired by his reflection on the resurrections. They will presumably put an end to the prolonged "stoppage" *(arrêt)* (III 918/vi 332) of his career. In a final summoning of confederates in the cause of involuntary memory, Marcel invokes the names of Chateaubriand, Nerval, and Baudelaire. They too put their faith in reminiscences. He steps forward "without hesitation."

And now comes the great fall. Marcel collapses into a dark pit of disorientation and uncertainty. In what the Narrator calls *"un coup de théâtre"* (a dramatic reversal) (III 920/vi 336), Marcel has not *found* his way but *lost* it. For one hundred pages he struggles in the swamp of mental paralysis: he cannot recognize the very people, here assembled as in the last ensemble scene of a ballet, whom he has known best and longest. Once again Proust has produced a scene both comic and tragic in almost every detail of disguise and revelation, advanced age, social convention, and genuine feeling. This is the famous *bal de têtes* or costume-ball scene, in which many of the cast reassemble disguised by age. Proust had sketched it out fourteen years earlier when he began the novel and then held it for the closing pages. It can be seen as an extended, melodramatic, and providential counterpart of the brief, muted, and incidental stumble in the book's second sentence (see above, page 64). Will Marcel now be able to complete his lifelong quest?

Yes he will. But not through a new upwelling of resurrections by involuntary memory. For we come now to a further principle of perception. As he has done many times before in his life, Marcel comes down some steps to enter a salon full of people. After a moment of hesitation, he realizes that the white-bearded, leaden-footed old man who greets him first must be the host, the Prince de Guermantes. Then we are treated to a four-page description of a doddering beggar played to perfection by an actor of genius—except that no acting is involved. For the personage turns out to be the Marquis d'Argencourt, twenty years after, Marcel's old enemy, the Marquis himself playing himself, "sublimely gaga" (III 922/vi 339), and, on final recognition, provoking Marcel's uncontrollable laughter. In order to find the pulse of this final scene, we shall have to return to the fertile field of optical imagery.

For Proust and the Narrator, the basic unit of subjective life is the image. It occurs in a variety of synonyms, including *instantané* (a photographic snapshot) and *pan* (section, patch, side, spot . . .). The latter takes on a special life in the *Search*. What Marcel's magic lantern cast on the wall at Combray was a *pan* of Geneviève de Brabant's château (I 9/i 10). In the opening pages, that image is subsumed in a more extensive one: all that remains of Combray in Marcel's memory is a *pan lumineux* (I 43/i 58) revealing a fragmentary view of the house and life within it.

What exalts and distresses Bergotte at the moment of his death in the art gallery is a *petit pan de mur jaune* painted by Vermeer (III 187 /v 245), symbol of every effect he was himself unable to capture in writing. In all three cases the tiny neutral syllable *pan* conveys the sense of an isolated visual fragment that retains the capacity to suggest something lost, something infinitely worth seeking. Alone, it remains a "still," unable to transcend itself, blocked. But life offers us a way out of this impasse. Two or more images of the same object seen at different moments, registering contrast or even contradiction, release use from stillness into succession, into narrative time.

Examples abound. Late in the novel, Marcel discovers that M. Verdurin, a rich and somewhat self-centered bourgeois, has hidden from everyone the admirably charitable action of helping a needy friend financially. Proust falls back on photography to describe the multiplication of images.

> Nevertheless, at the moment of my discovery, M. Verdurin's character offered me a new and unsuspected aspect; and I had to concede the difficulty of presenting a fixed image of a character as much as of societies and of passions. For character changes as much as they do, and if one wishes to photograph *[clicher]* its relatively immutable aspect, one can only watch as it presents in succession different appearances (implying it does not know how to keep still, but keeps moving) to the disconcerted lens. (III 327/v 440)

Though it remains the basic unit of observation and memory, the single image turns out to be an orphan, a meaningless fragment snatched out of the flux. The still camera must yield to other optical devices to provide metaphors for our pursuit of reality: the magic lantern, the kaleidoscope, the cinematograph. All three depend upon a succession of images and describe the flux by reproducing it in schematic form. They reflect time by partially submitting to its ceaseless modifications.

A succession of contradictory images going under one name and "passing," by convention, as a single person or sentiment or social entity—this is probably the most striking aspect of Proust's universe to the unprepared reader. In this respect Proust reveals himself a creature of his age, a fact that by no means strips him of originality in his literary work. He recorded discontinuity more insistently than continuity. The character Saint-Loup first appears as an insolent, unapproachable, exceedingly chic young aristocrat who will not deign to look at Marcel; within two pages he turns out to be the most loyal and considerate of friends. One paragraph later he reveals himself as not merely a republican suspicious of the aristocratic principles he first seemed to incarnate, but a socialist who has steeped himself in Nietzsche and Proudhon. Three hundred pages later we watch him in the role of the headstrong, jealous lover of the actress Rachel, and blind to the extravagance of his own behavior. In his next transformation, after an equal interval, he has become simultaneously a selfish and cruel husband and a philandering homosexual keeping mistresses in order to cover up his carryings-on with young men. Saint-Loup turns out in the end to be the only major character in the novel who is killed in combat, a patriot and a true hero.

A similar series of mutations is followed in practically every development of character and action. The stations of Swann's love for Odette begin and end in indifference, and between those terms his sentiments, still covered by the generic word "love," pass through multiple, overlapping stages: aesthetic appreciation of Odette's beauty, passive acceptance of her company, suffering because of being deprived of her company, urgent physical need for her, brief happiness in the satisfaction of that need, the torments of jealousy, social disgrace in her eyes because of his importunate behavior, a sense of physical and nervous sickness, despair at the recollection of his happier moments, incapacity to act in order to rescue himself, and the slow cooling of affection. Only afterward, when the subjective emotions of love have been exhausted, does Swann marry Odette, an insignificant event that takes place offstage, barely mentioned. Not one image: a multitude. The action of the first twenty-eight hundred pages out of three thousand can be seen as consisting in Marcel's gradual discovery and acceptance of the truth that no person, no action, no sentiment, no social phenomenon is ever simple or consistent. Most of the way through, the *Search* remains a book of dis-enchantments. Things are never what they seem.

During these sections of the work, however, the heterogeneity of im-ages, of *instantanés,* occasionally seems to graze a sense of order, to come into phase with itself. (The phenomenon is distinct from involun-tary memory and reminiscences.) Odette turns out to be (or have been) the "lady in pink" with whom Marcel's uncle consorted, as well as Elstir's mistress and his model in the costume of Miss Sacripant. Elstir turns out to be the "Biche" of Mme Verdurin's salon. Saint-Loup's mistress, Rachel, turns out to be the same "Rachel quand du seigneur" whose charms Marcel declined as a youth in a *maison de passe* with Bloch. These identifications suggest to Marcel some form of truth he does not yet un-derstand. On the other hand, two of his most grievous moments occur when an expected identification is *not* made: first when he fails to rec-ognize his grandmother the day he comes upon her suddenly and sees her as an old lady, and second when on her deathbed she fails to recognize him. (At the very last she appears to respond to his kiss, but her actions are ambiguous.) Meanwhile, Marcel has lived through a whole series of misapprehensions, which occur when he tries to verify the present against past experience or future expectation. Every name that has enthralled him loses its magic. Similarly his ideals. Love, the elect world of nobil-ity, memory, even the prestige of art and the sense of his own identity disintegrate into a set of fragmentary experiences. Marcel is reduced to living with a collection of meaningless "stills," and it is exactly thus that he describes himself at the end of the passage on page 106. His failure to recognize himself is as ludicrous as the puzzlement one feels before a mislabeled painting.

But the second half of the last volume, *Time Regained,* brings several reversals of mood and action. Following Marcel's prolonged absence from Paris and from the places and people he has frequented, he returns. As he crosses Paris in a carriage, he undergoes an interior shift in sensi-bility, an ascension (expressed in an airplane image) above both past and present. The spectacle of the Baron de Charlus in ruins brings him back down to earth. Marcel arrives in discouragement in front of the Prince de Guermantes' house, when unexpectedly, he experiences, five times in close succession, a *moment bienheureux* or resurrection. Soon thereafter, when he enters the salon of the Prince de Guermantes, he undergoes, ten times in close succession, a complementary but different experience. He comes upon ten assorted figures out of his past, all of whom he fails at first to recognize because of their "disguise" and travestied appearance. Yet he finally contrives to "give a name to the faces" (III 926/vi 344). The entire final sequence is foreshadowed by the invitation to attend this *matinée chez le prince de Guermantes*. After looking at the invitation, Marcel discovers that the name Guermantes has resumed its initial condition of "a name I did not recognize" (III 857/vi 241).

The remaining two hundred pages of the novel form the heart of the labyrinth and conceal the only egress from it. In an extended confrontation scene Marcel finally re-identifies the elements of the world that formerly had crystallized around that name of Guermantes. The essential point about these last pages, however, is not the fact that he stumbles back over his past and finds it, but the fact that in coming upon it again, his own subjective processes have to follow a new order of events. In the past, Marcel experienced a series of encounters with particularly alluring strangers who, after a number of wild surmises in Marcel's mind about their character and station, are finally identified by name as individuals of particular prestige and eminence in Marcel's universe. In this way he meets or sees at a distance Gilberte at Tansonville (I 140ff./i 197ff.), Mme de Guermantes in the church at Combray (I 174ff./i 245ff.), la Berma in the theater (I 448/ii 125), Charlus at Balbec (I 751ff. /ii 452ff.), and Elstir at Rivebelle (I 825/ii 553). In each case the incident terminates in an identification by name. (The first appearances of Bergotte and Saint-Loup entail slight variations.)

At the end of the novel, however, in the reversed order of events, Marcel begins with a familiar name and confronts at approximately the same time an individual "changed beyond recognition" to go with that name. Out of this dilemma he finally wins through to recognition. Each of the first ten cases following fast on Marcel's entry into the Prince's *matinée* (III 920–52/vi 336–83) observes this order with minor variations and irregularities. At the fourth repetition the nature of this little "act" has become perfectly clear to Marcel, and he states how much he must rely upon the cueing contained in a name.

> I made a determined effort to apply to the face of an entirely un-known woman the idea that she was Mme Sazerat, and ultimately I re-constituted the old familiar significance of her face, which would have remained utterly strange to me, wholly that of another woman who had lost all the human attributes familiar to me as fully as would a man who turned into a monkey, if her name and the assertion of her identity had not put me on the track of the solution, notwithstanding the difficult nature of the problem. (III 931/iii 351–52)

The ageless, unchanging Odette provides a comic variation on the es-tablished pattern of name, nonrecognition, recognition. Marcel comes upon her tenth among his encounters with the past, when his mind has begun to adjust itself to the visible passage of time in people's physical appearance. "In her case, if I didn't recognize her at first, it was not be-cause she had but because she had not changed" (III 948/vi 377). By this time a fundamental shift has taken place in the nature of a name, a sound that for the young Marcel could create the magic and prestige of un-known creatures. No longer a summation of mysteries, the name here acts only as a convenience or reminder, a means to a different end. That end is recognition, a final reconciliation and acceptance of conflicting images, not by any logical process but rather by an enlarged vision de-veloped in the long experience of life itself. The tiny defiant convention of a name kept over the years challenges this mature vision to find a unity in multiplicity.

We are ourselves now in a position to recognize *recognition* as the crowning mental operation of the novel and Marcel's long delayed achievement. There have been earlier hints. Swann's pleasure and pain in listening to *la petite phrase de Vinteuil* arises from the fact that he both succeeds and fails to recognize in those notes a part of himself to which he has no other access. But in affirming now that the ultimate meaning

of the *Search* lies in acts of recognition, I shall have to depart from
widely held interpretations of Proust's aesthetics and to restate my argument from earlier pages of this chapter.

The dozen or so unevenly distributed *moments bienheureux* produced
by involuntary memory contain what first appears to be the essence of
Proust-Marcel's sense of reality—a fleeting re-creation of the past in the
present, conferring a rare and pleasurable sensation of timelessness. The
sense of literary vocation seems to arise out of the desire to capture and
fix this experience. The case is clearest in the *clochers de Martinville* passage where the adolescent Marcel notes down his impressions on the
spot. But in the sudden and overwhelming sequence of *moments bienheureux* near the end, just before Marcel enters the Prince's salon (III
865–88/vi 253–79), any literary outcome is obstructed. In this latter passage he makes two references to the work before him: once to speak of
its great difficulties (III 870–71/vi 261) and later, in a meditation on
how to "fix" the "image" of these instants, to ask himself, "Now, this
means, which seemed to me the only one, what was it other than to create a work of art?" (III 879/vi 273). The sadness and reluctance of
Proust-Marcel's tone here, the very deviousness of the syntax in the
question, suggest that the sequence may not be complete after all. We feel
the need of some further development in the action to carry us beyond
these irresolute statements. The following thirty pages (III 888–918/vi
279–332) of discursive writing on literature do not contain any new incidents and were probably intercalated late in the composition of the
manuscript. Only when Marcel enters the Prince's salon does the action
move again, in just the series of arduous recognitions I have been belaboring. People, not objects or landscapes or sensations, fill these pages.
In addition to the new order of events that devalues the magic of name
in favor of a literal double take, these concluding pages establish a rising tension between Marcel's present circumstances and his literary vocation. His confidence on entering collapses into uncertainty.

Can Marcel's project survive in the face of the unexpected effort required of him to recognize the very creatures about whom he proposes
to write his novel? It is a crucial test. As the ten figures loom up before

him, he doubts once again every resolution he made a few moments earlier after the spasm of *moments bienheureux*. Yet a new realization comes to him gradually, a revelation that could not be made by the objects and sensations associated with the *moments bienheureux*, but only by people. He confronts the reality and meaning of death.

> And in truth, to "recognize" someone and, more especially, to work out someone's identity after not having been able to recognize him or her, means conceiving two contradictory things under the same denomination; it means admitting that what used to be here, the person we remember, no longer exists, and that we did not ever know the person who is here; it means having to penetrate a mystery almost as disturbing as death, of which it is, moreover, the preface and the forerunner. (III 939/vi 365–66)

The complex shuffling and sorting out of images that we call "recognizing" a person arises from the reality of disappearing selves, of death. Living consists in a precarious survival. The perpetual menace of death, instead of discouraging Marcel, spurs him on anew toward his "urgent, capital rendez-vous with himself" (III 986/vi 436). But he is not there yet. Marcel is now in effect going through the same set of reactions to himself as to everyone else he encounters. After the preliminary assertion of his new literary vocation during the *moments bienheureux*, he fails to recognize himself in that role any longer when he enters the salon. His masquerade as writer is no more convincing than anyone else's disguise. At least so it seems at the start.

Meanwhile, his sense of vocation has received two more setbacks, which prolong the suspense. Not having been given the essential clue of a name, he totally fails to recognize his childhood sweetheart, Gilberte, and afterward, the actress Rachel. He feels as if he had failed an examination (III 980/vi 427). The *matinée* moves toward its climax—or rather the climax of Marcel's life approaches in the grotesque zoological setting of elegant society. And we are carefully prepared for it. Gilberte goes to find her daughter, Mlle de Saint-Loup, to introduce her to Marcel. Four pages are devoted to establishing in her absence how she embodies the entire action of the book in its orientation between the *deux côtés*. And when at last Marcel turns his attention to the approaching girl of sixteen, he sees more than he has seen in any other person in his life. Since he has never met her before, he cannot recognize her—or rather, he can recognize only those aspects that reveal her relation to what he does know. Thus he recognizes in her "my Youth." In the very next sentence the innocent pronoun *elle* gently associates the physical person Mlle de Saint-Loup with his thoughts on time, and he recognizes her as an inspiration, a revelation.

> And finally, this idea of time had a further reward for me; it [she] was a goad, a stimulus, reminding me that it was time to begin if I wished to achieve what I had occasionally in the course of my life sensed in brief flashes, along the Guermantes way or while driving with Mme de Villeparisis, and which had encouraged me to regard life as worth living. (III 1032/vi 507)

Mlle de Saint-Loup incarnates a new idea of time, not death only, but youth. Her beauty as of a "masterpiece" is the spur to Marcel to begin his work. She is his vocation, not merely its symbol, but the work of art in the flesh, which he must have the courage to reproduce in its lengthy gestation and its final fullness.

This is the last sustained scene in the novel. Sixteen pages remain. Marcel simply disappears without stage stuff from the Prince's salon. The story is not yet over. Françoise, having grown into the figure of his faithful muse, will help him construct his book. In his hovering thoughts, Marcel once again overcomes the fear of death and of its counterpart, losing his mind. But one key element is still missing: finding the willpower to act on his good intentions. Everything pushes him toward his vocation; he hesitates nevertheless.

Only four pages from the end, Marcel recalls/recognizes the opening bedtime scene Combray. What the Narrator originally called "the first abdication" (I 38/i 51), that is, Marcel's parents giving in to his hypersensitive disposition, and thus marking "a sad date" in his life, now becomes his salvation. For that early episode reveals another trait in the boy. When his mother will not come upstairs to kiss him good night, he suddenly "resolves" (I 32/i 42) against all rules and precedents to stay awake until she comes upstairs after the guest leaves. And he carries out his resolve. Now at the end, Marcel recognizes and regains his long-lost willpower. For only the second time after nearly three thousand pages he resolves (III 1044/vi 525–26) to carry out a major course of action, to write his book. The *Search* ends in a recognition scene—better, in a scene of self-recognition—which incites Marcel to become the Narrator of his own *Search* and to settle down to work.

I have taken a long time in this rehearsal of the end of the *Search* for what I consider important reasons. The much touted *moments bienheureux* do not bring Marcel to his vocation or confer on him any lasting happiness. They represent an important step toward both those ends, or more accurately, they are the guideposts that show him the right direction without themselves taking him to his goal except by anticipation. The multiple sequence they contribute toward the end functions as a preliminary to the denouement of the book, not as its true climax. The attitude of passivity on which they rely and the tendency they have to encourage the substitution of pleasure for effort, and objects for people, prevent them from offering the key to Marcel's salvation. The ultimate moment of the book is not a *moment bienheureux* but a recognition. After the prolonged sequence of double takes in the Prince's salon, the final step brings Marcel to a true *self-recognition* and the resolve to fill that role.

It is revealing to imagine the different ways in which this end might have been accomplished. For instance, Proust could have turned the tables on Marcel and let him squirm while an old acquaintance fails to hide the difficulty he has in recognizing Marcel. This variant of the hunter hunted or the mocker mocked would have forced Marcel to acknowledge the whole apparatus of naming, nonrecognition, death of former selves, and identification as directed at himself. Or, in another equally comic version, Proust might have let Marcel glimpse a disturbingly familiar figure across the room—so familiar and so impossible of recognition that he pushes through the guests in pursuit of the mysterious personage. And after a fruitless search among the assembled ancients, Marcel would suddenly discern his prey as a clouded reflection of himself in a mirror half hidden behind the guests.

Still, there is something a little inept and contrived about both these possible incidents. At the end of a novel unflaggingly subjective in orientation, Proust chose to exteriorize and objectify this ultimate incident and to represent its full meaning in the flesh. In a young girl he has never seen before, Marcel at last recognizes his past and his death, his youth and his hope, his duty and his vocation. What distinguishes this final recognition from the *moments bienheureux* is that recognition entails an active participation of the mind.

Marcel now fully acknowledges the elusive being who has been growing steadily inside him, like a chrysalis. That chrysalis is a nascent writer, thwarted and abandoned at every turn. But his time has now come. He matures in the final pages into the Narrator, whom Marcel at last recognizes as himself—himself transformed, his alter ego, the other *I* in the double *I*. It's a long story. The *Search* turns out to be a metamorphosis that permits a self-recognition. (See Appendix III, page 265.)

VI

❦

ART AND IDOLATRY

IN CHAPTER IV, I SPOKE OF ART AS ONE OF THE FALSE scents that absorb Marcel's attention and energies without giving him a satisfying purpose in life. He speaks of his literary vocation as something estimable but beyond his reach. And I have insisted on the series of stages through which his sensibility develops in his search for himself: impressions, reminiscences, and (self-)recognitions—all closely related to optical imagery. This exposition will appear to many Proust readers and critics to slight the most important domain of all: art and aesthetics. There are reasons for holding off the discussion of art. The principal one is to avoid letting it interfere with an adequate consideration of the three stages just mentioned. The aesthetic has a tendency to encroach on everything around it.

Closely associated through his father and his brother with scientific developments in medicine, drawn by temperament to philosophy and its pursuit of general laws, Proust strove constantly to produce clear and distinct ideas. But he was dealing in his novel not with ideas primarily but with complex entities called human beings, who change over time in unpredictable nonmechanistic ways. And since art comes into being only through human beings, it too is changeable and complex. Consequently, it is little wonder that Proust's treatment of art through his long novel both honors its high stature and genuine rewards and treats the ways in which art may lead us astray. I believe it is a mistake to simplify the *Search* so drastically as to conclude that art is the ultimate value it expresses, the highest human activity, the refuge finally sought out by Marcel as he becomes the Narrator. Such an opinion contains a partial truth, yet leaves much of the narrative unaccounted for. I interpret Proust's ambivalence about art not as weakness but as an insight into its (and our) true condition.

Art

Approaching forty, when he should have been coming into his own, Proust fell very low. His gifts seemed to elude him. In the novel Marcel reaches an equally dismal point. In *The Captive,* Marcel loses confidence in the one talisman he has been carrying for many years, the experience of the madeleine. "Nothing assured me that the vagueness of such states was a sign of their profundity" (III 382/v 513). He has not yet reached the stage of recognition. Furthermore, his strongest insights lock him into a deeper solitude than ever. He can share these moments with no one. His inner life isolates him even more than the false scents of love and social climbing. "The universe is real for all of us, and different for each one of us" (III 191/v 248). It is a desperately forlorn sentence. Until very late in the story, Marcel's "difference," that is, his mnemonic gift, brings him a sense of isolation that dims the rewards of involuntary memory. Both Proust and Marcel survived these trials and attained a form of salvation in part because of art—literature in particular. We need now to examine what the *Search* tells us about the role of art, not only in discursive passages but also in the incidents of its narrative. It is not a simple message.

In the opening chapter, I touched on the perplexities and moral insecurity of Proust's existence as he entered his late thirties. He had no job, no wife, no firm social status, no sure sense of past or future accomplishments. His parents had died. He had published one book of youthful fragments, about which he had ambivalent feelings, two translations of an author whose intellectual posture he came to reject, and a few journalistic stories and articles. But the bulk of his writing lay buried in a stack of notebooks. By his own exacting standards he was a failure; by outward appearances he was a wealthy amateur and a social sycophant. Nevertheless, he kept trying. In the latter part of 1908 Proust announced to his friends that he was working on a new project: an essay, combined somehow with a personal narrative, on Sainte-Beuve's critical method. In the second sentence of the preface he drafted for the work, he states flatly that "past impressions" form "the only materials of Art" (*CSB* 211 / *OAL* 19). But after a brief discussion of the "resurrection" of three such impressions, he moves on into an ambivalent and unfinished disquisition on the role of the intelligence in literature. *Against Sainte-Beuve,* as this project came to be called, assembles the old materials once again and tries to arrange them in a rough circle around a half-dreaming consciousness in a bedroom. Proust put the project aside within a year— or rather he incorporated it into something significantly different. For, during the first half of 1909, Proust resolved his personal and artistic crisis and redeemed much of the writing he thought he had been producing to no purpose.

At this point Proust was traveling on two kinds of moral credit: his theories about the experience of involuntary memory (by now confirmed in his reading of Bergson's first two books); and the growing conviction that suffering and grief are ultimately salutary and provide a form of spiritual knowledge. Both sets of ideas turned Proust back toward his own past and encouraged him to see it with augmented relief, with depth perception in time. Both involuntary memory and the "agitations of grief" raise up out of the mind a landscape of thoughts and feelings that otherwise lies at too low a level to be seen (III 897 / vi 301). In one direction these clues led backward in time toward one crucial incident that held the germ of everything to come. They took Proust to *le drame du coucher* (the good-night scene), a play within a play enacting the ritual of desire and discontent that animates soul error. But the same forces of memory and grief also led Proust in the opposite direction, forward toward the future in its relation to the present.

What happened represented a distinct mental leap. Sometime in 1909 Proust grasped that the story he had to tell was embodied in the very process of failure and rediscovery that he was going through. His book lay at his feet. He had to watch and tread carefully. His present turmoil over memory and art projected his theme and offered both the message and the method of a novel. He reached beyond autobiography toward the transformation of his life into the shape of a narrative that could convey his deepest sense of self. He found he could stand back from himself. He discovered the device, or the design, of what could be called *a play outside a play*. By seeing his personal situation from outside as if it radiated a larger, generalized narrative action of loss and recovery, he transformed his failure into potential success and his isolation into communication. Thus he almost stumbled upon the unity of form fatally absent in *Jean Santeuil* and *Against Sainte-Beuve*. What the draft preface of the latter states vainly at the start, the *Search* affirms triumphantly at its close. "I understood that those materials for a literary work were my own past life" (III 899/vi 304). "Materials," not the story line. This insight of 1909 signifies a shift away from both autobiography and fiction (as pure invention) to *translation,* a term that keeps occurring in the final section of the *Search*. Henceforward, Proust became the author of his own life and also of a book that subsumed his life. Increasingly he gave priority to the latter, to his work, for which the former became a rehearsal, subject to observation and experiment. Proust produced a work of art representing as its subject the circumstances and vagaries of its own creation and the origin of its form.

In the novel there are two significant differences from autobiography. First, Marcel's conversion to literature as a vocation comes not in mid-career, as in the case of Proust, but very late—nearly at the end of the book when Marcel is described as an old man. Thus the dramatic effect is enhanced, and the body of the book is constructed as a long decline. My remarks in the preceding chapter about art as a false scent suggest how art conforms to that pattern in the *Search*. Painting and music keep

some of their savor, but as the story goes on, literature, representing
Marcel's first aspiration to transcend ordinariness and isolation, withers
to a dry husk. Even Marcel's long discussion with Albertine in *The Captive* about Dostoevski, Mme de Sévigné, Thomas Hardy, and Baudelaire dangles from the troubling thought that "Vinteuil's music seemed
to me something truer than all known books" (III 374/v 504). These discouragements begin soon after Combray and become one of the leitmotifs of the book until close to the end.*

The first difference, then, between the novel and autobiography is one
of timing. Marcel rediscovers his literary vocation near the end of his
life, not in his prime as Proust himself did. The second difference is that
what the circumstances of life tend to obscure—namely, the origins and
meanings of things—the novel tends to reveal. There lies its essence
and its purpose as a work of art. The earliest sustained reflections on literature in the *Search* develop precisely this aesthetic theory.

At the beginning of *Swann's Way* the reader comes upon several celebrated set pieces: the kaleidoscope of bedrooms in Marcel's life; the

---

*To launch this downward movement, Proust wrote a somewhat contrived six-page
coda for the end of *Swann's Way* as it was chopped off in the first Grasset edition in
1913. The mythological Bois de Boulogne, peopled with the most elegant creatures in
the world, collapses into its most paltry self, a mere woods. Six pages of romantic despair lead up to a muted allusion to Horace in the closing lines:

". . . the memory of a certain scene means nothing more than the loss of that instant;
and the houses, roads, and avenues are as fleeting, alas, as time itself" (I 427/i 606). The
spinning of the story goes on, but deprived now of the hope that memory or art can
transcend the flux.

Is it really so? as Proust himself would immediately have asked. In a significant letter written to Jacques Rivière just a few months after publication of *Swann's Way* in
1913, Proust states that this coda is merely "a screen to finish off the volume within the
limit of 500 pages" and that the thought expressed there is "the contrary of my conclusion." But at that point in the narrative, the despair is convincing and authoritative.
Proust here initiated a prolonged and seemingly irreversible descent. The weight of the
evidence continues to bear it out, not just through a few hundred pages as Proust originally planned, but through two thousand more pages, before the contrary movement
begins in *Time Regained*.

good-night kiss withheld and granted; and the madeleine dipped in lin-
den tea. And what then? Aunt Léonie. The village church and steeple.
The two ways. Each one has high definition. Are we reading a novel
composed of detachable parts? Not really. The pages of "Combray"
form a radial unity, which it is unwise to cut up into scenes and segments.

Still, one sequence stands apart because it casts everything else into
doubt and jeopardy. The Combray world that displays convincing color
and strong personality dims temporarily when seen from another
perspective. The shift occurs when Marcel is reading in the garden
(I 83–88/i 113–21). This carefully reasoned yet poetic passage places us
suddenly inside his world looking out. Marcel's faith in the special world
of childhood weakens briefly in the face of a competing faith—the reality of a book. Art makes the challenge. Marcel describes his long
Sunday afternoons of reading as forming a single consciousness "simultaneously dappled with different states." He has become only mar-
ginally aware of the world around him. ". . . my most intimate thought,
the constantly shifting control that regulated everything else, was my belief in the philosophical richness and in the beauty of the book I was
reading and my desire to appropriate them for myself" (1 84/i 115).
And we are told why. Being not opaque flesh-and-blood people, but
images made out of words, the characters of such a story can be transparent and can reveal their feelings and motives to us. As images they can
also concentrate the actions of a lifetime into a few hours' reading, thus
making perceptible what we cannot observe at the slow pace of living.
The transparent image of fiction is doubly revealing compared to life,
and hence more alluring than life. Furthermore, the Narrator explains in
this passage that the "magic" of the fictional world consoles Marcel for
the apparent mediocrity of his own life and releases the constant gush-
ing forth *(jaillissement)* of his consciousness toward other things and
other beings. These beautiful Sunday afternoons, characterized as
"silent, sonorous, perfumed, and limpid," transform Marcel's life and anticipate the final return to art. They do not destroy Marcel's basic faith
in his childhood experiences, but they shadow it. These six pages on

reading offer a superb example of how Proust's prose interweaves a narrative sequence of Marcel taking his book out into the garden, a double description of both a topographical and a mental landscape, and a careful step-by-step philosophical argument about the nature of reading—a full-fledged epistemology of reading.

As a reader, then, Marcel lives through a few afternoons that transcend the magic of childhood. Yet, like the impressions and resurrections, they do not last. Instead, they lead into the inadequate attitudes toward art of Swann, Bergotte, Charlus, and Marcel himself. However, this first sustained aesthetic meditation presents art as a form of revelation and communication that importunes our inmost being. Like the madeleine sequence in the domain of memory, it remains a talisman in the domain of art.

Art is never far from the narrative line of the *Search*. Marcel lives surrounded by the mythological presences of art, in the double form of the masterpieces of Western culture and of several characters in the story who practice one of the arts. The three major artists represent a kind of progress: Bergotte, the most compromised by the world, society, and his own temperament; Elstir, who seems to work directly with the phenomenon of vision rather than to render reality; and Vinteuil, depicted as a martyr-composer. It is Elstir who means most to Marcel after he has passed adolescence. ". . . if God the Father created the things of the world by naming them, it is by depriving them of their names, or by giving them new names, that Elstir re-created the world" (I 835/ii 566). Marcel gleans lessons like this one and many more along the way. However, such insights become less frequent and more fragmentary with time. Art takes the same downward path as memory. It is not until we are well into the fifth volume that Marcel has another experience of art as intense and as carefully described as the Sunday afternoons in Combray. The fifteen pages devoted to the Vinteuil septet in *The Captive* (III 248–65/v 331–53) carry Marcel through a series of stations along the path to understanding art. Taken unawares by the music, he first hears it as a description of a seascape and then associates it with his love for Albertine. After thinking of the piece as an expression of Vinteuil's troubled life, Marcel goes on to discover in the music something "ineffable": a sense of individual being and "the communication of souls" (III 258/v 344).

Proust has written a profound meditation on music as a progressive experience engaging one's whole consciousness. The passage is less about music than about coenesthesia, the organic sensation of existence, released by a full encounter with music. Within the context of Marcel's story, however, the incident falls short of changing Marcel's life. He hears the music as a "call" away from the "emptiness" of his life. He cannot answer that call, possibly because he remains a hearer or spectator, possibly because it is a musical rather than a literary experience. Nevertheless, this scene takes so long a step toward divulging the outcome of the novel that Proust saw fit to lead us back into a swamp of misunderstanding and disappointment before the end comes. When Marcel reads the Goncourt brothers' journal (see above, pages 77–78), he has lost his aesthetic bearings so thoroughly that he all but renounces his ambitions as an artist along with his hopes of grasping the significance of past events in his life.

After so many tribulations the conclusion of the novel may begin to look strained. When impressions, reminiscences, and art have lost their power to sustain Marcel, how is it that they return miraculously and more compellingly than ever in the long culminating scene? What accounts for this melodramatic turn of events? The basic reason has a sturdy simplicity about it. At long last Marcel comprehends the crucial interrelation between these three elements of his experience. Earlier, he barely associated them. The impressions faded as soon as they occurred. The reminiscences might or might not lead him back to their source among forgotten impressions, and did not reach out toward artistic creation. Art took refuge in prestige and snobbery. The one exception to this compartmentalization turns up fairly early in the story. I am referring to the scene in "Combray" when Marcel scribbles out on the spot a description of the beautiful slow dance of the Martinville steeples on the horizon as seen from Dr. Percepied's fast-moving carriage (I 178–82/i 251–57). Yet nothing in this carefully composed sequence encourages the reader to regard Marcel's product as a work of art. "I never thought about the page again," the Narrator says. As I pointed out earlier, he ridicules the whole affair by telling us that Marcel began to cackle like "a hen . . . that had just laid an egg." There is little here to convey any lasting faith in impressions, reminiscences, and art, or to bring them together.

No such flippancy marks the last two hundred pages of the *Search*, even though it contains the great mock apotheosis of Marcel's failure to recognize his oldest friends and many smaller comic touches. Five successive resurrections impel Marcel to collect the thoughts and experiences of a lifetime into a final meditation. The fifty-page philosophical-poetic sequence does not reflect *on* the action at this juncture. These pages narrate the action itself and reconstitute every theme in the novel. Joyce seeks a similar effect in Molly Bloom's great affirmative monologue at the end of *Ulysses*. Marcel's monologue that opens the final sequence follows a basic argument as clearly articulated as that of the passage describing the Sunday afternoon readings in Combray. The opposite of a denouement, it knots together the several strands that have hung slack and barely intertwined during the central portion of the novel:

1. Though they bestow a sense of "the essence of things" and of "our true self," resurrections such as those just experienced by Marcel are of fleeting effect (III 866–75/vi 254–68).

2. The only means to arrest and transfix their elevating impulse is to capture it in a work of art (III 876–88/vi 269–80).

3. The writer does so by creating a metaphorical link or loop between ordinary, lived "reality" and the "vision" of a work of art. This aesthetic loop encompasses the analogous loop between past impression and its resurrection in the present (III 889–96/vi 281–300).

4. The understanding of art as a creative process permits Marcel to embrace his literary vocation and to see the carefully defined role literature gives to intelligence and general laws, and to suffering. He also speaks of the role and the rewards of the reader (III 897–917/vi 301–32).

The last two parts of the argument, especially part 3, need elucidation. In approaching what he considers to be the essential function of a

work of art, Proust relies heavily on the French word *rapport:* relation.
In the crucial paragraph of his meditation (III 889/vi 289–90), he describes a set of interlocking relations connecting all parts of his universe
and based on the "natural" phenomenon of seeing one thing in another
through association or analogy. The analogy that links past and present
experiences through memory confers on them a sense of "reality," of
"true life." Resurrections create a kind of relief or depth perception in
time. This reality is in turn related to art through the analogy of
metaphor. The transparent, accelerated image of fiction can capture what
is opaque or imperceptible in life. Thus art forms a second loop in a different dimension, reaching out of reality and time, yet also flowing back
toward them. When Proust describes the writer discovering the *rapport*
between art and life, he does so in the context of a now familiar incident.

> If I tried to analyze for myself just what takes place in us at the mo-
> ment when something makes a certain impression on us—as, for ex-
> ample, that day when as I crossed the bridge over the Vivonne, the
> shadow of a cloud on the water made me exclaim, "Gosh, gosh," as I
> leaped for joy . . . —I perceived that, to describe these impressions, to
> write that essential book, the only true book, a great writer does not
> need to invent it, in the current sense of the term, since it already ex-
> ists in each one of us, but merely to translate it. The duty and the
> tasks of a writer are those of a translator. (III 890/vi 290–91)

Involuntary memory links past and present into reality. "Translation"
links that reality, focused in reminiscences and impressions, to the work
of art. A little further on, Proust adds a third loop: reading. The reader
ultimately reads *himself* in the work of art and gains an insight into his
reality by retrospection or anticipation.

In the hope of clarifying my exposition, I have constructed a diagram
of the operation of Proust's literary aesthetic as I comprehend it (see Diagram V). It can offer only a clumsy simplification. The significant aspect of this vision of things is that every element is linked by a universal
principle of analogy or relation. Literature and, by implication, the other

V. The Loops of Art

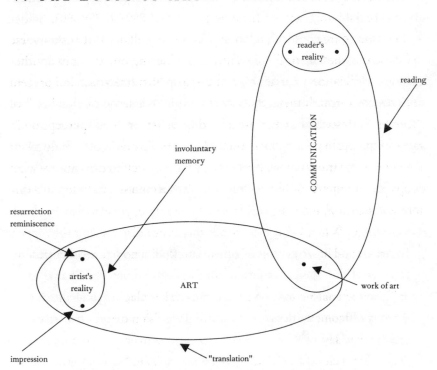

arts play a key intermediary role between one person's reality and that of another. The word that best sums up Proust's philosophical attitude in this context, encompassing both an epistemology and an aesthetic, is "communication." In 1905, when toiling to find his way beyond Ruskin, Proust had spoken of reading as "that fecund miracle of communication in the midst of solitude" (*CSB* 174). For social conversation distracts the mind; solitude strengthens it. Directed toward a work of art, reading brings communication without social distraction. Yet Proust went on to insist that reading constitutes an "incitement" to the true life of the mind, and not the full realization of that life (*CSB* 178). We shall gradually understand why he made that qualification. Part of the same train of thought about solitude reappears in *The Guermantes Way* when the Narrator passes harsh judgment on friendship, "all of whose effort is to make us sacrifice the only part of ourselves which is real and incommunicable (except by means of art) to a super-

ficial self which, unlike the other, finds no reward in its own being"
(II 394/iii 540).

The work of art holds the secret of communication. But at this point
in the narrative, that truth is confined in a parenthesis of suspended an-
imation, while society carries Marcel along in its distractions. The secret
declares itself again during the Vinteuil septet when the ultimate power
of music is described as that of allowing us to see "with other eyes,"
something approaching "the communication of souls" (III 258/v 344).
One of the most expansive passages in the last meditation leaves little
doubt that art provides the antidote to Proust's complaint, to the solitary
confinement of the human condition.

> By art alone can we get out of ourselves, find out what another per-
> son sees of this universe which is not the same as ours. . . . Thanks to
> art, instead of seeing only one world, we see it multiplied, and we have
> as many different worlds at our disposition as there are original artists.
> (III 895–96/vi 299)

Proust rarely allowed himself such flights when speaking specifically
about literature. In the following pages the communication a book affords, its "incitement," is compared to that of an optical instrument that
"the author offers the reader in order to allow him to discern things
which, without the book, he would possibly not have seen in himself.
The reader's recognition in himself of what the book says is proof of the
book's truth, and vice versa" (III 911/vi 322). True reading of a worth-
while book takes us just far enough out of ourselves and our solitude to
return to them restored. Art affords this communication with our own
life through self-recognition.

In sum, art springs from life and in turn serves it through the interlocking *rapports* or loops of communication. Yet there remains an underlying inconsistency between the affirmation that art belongs to life
and Proust's thoughts on solitude and society. Everything he says about
social life and friendship and snobbery as contrasted to reading and meditation establishes the vanity of social intercourse next to the true rewards

of solitude. To converse with a friend is "a self-abdication" (I 906–7/ii 664). Marcel prefers to read and look at pictures alone; on country walks he drops behind his friends when he wants to commune with a hawthorn bush or a view of the ocean. The deepest experiences of memory and art appear to be excluded from that portion of our lives spent with other people. Few divisions in Proust's universe go so deep as this cleavage between the integrity of solitude, associated with memory and art, and the distraction of society, associated with superficiality and snobbery.*

Yet the close of the book brings an unexpected shift in Marcel's attitude. Most of the dramatic developments at the end, concerning art and memory and vocation, have been anticipated many times over in earlier passages. But on the matter of society and solitude, Marcel and the Narrator have kept their secrets of state very successfully. Directly after the fifty-page meditation on the nature of art and its relation to memory and to life, Marcel is told that he can enter the salon and join the other guests. Brought back to himself and his surroundings, he seems to have found a new calm.

> But in the line of thought upon which I was embarked I was not in the least disturbed by the fact that this fashionable gathering, my return to society, might have provided me with that point of departure for a new life which I had been unable to find in solitude. There was nothing extraordinary about this fact, there was no reason why an impression with the power to resuscitate the timeless man within me should be linked to solitude rather than to society (as I had once supposed and as had perhaps once been the case, and as perhaps would

---

*During the madeleine resurrection, Marcel's mother is with him and in fact supplies both the tea and the cake. However, the passage does not indicate that she either shares the experience or receives an account of it from her son. He becomes totally rapt in his own mental processes and never mentions her again, not even at the end of the sequence. During the Martinville steeples impression, the coachman, next to whom Marcel was sitting, refused to talk with him. ". . . I was obliged, for lack of any other company, to fall back on myself" (I 180/i 255).

still have had to be the case had I developed harmoniously instead of going through this long period of arrest which seemed only now to be coming to an end) . . . I felt that the impulse given to the intellectual life within me was so vigorous now that I would be able to pursue these thoughts just as well in the drawing room, in the midst of the guests, as alone in the library; it seemed to me that, from this point of view, even in the midst of a numerous gathering, I would be able to maintain my solitude. (III 918/ vi 332–33)

Undistracted, no longer deceived by the false prestige of noble names and celebrated faces, sustained by the sense of his own life as worth living, Marcel will pass among the guests and watch the scene around him as if it were part of a play or a painting. Marcel will achieve the familiarity and the detachment to behold these other people without soul error, without the abdication of self that has always beset him before in a social context. His equanimity and powers of recognition will allow him at last to enter into his own existence as into a work of art, briefly transcending intermittence by fusing solitude and social intercourse. Marcel can now return safely and even profitably to his old haunts.

But we are reading Proust. No such simple triumph can be allowed to happen. It must be thwarted, or at best postponed. When he tries to join the party, Marcel recognizes no one and repeatedly loses his bearings. What ensues is a magnificent comic scene revealing the tenacity of general and individual human traits beneath the grotesque masquerade of age. Odette and the Prince de Guermantes and the rest are incorrigibly themselves to their last breath—which seems very near. Marcel has to perform an extended double take.

Presumably Marcel could now find the rewards of old age in the same social milieu that for years arrested his development. Yet it is not to be so. Marcel the writer realizes that he must devote the time remaining to him to composing the book he feels alive within him as the true fruit of his experience. Having attained an inner equilibrium of solitude and society, he will not have time to enjoy it. Here is the final irony. Attended only by Françoise, Marcel must turn resolutely to his solitary work as an artist.

Even though it opens a place for the reader, Proust's aesthetic raises an uncomfortable question: Is illumination by art reserved for the creative artist? The three major artists in the book play the role of collective godfather to Marcel. Until he finds his own vocation, they take his vows for him and guide him on his way. Conversely, the gifted amateurs—Swann, Charlus, even his grandmother—often lead him astray. When Marcel comes back to art at an advanced age, he does so not as an amateur or appreciative spectator but as a novelist. The hierarchy of functions is fully declared. Yet there are a few glints of hope for the nonartist and ordinary citizen. The basic materials of art, meaning impressions and possibly reminiscences, exist in all of us, available for translation into art. The true motif is life itself, if only we know how to approach it. Art is a matter of vision and revision. In his final meditation, Proust develops this thought and dramatically closes the loops between life and literature. Realism depicts only the surface of things, he states; both life and art lie "underneath." The key passage sounds like a manifesto.

> The greatness of true art . . . was to find, grasp, and bring out that reality which we live at a great distance from . . . that reality which we run the risk of dying without having known, and which is quite simply our own life. True life, life finally discovered and illuminated, is literature; that life which, in a sense, at every moment inhabits all men as well as the artist. (III 895/vi 298)

"All men" does not equivocate; "in a sense" holds something back. The stuff of literature is there for all to find and take. Few people find it; fewer still translate it into a work of art. But it is precisely that literary work which may help the less gifted to find their true life. They do so not vicariously, by seeking to identify with another life, but indirectly, by the reciprocating movement of literature, which propels them first toward clearly visible beings in a novel and then back toward their own existence insofar as they recognize themselves in the story. But only the writer-artist has the task and the reward of extruding a work of art out of his own experience. According to Proust's mature aesthetic, which is also his ethic, the writer draws both on an exceptional memory (encompassing impressions and reminiscences) and on a logical-imaginative insight that relates these mnemonic experiences to, and in, the work of art—process and product as one. The shape and the content of the *Search* derive from this aesthetic insight. The novel depicts the artist very much in the role of the Prodigal Son. After a long journey and many trials, a joyful return. It is primarily the obbligato motifs of suffering and work in the artist's life that keep the conclusion from sounding prideful. Within that obbligato, furthermore, one detects the quiet but unmistakable suggestion that each one of us—particularly a reader of Proust—is potentially the artist of his own life.

Now the quotation examining "the greatness of true art" is better known for another affirmation it contains, an affirmation sometimes truncated to a formula: "True life . . . is literature." Isolated from the surrounding argument, which is as much concerned with the nature of life as with the nature of art, the statement appears to be a categorical declaration of the aesthetic position referred to in the Introduction. According to this view, literary art carries a higher value and exists on a higher plane than ordinary living. Before we examine the merits of this conclusion about Proust's treatment of art, we need to look at another chain of ideas on the subject.

Idolatry

Marcel does not remain an intellectual-aesthetic version of Voltaire's character Candide for three thousand pages. But knowledge does not come to him easily or all at once. He has to penetrate a sequence of historical events along the false scents of temporal order before attaining some understanding of places and people and time. Wisdom is not given but earned, achieved. The *Search* relates a journey, a progress that cannot be discounted just because it reaches its destination against all expectations. There is no substitute for living, for the thickness of human time traversed. Proust's prolonged narrative and oblique, flickering presentation of character resolve into a courageous personal morality rarely discerned: we must create our own character by living, by surviving the succession of errors that is our lot. When he comes to declare himself directly on life and art in one of the capital passages of the book, Proust significantly frames it by attributing it to the painter Elstir as he and Marcel approach his studio on foot. Marcel has just reminded him of some very smug and stupid behavior in Elstir's early days. Elstir's exceptional little sermon in reply is identified as "the lesson of the master" and, paradoxically, contradicts itself.

> "There is no man," he began, "however wise, who has not at some period of his youth said things, or lived in a way the consciousness of which is so unpleasant to him in later life that he would gladly, if he could, expunge it from his memory. And yet he ought not entirely to regret it, because he cannot be certain that he has indeed become a wise man—so far as it is possible for any of us to be wise—unless he has passed through all the fatuous or unwholesome incarnations by which that ultimate stage must be preceded. I know that there are young fellows, the sons and grandsons of famous men, whose masters have instilled into them nobility of mind and moral refinement in their schooldays. They have, perhaps, when they look back upon their past lives, nothing to retract; they can, if they choose, publish a signed account of everything they have ever said or done; but they are poor creatures, feeble descendants of doctrinaires, and their wisdom is negative and sterile. We are not provided with wisdom, we must discover it for ourselves, after a journey through the wilderness which no one else can take for us, an effort which no one can spare us, for our wisdom is the point of view from which we come at last to regard the world. The lives that you admire, the attitudes that seem noble to you are not the result of training at home, by a father, or by masters at school; they have sprung from beginnings of a very different order, by reaction from the influence of everything evil or commonplace that prevailed round about them. They represent a struggle and a vic-

tory. I can see that the picture of what we once were, in early youth, may not be recognisable and cannot, certainly, be pleasing to contemplate in later life. But we must not deny the truth of it, for it is evidence that we have really lived, that it is in accordance with the laws of life and of the mind that we have, from the common elements of life, of the life of studios, of artistic groups—assuming that one is a painter—extracted something that goes beyond them." (I 864/ii 605–6)

Read attentively in the light of the entire novel, this page needs little comment. It is as personal and as universal an affirmation of individual experience as Montaigne's superb essays "Du repentir" and "De l'expérience." Elstir tells Marcel (to whom it all means very little until much later, when he has learned for himself) that life cannot be dispensed with and cannot be taught; it must be lived. One has to find out for oneself, and what one comes to is a "point of view" on one's own experience. Here lies true wisdom. The victory may belong to an instant, but it cannot be attained without lengthy combat. In this attitude of self-reliance the novel reaches beyond any set code of behavior such as that of Françoise and Norpois to assert a faith in the process of life as discovery.

We can now better understand Proust-Marcel's profound preoccupation with and reverence for age. A genuine prestige attaches to the mere fact of a person's having passed through a certain segment of time. This attitude forms one of many biblical elements in the *Search*. Tolstoy takes the same blunt attitude toward the irreducible, irreplaceable process of living. Near the end of the novella *Family Happiness,* Sergei finally explains to his wayward wife why he did not use his authority or persuasion to keep her from the temptation of worldly society.

"Yes," he began, as if continuing his thoughts aloud, "all of us, and especially you women, must have personal experience of all the nonsense of life, in order to get back to life itself; the evidence of other people is no good."

And the reason why Pierre occupies the center of interest in *War and Peace,* gradually displacing Andrew and Natasha for all their allure, is that he pursues so many false scents. We feel the full force of his experience, his restlessness, and his impatience with shoddy answers. No one answers Pierre's mighty questions; he simply takes time to discover his being and to assume himself.

Now, for all the rugged strength of this attitude toward life, it confronts us with a great dilemma regarding literature. Does it not seem that these two masters of the novel confound themselves by denying any final value to their own work? If we must learn through personal experience, following a progress of self-realization that cannot be hastened or influenced without some kind of damage to what we really are, *what is the purpose of literature?* Why read a book that, according to the deepest convictions of its author, we cannot substitute for life truly lived? The question is not specious. On the contrary, it probes toward the essential nature of literary experience and artistic experience in general. To put the question in terms of the *Search,* if what Marcel learns by living through a lifetime of disappointments and missteps comes clear to us as readers but cannot serve us as it serves him, what, then, are we doing here? I shall defer until the last chapter my attempt to answer the question, both because the appropriate terms will emerge later and because ruminating over the question a while may induce better understanding of it.

Because there are few passages so insistently didactic as the one I have just quoted, Elstir appears to be talking for Proust. In spite of all the special powers Proust has assigned elsewhere to art—to translate and to communicate the special experiences called impressions and reminiscences and recognitions—he here has the dedicated artist Elstir subordinate art to life. And I shall bring up several more passages and scenes that diminish the status of art, both as a way of life and as a collection of artifacts.

A dilettante and aesthete in his youth, Proust gradually developed his own convictions in his early thirties when he won his independence from Ruskin. In the postscript he added to his introduction to *The Bible* *of Amiens,* and in the later introduction to *Sesame and Lilies,* a series of references singles out as "intellectual sin" (*CSB* 183) what begins as a form of artistic "snobbery." This "essential infirmity of the human mind" (*CSB* 134) is attributed to Ruskin as well as to the Comte de Montesquiou, Proust's two intellectual heroes at that time. They are guilty of aesthetic "fetishism" (*CSB* 117), a veneration of the symbol instead of the reality it represents, a worship of aesthetic beauty without approaching the "discovery of truth" (*CSB* 132) that gave it birth and significance. "Idolatry" was the word Proust finally settled on to carry his full condemnation of this aesthetic attitude (*CSB* 129–41). The harshness of the word testifies to the rigors of his struggle to liberate himself from that attitude.*

In the *Search* we are given so much varied discussion of art that it is difficult to sort out false or provisional attitudes from the deepest insights. A sensitive and intelligent amateur of the arts, Swann is nevertheless a victim of "idolatry of forms" (1 852/ii 589) because he tries to arrange his life—even his love life—according to the narrow beauty he sees in art. Bergotte, a genuine though limited artist in his writings, has, when he dies, a glimmering sense that he has taken the wrong course, that he has been "imprudent." Looking at a little yellow patch in the Vermeer painting he has gone to see ("That's how I should have written"), he has a heart attack. "A celestial scales appeared to him which carried on one side his own life and on the other the little patch of wall that was so beautifully painted. He felt that he had imprudently given up the former for the latter" (III 187/v 245). He has been a fetishist of art, and he dies as one. He has neglected "his own life." In the curious image that follows, his books are displayed by threes in bookstore windows, "like angels with unfurled wings . . . the symbol of his resurrection" (III 188/v 246). Resurrection by art? By books in a window? We must read carefully. Such a resurrection could take place only among the cultists of aesthetic

---

*A close equivalent in English of the above passages can be found in the translation by Jean Autret and William Burford of Proust's *On Reading,* (New York: Macmillan, 1971), 47–49.

idolatry. Proust's tone is deeply ironic here. Bergotte had wasted his life and therefore compromised his art. It is a tainted resurrection.

A scene late in the novel returns to this line of thought. Therefore, I shall document it further. Though there are long passages of conversation in the novel, Marcel's words are rarely given in direct discourse. What he says is barely summarized, and often passed over in silence. (Possibly this is further evidence that we cannot be ourselves with others.) Exceptionally, Marcel is quoted at some length in a conversation with Charlus, who is bemoaning the wartime destruction of the Combray church. "The combination of surviving history and art that represents France at her best is being destroyed" (III 795/vi 154). (It also represents Marcel's childhood.) Charlus goes on to wonder whether the statue of Saint Firmin in Amiens has also been destroyed. "In that case," he adds, "the highest affirmation of faith and energy in the world has disappeared." Marcel raps his knuckles.

> "Its symbol, Monsieur," I answered. "And I adore certain symbols as much as you do. But it would be absurd to sacrifice to the symbol the reality it stands for. Cathedrals should be venerated until the day when, in order to save them, one would have to renounce the truths they teach. The arm of Saint Firmin raised in a gesture almost of military command, proclaimed: Let us be broken if honor requires it. Do not sacrifice men to stones whose beauty has caught for a moment a few human verities." (III 795/vi 154)

There is no other passage quite like it in the book. The Author has thrust his head through the text in order to speak to us directly. In his desire to refute idolatry, he violates the conventions of his own work. As a character, Marcel is never so resolute and categorical as this speech suggests. Even the Narrator speaks more softly. And these are not Marcel's convictions: they are Proust's. Marcel inherits from Swann and Bergotte a sense of the privileged status and calling of art. Its elevated position has made it impossible for him to believe he could ever become an artist. How could he ever lift his lowly insights and impressions to the

exalted regions of literature? Aesthetic snobbery, or *idolatry*, has kept
him from pursuing his own vocation. No, in this passage Proust is using
Marcel as a ventriloquist's dummy to condemn idolatry.

But in the scene of Marcel reading the Goncourts' journal, it is the
Narrator's voice, not Proust's, that we hear. (See pages 77–78.) This
book-within-a-book device offers a wholly new point of view on the familiar Verdurin clan. Unexpectedly, the story turns back to look at itself,
like a passenger catching sight of his own train going around a curve.
Marcel's dilemma is devastating: either he has misjudged those characters as ordinary, or the prestige of literature has given them a status they
do not deserve. In any case, the Narrator matter-of-factly employs the
phrase "the illusory magic of literature" (III 723/vi 46). There is no
authorial intrusion here. The events of this long tale of Marcel's search
for a vocation give him a jolt and oblige him to associate literature not
with truth but with illusion.

The clinching passage on establishing the legitimate claims of art
comes in the middle of the long philosophical meditation on memory and
art that Proust himself referred to as "Perpetual Adoration." The Narrator carefully explains that "artistic joys" arise from a "double impression" linked both to an external object in nature or a work of art, and to
an elusive inner trace or state of mind much more difficult to discern.
Those who celebrate the exterior work of art without seeking the inner
link in their own lives the Narrator calls "Bachelors of Art"—a double
pun in English. *Célibataires* in French suggests sterility and solitude.

> They become more exalted over works of art than artists themselves,
> for, their exaltation not being the result of the hard labor of explo-
> ration in themselves, it overflows toward the outside, animates their
> conversation, reddens their face; they think they have made an im-
> portant contribution by shouting "Bravo, bravo," after the perfor-
> mance of a work they love. (III 892/vi 293)

And the Narrator goes on to compare these "aging art-lovers" to
early airplane models that could not lift off the ground. Such amateurs

cannot grasp that the domain of art does not exist exclusively or even primarily outside us in great masterpieces, bound in books and displayed in museums, but rather in our responses to it, and in our good-faith attempt to track that response to our inner life—impressions, memory traces, parallel experiences.

Permanently sensitized by Ruskin, Proust would never allow art to present itself as a substitute for life, even for the life of the mind, but only as the exercise of communication that leads us back into life. When Marcel's Sunday afternoon reading in Combray tempted him to turn away from his existence in dissatisfaction and desire, he was misusing art as an escape and not discerning himself through its lens. In a boy this is natural enough. It may take the better part of a lifetime to discover that reading can augment rather than diminish one's own life and circumstances.

All these qualifications and scruples about the role of art in the *Search* are consistent with the final affirmation, by both Marcel and the Narrator as they become one voice, of "life as worth living" (III 1032/vi 507). Elstir's advice about personal experience, the lessons of the Goncourt journal, Charlus' overvaluation of the statue of Saint Firmin, the bachelors of art shouting bravo and missing the essential—all these episodes testify to the fact that the action of the novel, backed by many of its expository passages, does not assign to art and works of art the power of eminent domain. That ultimate power resides in life, in men and women trying to come to terms with everything around them and with one another. In a closed loop or arabesque, literature departs from life in order to lead us back to it with new understanding.

As the Narrator settles down in the last fifteen pages to write his book—presumably this very novel—he appears to withdraw from the world in order to work. But that withdrawal allows him in reality to devote himself to life. For we have now learned that the role of literature is instructive, didactic. I am not talking about clumsy precepts and the lives of saints. Proust teaches by parables and lives gone astray. A work of art does not exist in a realm separated from life by the laws of aesthetic autonomy. It allows us to find our own life through its finely ground lens. Proust loved that image of the artist as optician and used it many times.

At the end of his novel, Proust was so intent on proclaiming the vital tie between life and literature that he suggested that our very survival depends on it in the face of imminent death. The work of literature to which he gives the key role in the final pages is not a major European classic or even the Bible. The Narrator says not only that his book will run as long as *A Thousand and One Nights* but that it will, like the Arabian masterpiece, prolong life. By telling stories to stay the cruel hand of Shariar, Scheherazade saves her own life and that of many other potential victims, and converts the Sultan to love for his family and a new benevolence. Very gradually and by indirection behind its extravagant adventures, *A Thousand and One Nights* reverses its opening situation of deceit and murderous revenge and suggests that a good woman can be trusted and a good man can be tamed.

Proust's *Search* teems with places and characters and plots that are endangered, not by a Sultan's daily massacre of his consort, but by the blandishments of high culture, including the idolatry of art and literature. The novel unfolds a lifetime of experience, which enlarges our understanding of love and nature, memory and snobbery. One of the principal messages that emerges is that literature, with its marvelous advantages of transparency and structure and timing, does not stand superior to life: it serves life. Proust's instructive novel seeks to show us the springs of life—not in a work of art but in ourselves.

VII

THE STRUCTURE OF
SHEER LENGTH

Finding a Form

I N 1912 PROUST HOPED TO PUBLISH HIS FINISHED NOVEL IN two volumes of 650 pages each. After several rejections, the best arrangement he could obtain was a contract for one volume of 500 pages—at his own expense—and the rest to appear later. This serial publication meant that the first volume would not convey the sense of the whole, the overall unity, to which Proust attached great importance. "I feel like someone with a tapestry too large for any of his rooms," he observed in an interview, "and who has to cut it up into sections." And there was another problem. In the five-year interval imposed by the war and during the four further years of Proust's life, the tapestry kept growing to more than double the size originally projected.

Through the prolonged vegetable growth of the novel to some three thousand pages, working mostly in bed, Proust displayed astonishing organizational powers over his proliferating notebooks and drafts and typescripts. To his friend Louis de Robert he insisted on the novel's "very strict composition, though not easy to grasp because of the complexity." He appeared to falter only at the very end. A few months be-

fore he died in 1922, he wrote his editor and publisher that he had no
trouble composing the narrative. "But patching things together and tying
up the ends—that's more than I can handle." We need to look beyond
such statements, however, in order to discover to what degree Proust
succeeded in finding an adequate structure for the *Search* and how he
may have done so. I shall examine three elements of structure in the
Search in an order of increasing complexity and importance.

I have already mentioned one device Proust adopted to express and almost to embody conflicting principles of fragmentation and unity in
registering experiences: namely, the double *I*. Inside that simplest and
most elusive of words, Marcel's clumsy projects keep going astray and
collapsing under the detached, ordering, sardonic gaze of the Narrator,
who is Marcel's older ego. The double *I* projects a stereoscopic perspective and creates a narrative relief or depth perception on the events related. This narrative device arises from Proust's style, from his use of the
first-person singular pronoun with two edges on it so that it cuts two
ways. We are carried back toward a protagonist growing up and forward toward a mature adult watching his (own) progress. That stylistic
device also operates structurally to permit asides, recall related events,
and remind us how far we have traveled in this seemingly infinite itin-
erary.

The second unifying device begins as topography, expands into social
relations, and ends as metaphysics. We learn early in the opening volume
that all Combray is divided into two parts, into two possible directions
in which the family members may take their daily walk. These "two
ways" distinguish two kinds of terrain and two social strata. Swann's
way leads to Swann's bourgeois estate and toward less respectable zones
represented by the cocotte Odette and the lesbian Mlle Vinteuil. The
Guermantes way leads toward the historied château of the noble Guermantes family, never reached because beyond walking distance, yet constantly occupying Marcel's imagination. This entirely local division of
the countryside gradually develops into an analogy for Paris society also
and for unexpected exchanges that will develop between the "two ways."
By the end of the novel the narrative voice, speaking for both Marcel and

the Narrator, reflects on how he was once shut up in the Combray basin and on how he now sees that its "two ways" extend "into the ocean of the 'wide world' " (III 969/vi 410). The map of Combray with its two ways that Proust gives us at the start will continue to serve Marcel as he journeys out into the world beyond Combray.

The geographical division of "two ways" gradually comes to stand for two important dualities in the overall action of the novel.

The first duality is that of two kinds of snobbery that fascinate Marcel as he grows up—the lure of the higher aristocratic levels of society, and the lure of the basest, most vulgar, and most depraved levels. He has little but scorn for anything in between. It is this double snobbery that causes Marcel's original indifference to Albertine (I 844/ii 578) and arouses his desire for Baronne de Putbus' maid and for the wellborn girl who frequents a brothel. He has laid eyes on neither (II 723/iv 166). Marcel has to acknowledge the aptness of M. de Charlus' terse metaphor for this preference for the extremes. "No middle ground. *Phèdre* or *Les Saltimbanques* " (III 830/vi 203).

The second duality represented by the "two ways" consists of the two paths of knowledge that for years determine Marcel's response to any event or sensation. What he has himself already experienced seems inevitably trivial, whereas all the mystery and promise of life appear to lie in a wider, higher realm not yet explored. We are very close to soul error. With his grandmother in Balbec, Marcel spends a good deal of time with the frumpy Mme de Villeparisis. Though she is a marquise, she makes a poor impression on Marcel because, among other things, she likes oysters. Then he learns that the old lady is closely related to the Guermantes, most aristocratic of families, none of whom Marcel has yet met. He reacts immediately and in terms of the duality that still holds him in thrall. How can Villeparisis contain Guermantes? "How could I be expected to believe in a common origin uniting two names which had entered my consciousness, one through the low and shameful gate of experience, the other by the golden gate of imagination?" (I 698/ii 377).

The familiar and the unknown seem to represent opposite poles of experience. The immense geographical polarity of the "two ways" contains this duality as well and extends it over the social fabric of the entire novel.

At the very end the "two ways" and corresponding dualisms of snobbery and knowledge fuse into an enlarged understanding of human experience. But this local-universal division of the landscape has helped to orient us within the vast narrative. And the "two ways" come to function as a metaphor for metaphor itself—for the way in which apparently opposed elements reveal similarities and fold into one another.

The action that comes to dominate the *Search* is the action of metaphor: to reconcile a duality or, in more complex cases, a multiplicity. The action encompasses all aspects of the book, from the facets of personality to levels of society to the stereoscopic assembling of past and present. Marcel finally understands that he has himself produced this great fusion by growing up, by recognizing himself, by living his own life as no one else could live it for him, and by heeding the vocation of literature. The circle of this extended metaphor closes only in the last two hundred pages and is certified by the apparition of Mlle de Saint-Loup, the final flesh-and-blood symbol of the "two ways," barely fifteen pages before the end.

There is a stylistic question to raise about this culminating moment of the novel's action. The crucial paragraph on Mlle de Saint-Loup runs to only half a page, begins with the simple sentence "I saw Gilberte approaching me," contains no sentence over five lines long, and closes with another modest sentence, "I found Mlle de Saint-Loup beautiful . . . she resembled my youth" (III 1031–32/vi 506–7). Do we expect more here? Is it incumbent on Proust, after three thousand pages of prose that unrolls like a rich brocade, overflows with metaphor, and uncoils vine-like syntactic structures, to surpass himself at this point? Does the occasion require that he break into poetry or into song? In the last chapter of *Proust's Binoculars*, which was published in *1963*, I declared that he has partly failed us by not producing a needed stylistic leap.

Today I would maintain that the simplicity, the muteness even of this key paragraph, is fully appropriate to the context. Marcel's revelation is intense yet sober. Dazzling effects would be out of place. It is true that at a comparable point near the end of *Ulysses*, Joyce lifts his constantly shifting prose one notch higher to the final interior monologue of Molly Bloom. The narrative devices of earlier sections do not match her swelling affirmation. It is also true that in the final Canto 33 of the *Paradisio*, Dante does not have to outstrip himself with a burst of dazzling poetry. The momentum of a hundred cantos sustains us. A certain stillness, a certain silence suits the occasion in Proust as in Dante.

The first professional opinion of Proust's novel (written for the Fasquelle publishing house in 1912) was based on one-eighth of its final length. Little wonder that the reader found it "wandering" and asked irritably in his report, "What's it all about?" He concluded that the book was written by a "pathological case." And even recently, with the full novel available to him, in a widely reviewed book, *Proust et les signes* (1964), Gilles Deleuze has this to say about the architecture of the *Search:* ". . . it brings with it fragments which can no longer be restored, pieces which do not fit into the same puzzle, which do not belong to a preceding totality, which do not emanate from the same lost unity." To my mind, Deleuze is blind, particularly to the third structural element, which encompasses more than the double *I* and the "two ways." Here my exposition will have to cover familiar ground as well as enter new territory.

The opening 180-page section of the *Search* moves through three distinct stages. The first three pages record the thoughts of an unidentified and unlocated consciousness trying to orient itself while wandering on the frontier between waking and sleep. As it seeks its identity, it describes a movement backward and downward in the evolution of consciousness through sickness, childhood, Edenic innocence, the ignorance of a caveman, and animal existence—to nothingness, *le néant*. When rescued by memory from this collapse, the narrative voice says, "In a second I passed through centuries of civilization" (I 5/i 5). In the most literal and direct sense, the *Search* opens, like *Alice in Wonderland*, with a fall. Consciousness tumbles all the way back to a point before creation itself, to the void. The book recoils to zero. Then, out of the swirl of images, one scene comes clear.

That scene is narrated in the second stage of thirty pages. A child in

Combray is anxiously awaiting his mother's good-night kiss and finally
has his way. But that vivid spot of awareness cannot expand beyond a
strict limit. It remains blocked until the spell is broken. Through the unexpected intervention of the madeleine incident, a whole segment of the
past floods back and gives the protagonist a firm identity, the start of a
life, and a story to follow. This is the third stage.

Correspondingly, in the final two hundred pages of the novel, the
narrative comes to a conclusion in three stages. After long wanderings
Marcel arrives at the last Guermantes reception and experiences a series
of reminiscences (III 866ff./vi 254ff.) echoing the madeleine sequence.
They too seem to array the past around him, this time as available material for his literary undertakings. For the first time he has positive
thoughts about his career as a writer. The most sustained reflections on
literature in the book lie in this fifty-page section. The second stage carries him into the salon. Suddenly, all his projects fall apart because he
cannot recognize anyone. For an agonizing interval he is locked back into
the present, into contingency. It takes well over a hundred pages for
Marcel to readjust his sights and to focus on past and present together.
Then the apparition of Mlle de Saint-Loup lifts Marcel and the Narrator (now fused in a single *I*) into a kaleidoscopic swirl of images—settling down to write with Françoise as Muse, the menace of death, the
stilts of time. The brief closing section portrays both the precariousness
of advanced age and the strong impression of something still in progress,
like a pot cooking on the stove.*

What can we now make of Proust's insistence in many letters that the
last pages of the novel were written immediately after the first pages
and "come back exactly to them"? A little reflection shows that the three
stages of the opening and those of the close occur in reverse order. In the
opening section: wandering consciousness seeking identity; the clear

*My analysis here owes a good deal to the chapter on Proust in Jean Rousset's
Forme et signification. However, where he sees two stages I see three. And we have
markedly different ideas about the relation between the opening and the close of the
novel.

outlines of one confining specific scene; and release into the varied experiences of Combray and the wide world. In the last section: a welling up of reminiscences spanning the entire book; the scene of Marcel failing to recognize his oldest friends; and a detached consciousness resolving to accept its literary calling. In both sequences the second stage works as an obstacle. Marcel (at the opening) and the Narrator (at the end) are held captive in a restricted segment of contingent time until a new development releases them. But the narrative movement in these two segments is flowing in opposite directions. The first two hundred pages open out like a megaphone or a river delta to project Marcel's budding consciousness toward the wide horizons of adult life. The last two hundred pages close the action down like a funnel and concentrate that flow into the mind of an author bending over his lifework. The cycle of expansion and contraction approaches mirror symmetry of form over a very long interval.

In a letter to Mme Scheikévitch in 1915 Proust transcribed nearly verbatim from his novel in progress a description of the way Marcel fell in and out of love with Albertine (III 558/v 753). "Before forgetting her completely, like a traveler who comes back to his point of departure by the same route, . . . I had to pass through all the same feelings I had already gone through—but in reverse order." The shape of the action now comes into view. The beginning and the end of the novel are firmly in place, the former leading us into and the latter out of the narrative. In between comes a malleable and infinitely expandable section, which more than doubled its original size. This vast median segment has the resilience of life itself. Only a few incidents seem absolutely essential: all are significant when related to the rest. The opening and the close establish beyond challenge an overarching movement that encompasses all digressions and meanderings. After the initial and transient hope of salvation in childhood, the *Search* follows a downward slope toward error, perdition, and death. Only at the end does the action turn out to be a resurrection and self-recognition. And now we may be able to discern why Proust insisted not on the distance but on the closeness between the first page and the last.

A number of modern novels concern a character who is at work writing a novel. A literary convention has grown up implying that we are reading that fictional novel. The convention has something both obvious and contrived about it. A few years after Proust's death, Gide's *The Counterfeiters* and Huxley's derivative *Point Counter Point* developed the scheme into a sustained testing and spoof of the novel form. They imply the infinite regress of the figure on a Quaker Oats box: "This is a novel about writing a novel about. . . ." Sensing the fragility as well as the fascination of that theme of infinite regress, Proust held it off until the very end of his work. Marcel, we are repeatedly told, will never be a writer. Yet when, at the end, against all odds and expectations, he metamorphoses into the Narrator of his own life, a whole new state of things appears. Proust's ending leads us firmly out of the *Search* as *Marcel's* story of growing up and across into a symmetrical mirror-novel, consisting of all the same words and incidents, this time recording the *Narrator's* story of recording Marcel's story. A new circumambulation begins, this time not of living the events but of writing them. As Proust's *I* contains two persons, his novel contains two stories.

Proust's construction of his novel could now be traced out in graphic form (see Diagram VI). The firmly established paths marking the opening and close permit almost limitless latitude in the intermediate sections. Indeed, the figure looks like an inflatable balloon. And the careful alignment of entry with exit, retracing similar steps in reverse order, leads us over into a second reading or interpretation of the same work seen not as Marcel's benighted wanderings among false scents but as the Narrator's recognition and portrayal of those events as revealing, as meaningful experience. The fact that many readers of the *Search* report an impulse to read it a second time testifies to this two-tiered nature of the novel. It tells two stories in one—a failure and an achievement.

Occasionally, as we read A, Marcel's story, we become aware of B, the composition of that story, called to our attention by the Narrator ventriloquizing through the double-bottomed *I*. We watch love and friendship, social success and even art disintegrate as Marcel reaches them. Only at the very end does the reader follow Marcel in performing a great

VI. The Shape and Trajectory of the *Search*

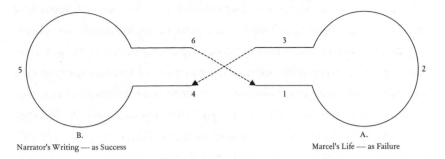

B.
Narrator's Writing — as Success

A.
Marcel's Life — as Failure

A. *Life*   1. Three stages of *Combray* (first 50 pages)
    as   2. Vagaries of Marcel's life
    Failure 3. Three stages at the close of *Time Regained*
                  (last 200 pages)

B. *Narrative* 4. ⎧The same incidents as 1, 2, and 3 seen
    as   5. ⎨not as Marcel's life but as the Narrator's
    Success 6. ⎩self-recognition

double take on what has happened. No major new initiative reverses the action. Chance intervenes in the humble form of paving stones and spoons and water pipes. Yet everything Marcel has gone through has imperceptibly shifted the odds in his favor until chance has the force of fate. He lives surrounded by signs and secrets. Suddenly, after further delay and the final encounter with an unknown young girl, *qui perd gagne: loser takes all.* By an act of recognition that incorporates rather than rejects lived experience, Marcel sees the past anew as his own, as himself. It is the moment in which he becomes the Narrator, thus finding the vocation he had presumed totally lost.

    This metamorphosis in Marcel brings about the transition from A to B in the form of a setting to work. Retroactively it transforms every event of A into a new pattern of *success,* the systematic changing of signs permitted by the vantage point of age and retelling. This new light shed back over the entire action implies a second reading, this time not of A but of B. Yet a skilled reader will read A and B simultaneously.

It is precisely this firm construction that is lacking in Proust's earlier attempts at large-scale fiction. Having only a highly contrived beginning and no end, *Jean Santeuil* gives the effect of being all middle. A motley of texts lumped together under an awkward title, *Against Saint-Beuve* reveals Proust's impatience to find a form that would contain both events and reflections on events. The preface he drafted for that project shows how far astray Proust still was in early 1909, even though he had collected most of his essential ideas and incidents, including the resurrections. He opens the preface with three rapid pages narrating the three classic resurrections: toast dipped in tea, uneven paving stones, the clink of spoon on a plate. The incidents barely receive their due, and the exposition quickly moves on to other matters. It appears that Proust did not know what use to make of these importunings of involuntary memory and simply blurted them all out at the beginning. Within a few months, however, he had changed his scheme completely and saved all but one of the resurrections for the *end* of a story that he would eventually name *In Search of Lost Time*. In order to give the reader one clue to go on, one anticipation of the end, Proust left the tea and toast (or madeleine) sequence in place, near the opening. The others are transferred to the new location. Now we can see that the first pages of the preface to *Against Sainte-Beuve* contain in germ both the opening and the close of the *Search*, but with no sense of a life lived in between. They read like a manifesto on memory and create no undertow of narrative.

For the *Search*, Proust found the arrangement that allowed him to tell a story. The theme of great expectations runs very strong at the start and then diminishes, leaving us adrift on the ocean of Marcel's desultory life. The ocean seems to go on forever, until, when we have given up hope of any further movement, we find that the current is running again and has carried us back to shore—the same shore we left—now transformed by the passage of time.

This narrative line makes strict demands on the timing by which things can be divulged. The truth must not come out too soon. The limitation goes far beyond that of Marcel's age and experience. The end of the story controls all other sections. For example, in the opening volume,

Swann's Way, one of the guests at the Verdurins' dinners is a vulgar, ambitious, seemingly untalented painter called Monsieur Tiche or Biche. In later volumes the dedicated artist Elstir initiates Marcel to the genuine rewards of painting. Toward the end of *Within a Budding Grove*, Marcel discovers that Tiche and Elstir are the same man. While revising *Sodom and Gomorrah*, Proust decided that this discovery comes much too soon and made an urgent note for himself.

> *Nota Bene.* Don't say in this volume that Mme Verdurin called him Monsieur Tiche, nor, secondly, that I [i.e., Marcel] understand it's the same man whose life I learned about earlier. Keep the first for the Goncourt passage, and the second for the last chapter. (II 1200 / ——)

He never had time to make the necessary changes, but the sense of narrative shape he was aiming at is clear.

At the same time Proust could not abandon his readers entirely to Marcel's shrinking world of false scents and disappointments. At intervals along the spiral stairway of the narrative, we come upon a narrow window in the tower from which we can see a fleck of the countryside that later we will see in its full expanse from the top. These anticipatory glimpses do not fit together into a single picture, but they encourage our climbing. The first such window occurs early when Marcel flees from the scene in which his great-aunt exasperated his grandmother by urging his grandfather to drink more than he should. "Alas! I didn't know that, much more grievously than these little weaknesses of her husband, my lack of will power, my delicate health, and the uncertainty they shed over my future, preoccupied my grandmother as she incessantly paced about morning and evening" (I 12/i 14). Narrative has its own form of preterition. Proust's "I didn't know" is a fairly crude way of smuggling a fragment of contraband information into the text. He can do better. The concert of Vinteuil's septet, arranged by the Baron be Charlus in Mme Verdurin's bourgeois salon, two-thirds of the way through the novel, is a subtle and ambitious extension of the same hortatory device. When both the reader and Marcel need it badly, the scene anticipates aesthetic rewards still to come.

Aside from these brief remissions to keep us moving along, the *Search* flows powerfully within the confines of its double loop. Marcel and the Narrator attain their respective goals, the one of finding and assuming his full identity, the other of writing an account of that achievement. As Diagram V seems to say in its very appearance, this circular construction does not appeal beyond life fully lived to any higher domain—a world of eternal verities, art for art's sake, a divine being, or the historic destiny of man. Proust's story of self-rehabilitation makes a very human and earth-bound document. It does not hesitate to invoke any resource men have tried in order to sustain their faith, including the transmigration of souls and the legend of *le peuple éternel*. However, they are transient appeals. The reflexive architecture of the novel informs us that memory and art will lead us not out of life but back to it.

Lost and Found

Proust knew the drawbacks of excessive length in writing, particularly for fiction. The era of Victor Hugo's blockbusters lay in the past. Even the newly translated Russian novelists tended to stop short of a thousand pages. In all probability Proust was cognizant of two voices, one ancient and one modern, that had spoken firmly in favor of limits on size of works of art. Aristotle in the *Poetics* decreed for tragedy "a certain magnitude" that must not exceed what the eye or the mind can take in all at once. This human scale makes tragedy superior to the epic. In order to obtain the essential unity of effect, Edgar Allan Poe imposed on a poem the limit of being readable in one sitting—with similar implications for prose fiction.

But Proust was not listening to Aristotle and Poe. Increasingly, as the interval of the war afforded him more time, he felt the novel growing within him, held in place yet not confined by his early laying down of its beginning and its end. Somewhat less evident, I should say, is the fact that the novel has a middle—not prominently marked, but discernible as a linked succession of major episodes. These five hundred pages within the bildungsroman present Marcel's triple rite of passage into maturity and into a new perspective on his goal in life.

The major scenes in the middle section take place in an alternating order similar to the montage of a film. The order of things seems to arise both from contrast and from chronology. First, Marcel witnesses from close up the illness and death of his beloved grandmother without registering their effect on his deepest self (II 314–45/iii 427–71). When Marcel is invited to an elegant sit-down dinner given by the Duc and Duchesse de Guermantes, his fantasies about the magic world of aristocracy wither into disenchantment at their empty rituals (II 416–547/ii 570–749): it is the longest sustained scene in the book. From a window, Marcel observes the sexual encounter of the imposing Baron de Charlus, a Guermantes, and Jupien, a tailor, and Marcel's eyes are opened to understand the Baron's aggressive and enigmatic behavior (II 601–32/iv 1–44). Climbing even higher socially, Marcel attends an immense reception that the Prince and Princesse de Guermantes host and finds himself surrounded by homosexuals and by discussions of the Dreyfus affair (II 633–725/iv 45–170). And finally, traveling to the seaside resort of Balbec, Marcel, first in a dream and then at the sight of apple trees in full bloom with their roots in the spring mud, responds both to the terrible loss of his grandmother and to her survival as a moral and almost physical presence in his life (II 751–81/iv 204–45).

These 500 middle pages recount, in the two short framing sequences about the grandmother, Marcel's first encounter with the death of a beloved family figure. That split incident of delayed action frames the two scenes depicting the sumptuous yet empty rewards of social ambition. Centered in this double frame sits the scene that Proust always referred to as "indecent": the explicit revelation of Charlus as a predator. From here on, the direction of the novel becomes unmistakable—a long decline until the story comes to a standstill before the new beginning of the closing sequence. At the furthest extent of his narrative reach, Proust has constructed a sequence of scenes forming a 500-page unit that serves as the novel's pivot, its turning.

Partially hidden because it straddles two volumes, this high narrative plateau in the middle of the *Search* adds strength and articulation to Marcel's saga. It is as if Proust here brings the narrative machinery, like an immense optical instrument, into focus on three essential plot lines: the grandmother's incorruptible presence and absence; the limits of life in high society; and Charlus' corrupting behavior. These pages contain the major load-bearing posts and beams of the novel's structure apart from the beginning and the end. There is nothing desultory or self-indulgent about the writing. Even when expatiating on trivial genealogies of the nobility, Proust knows where he is going.

But the nagging question remains: Why, knowing the price and the perils, did Proust submit to—or work steadily toward—a novel of so great length? It has to do, I believe, with his way of telling a story, a talent, along with his mimicry, for which he was highly prized as a salon guest. For Proust, the secret of narrative lies as much in what is withheld as in what is related. In order to sustain anticipation, full divulgence must come as late as possible. Timing is all. And timing extended will increase the element that guides the dimensions of Proust's novel as much as it guides the length of his sentences: *suspense*. It should be evident that, at least up to a subtle point, and depending on the author's narrative skill, increasing a novel's length will enhance the suspenseful effect of deferred divulgence.

Does Proust exceed this point and fail as a novelist? Or does he extend it and establish a new marathon course for the novel? Has he violated or observed Aristotle's strictures on magnitude? Having published the opening, which both lights the narrative fuses and begins the great *arrêt* of the middle sections, Proust was unexpectedly given five war years to do what the original conception of the story both allowed and called for: namely, to extend the middle section of the novel while leaving the beginning and the end in place. Does the consequent doubling from thirteen hundred to three thousand pages amplify the dramatic effect of the final reversals and allow Proust to strengthen his aesthetic of suspense? Or does the novel stall out under the burden of a whole new set of rowdy characters and of obsessive themes such as jealousy and lying?

The evidence is not easy to assemble and interpret. Nevertheless, I believe the answer to these two questions is unambiguous. The novel approaches collapse, yet goes on to finish and to win the race. Just before Marcel's return to Paris after his third stay in a *maison de santé*, the action and the forward movement of the novel come to a standstill. We and he can go no farther. The Narrator's observations about elections, the bull market in diamonds, and the victims of Bolshevism after the war have lost their purpose. Proust marks this collapse, this rent in the fabric, by breaking off the story in midsentence (III 854/vi 238). The long voyage has ended in disaster and defeat. The unusual break in the printed text signifies an abandon ship. In rhetoric, the term for this effect is not the mild-mannered "ellipsis" but *aposiopesis*—a dramatic collapse in midpassage, the utter incapacity to continue.

But behold! We have come within sight of our destination. The novel's ending, sketched out years earlier, is waiting there to take us in (III 854–1048/vi 238–532). We have come through. The rescue that follows this narrative wreck represents the resolution of the long suspense created by 2,800 preceding pages. In Proust's mind the theatrical effect of extended decline and final reversal provided sufficient reason to brush aside the arguments of Aristotle about "a certain magnitude" and Poe's insistence on confining oneself to the dimensions of a reading in a single sitting. Proust could keep on adding until the end of his life, because the conclusion of his novel was already there, in place, ready to confer retrospective order and meaning on all that accumulating narrative.

The three opening pages of the *Search* relate how a human consciousness lost in a whirling confusion of images and memories finally focuses on his true identity. On the daily walks around Combray, Marcel's father loves to lead the family far afield in the dusk on unfamiliar paths. Then, when they admit to being utterly lost, he reveals that they are standing outside their own garden gate and have already arrived home. Launched into the adult world, Marcel wanders for years along the paths of snobbery, misplaced love, and aesthetic excess. Happily, the "lost and found" motif operates as well on this larger scale. For when Marcel thinks he has lost everything, his wastrel life has brought him home and he has found himself. As I have said, there is something of the Prodigal Son parable in the *Search*, without the figure of the loving father at the end to take him in. Marcel is able to recognize himself and to come home as the Narrator of his tale. Everyone's perseverance, including the reader's, is required for sheer length to attain its full effect.

VIII

CONTINUING DISPUTES

Too Much of Proust?

I T SHOULD BE CLEAR THAT THE INTERVAL OF WORLD WAR I reinforced Proust's natural inclination to expand his work. By the time the full novel appeared in 1927, it had grown to thirteen physical volumes. To read Proust in that paperbound, uncut, unannotated form requiring a paper cutter, as was necessary for three decades, carried the challenge of exploring an unmapped continent without a reliable compass. In 1954 the French Pléiade collection brought out the full novel in three compact volumes with indexes and résumés and essential notes. U.S. and U.K. publishers consolidated Moncrieff's translation into two large readable volumes in 1934. In these editions one can, with attentive reading, perceive the underlying shape of the novel sustaining its great length. In subsequent years scholars produced a series of substantial biographies, from George Painter's in two volumes to the 900-page *Marcel Proust: Biographie* (1996) by Jean-Yves Tadié. Meanwhile, Proust's correspondence has appeared in twenty-one volumes.

When Proust's novel fell into public domain in 1987, three Paris publishing houses were ready with new editions that had been in preparation for several years. They all carry the same basic 3,000-page text with few variations. The differences lie in packaging and presentation. Laffont-Bouquins chose to publish three fat volumes prefaced by elaborate historical and biographical materials. Garnier-Flammarion produced ten pocket-sized volumes competently edited by Jean Milly. The new Pléiade edition, published by the original copyright holder, Gallimard, made the boldest, most ambitious, and most expensive bid to claim the market. In a combination of editorial, literary, and commercial decisions, Gallimard proposed to influence the way we read Proust and, to some degree, the way we approach all great literary works.

The difference is immediately visible and palpable. The Pléiade edition of *A la recherche du temps perdu* grew from three compact leather-bound volumes totaling 3,500 pages to four bulging volumes totaling 7,300 pages. The added pages include expanded apparatus and, most prominently, newly introduced sketches, drafts, and variants in tiny print. These *esquisses* add up to some 1,250 pages, equal to almost half the length of the novel itself. Eight inches on the shelf instead of three. A price of several hundred dollars. Is there someone somewhere who believes that this elephantiasis is appropriate to Proust's novel? Three thousand pages are daunting enough. What past mistakes or what new discoveries explain this more than doubling of the product we are to pay for and hold in our hands? Other shorter, far less expensive, and fully satisfactory editions in French and English await one in the bookstores. Nevertheless, Proust scholars working with the original French have generally elected the new 7,300-page Pléiade as the authoritative version to be cited.

The leading proponent of this edition is Jean-Yves Tadié, author of the biography and of earlier studies of Proust's novel. His scrupulous scholarship and immense knowledge of Proust's life and writings qualify Tadié to be the dean of Proust studies. When he began on the new Pléiade edition, he was powerfully drawn toward what is known as genetic criticism—the study of the evolution of a work out of earlier outlines and drafts and sketches into its (presumably) final state. An author like Montaigne lends himself beautifully to such an approach. He himself published the second and third editions of his *Essays*, which incorporate the earlier versions interspersed with extended additions. Up to a point, he kept everything and rejected nothing. (As George Hoffmann has shown in *Montaigne's Career*, he had commercial, literary, and personal reasons for publishing his books this way.) But most authors, including Proust, work toward a final version for publication. In that process they may write and reject a mass of drafts and revisions. Prolonged obsessive attention to these exploratory materials tends to undermine a scholar's respect for the final version. We have become enamored with "the creative process." The most revealing and misguided statement from a genetic critic was made twenty years ago by Jacques Petit: *"Le texte n'existe pas."*

In Europe and the United States today, genetic criticism has expanded rapidly and opened up lush new fields for scholars, particularly studies of major modern authors with well-furnished archives. Most of Proust's working papers and drafts became available at the Paris Bibliothèque Nationale in the 1970s. They provided a scholarly bonanza. As head editor of the Pléiade volumes, Tadié persuaded himself, along with a crew of young scholars he had recruited and the responsible committees at Gallimard, that the new edition should contain extensive selections from Proust's working drafts as well as enhanced editorial apparatus.

And thus it is Tadié who, at the end of his 100-page general introduction, provides the justification for this remarkable expansion. Traditionally, the highly respected and widely sold Pléiade collection (a complete library of several hundred titles representing world authors, classic to modern, and including its own encyclopedia and other reference works) has presented a reliable text of an author's work or works along with brief introduction and basic notes. They are reader's editions, as distinct both from critical scholarly editions and from cheap popular editions. But Tadié's Proust shifts the undertaking from a reader's edition to a full-blown critical edition in which the actual text of the work occupies less space than the apparatus surrounding it. Many a miniature painting hangs in a frame distinctly larger than the tiny picture it contains. We accede to this summons of our attention to something so concentrated. But Proust's *In Search of Lost Time* cannot pass for a miniature. Like Monet's water lily series, it needs the most modest frame possible. Yet between the 1954 and the 1989 Pléiades, the editor has enlarged the frame from 500 to 5,000 pages. How are we to deal with this instance of physical and intellectual giganticism?

Proust is an exceptional author. The intelligent general reader will need some guidance. The other new French editions, and increasingly those in English, provide that guidance without intrusiveness. Therefore, we must carefully examine the sheer dimensions and specific content of the Pléiade phenomenon for the implications it contains concerning the status of a literary work and the future of literary studies.

THE SWEEPING ARGUMENT Tadié builds in the last six pages of his general introduction turns in part on an ambiguity of the French word *oeuvre* as used in the context of literature and art. It can mean a single, clearly defined, unified work—sonnet, tragedy, novel, painting—by a single author or artist. It can also mean the entire corpus of a writer's work, a lifetime's accomplishment. (In the latter sense, it is often given the masculine gender.) Tadié observes that in certain mechanical and superficial ways the last three volumes of Proust's novel (composed of seven in all with different titles) were left unfinished at his death. Then he adds emphatically, "But if *In Search of Lost Time* is unfinished in some details, it is in no fashion an incomplete work *[une oeuvre incomplète]*" (ciii). Four pages later in closing, he states that in this new edition the reader will be able to reconstruct Proust's entire *"oeuvre,"* meaning everything he wrote. This subtle shift from one meaning of *oeuvre* to another cannot be ignored. Tadié beckons us away from the universally recognized 3,000-page novel to consider a very different entity: Proust's entire output. Do we wish to follow him?

Tadié begins this closing section by recalling Proust's discussion in *The Captive* of the "retroactive unity" projected back over their earlier works by certain nineteenth-century writers such as Balzac. Even though Tadié claims that this discussion "defines Proust's poetics" (civ), he goes on to demonstrate the opposite. Proust did not find his "circular structure" after the fact. "Deciding from the start to link his first and last chapters, Proust avoids the incompleteness of the great nineteenth-century books" (cvi). Tadié argues that the special effectiveness of Proust's structure lies not in the fact that he imposed it retrospectively but that he waited until the end to reveal it. I have insisted myself on the role of suspense in the *Search*.

Unexpectedly, in the middle of a paragraph, Tadié insists that what Proust tells us about the order and structure of his novel has led to "the principles that direct the present edition" (cv). Tadié cites without transition the early abandoned novel *Jean Santeuil* to introduce Proust's taste for unpublished writings and concludes, "for the *amateur*, nothing that has fallen from Proust's pen, above all if it has to do with the novel, is indifferent" (cv). In one sentence, Tadié has vaulted from the unifying structure of the novel to the mass of materials omitted from it in order to create that unity. A bit later, Tadié tells us how much affection Proust felt for the word *esquisse*, meaning "sketch" or "draft."

Proust's three fictional artists are now summoned to testify in favor of successive, stacked-up, unfinished *inédits* of the kind Tadié wants to include in his edition. The *inédits* resemble the built-up layers of glaze seen by the writer Bergotte in Vermeer's patch of yellow wall in the *View of Delft*. (But glazes are integral to the final painting, not preliminary trial runs separate from the work.) The posthumous editor of Vinteuil's music, Tadié argues, makes sense of his "indecipherable notations ... by presenting the successive layers which, once unfolded, permit us to understand the composition of the work, the depth of its material" (cvi). (But in Proust's novel Vinteuil's editor, rather than laying out all the prospective versions, winnowed them down to the firm line of the work's unity.) And the painter Elstir sometimes preferred an early sketch to the final product. And then Tadié makes his final declaration of principle about his editorial method, about the true status of literature, and about the final meaning of the word *oeuvre*.

The *oeuvre*, daughter of time, does not assume its full relief unless one superposes its different stages, does not reveal its full depth unless, from the "ground plan," one descends to the crypt of the cathedral.

It is a great privilege to be present at the birth of a work. The drafts must therefore not be considered frozen and lifeless, but read as Swann listened to the motifs of Vinteuil's sonata: "Swann listened to all the scattered themes which would contribute to the composition of the phrase, like the premises of a necessary conclusion, and he witnessed its birth." Thus casting on the full set of Proust's published works and on the even more considerable mass of his unpublished writings a "retrospective" gaze, similar to the gaze the novelist himself cast on *Pleasures and Days*, the prefaces to Ruskin's works, *Jean Santeuil*, *Against Sainte-Beuve*, on his articles, rough drafts, and letters in order to compose *In Search of Lost Time*, thus the reader reconstructs the work *[oeuvre]*—in time.*

In other words, the *oeuvre* you have undertaken to read in buying these four volumes has become something far vaster than the novel Proust composed and published. In order to locate its mysterious genesis, you must take on his entire written output. The proliferation of sketches and drafts, which the author eliminated in order to obtain his circular structure and to maintain a certain order of magnitude, the editor now salvages and reintegrates, not into the text proper of the novel but as close to it as possible. This editorial decision and the arguments justifying it constitute a far-reaching redefinition and redistricting of literature. The author's decisions are now virtually overruled. The boundaries of a work of literature disappear by editorial fiat. The search for a creative process extending backward in time coterminous with the time of the author's biography usurps the unity of a work as a finite freestanding whole.

In arguing so insistently against the inclusion of extensive *esquisses* and elaborate editorial notes in the new Pléiade edition, I am not arguing against their publication separately in specialized collections annotated by scholars for scholars. Having taught and written about Proust for over thirty years, I find many of Proust's drafts absorbing for all the

---

*Deliberately and elegantly the concluding sentence echoes the concluding sentence of Proust's novel.

reasons Tadié supplies and for further reasons concerning the evolution of Proust's style. But such sketches can be distracting. At least four *esquisses* in volume III of the Pléiade edition concern an alluring "girl wearing red roses" who temptingly brushes up against Marcel at a reception. Subsequently he cannot find either her identity or her person, and she becomes an obsession. One can easily begin to remember the girl wearing red roses as a character in the novel. But Proust did not include her. The ordinary reader has enough to keep track of without adding this confusion not essential to the novel. I would welcome her in a separate volume of the Pléiade devoted to Proust's drafts and revisions, or more appropriately in a scholarly publication with a larger format.

It is difficult to attribute the hypertrophied Pléiade-Proust edition to commercial motives. Widely recognized but not a best-seller, Proust is unlikely to conquer new markets in a costly four-volume edition. What prompted the publishers of the Pléiade to approve for Proust an order of magnitude far exceeding his plans or expectations was the hubris of literary scholars, armed with a theory. The genetic critics, particularly when led by so disciplined and informed a figure as Jean-Yves Tadié, were able to do something the deconstructionists never succeeded in accomplishing. They unmade a work of literature. Intending to carry *In Search of Lost Time* to its final apotheosis in their sumptuous 7,300-page edition, Tadié and his associates have in effect buried Proust's novel in trappings and distractions and commentary. The volumes honor scholars' decisions about what to include more than they honor Proust's decisions about what to exclude. The miraculous construction of a coherent roman-fleuve out of an ocean of drafts and sketches is reversed by plunging the work back into that amorphous solution. The project is undertaken in the name of finding the genesis of the work, a genesis not recognized in Proust's choices for inclusion and exclusion, but tracked back into his whole extended life as a writer. We have no common word for this operation, the reverse of cutting or editing. Hypertrophize? Whatever we call it, we should not confuse this intended tribute in the new Pléiade with an acceptable way of honoring an author's accomplishment. It shrouds and demeans the author's work.

Here in the United States we stand forewarned against such an attempt. In the 1960s the Modern Language Association's Center for the Edition of American Authors began publishing Emerson, Melville, Hawthorne, and Howells in elaborate volumes edited with full apparatus and manuscript variants by committees of five to eight scholars. Each major author was assigned around forty such volumes, each called "An Approved Text." In a stentorian polemic, "The Fruits of the MLA," published in the *New York Review of Books* (September 26 and October 10, 1968), Edmund Wilson denounced the new editions as top-heavy with "rejected garbage," as offering unreadable texts, and as representing a barefaced academic "boondoggle." Wilson pointed to the first 1954 Pléiade edition of Proust as a model solution to editorial problems for such an undertaking. One volley was enough. Thanks in great part to Wilson's intervention, we have today not the MLA hypertrophized editions but the generally competent, well-presented titles in the Library of America.

Proust himself warned us about the present juncture. In the spring of 1922, only a few months before his death, he considered selling the manuscript and the corrected proofs of *Sodome et Gomorrhe* to the great couturier and collector Jacques Doucet for 7,000 francs. In July, Proust wrote to his English friend Sydney Schiff (who published fiction under the pseudonym Stephen Hudson) that he did not regret that the transaction had fallen through. For he had learned that Doucet's collection would become public.

> Now the thought is not very agreeable to me that anyone (if my books continue to interest people) will be able to paw through my manuscripts to compare them to the definitive text, to form suppositions, which will always be wrong, on my work methods, on the evolution of my thought, etc. All that bothers me a little, and I wonder if I wouldn't do better to cut back 5 or 7 thousand francs in my expenses rather than to expose myself to this posthumous indiscretion. (*Correspondence*, 21:372–73)

In his biography, Tadié quotes the first of these two sentences and concludes tersely, "Proust had foreseen everything" (882).

In addressing the 1998 meeting of the French Literature Conference at the University of South Carolina, I felt an obligation to draw conclusions that I renew here.

> I propose that we boycott the overblown, misconceived, and over-priced new Pléiade edition. It saps and traduces Proust's life-long devotion to a single work. It includes materials of concern primarily to scholars, four thousand pages best published in a separate scholarly edition keyed to a reader's edition. Every time we cite the new Pléiade edition, we are endorsing a scholarly enterprise that seeks not to identify and present the text of a major literary work but to blur and smear it back into a congeries of manuscripts. The new four-volume Pléiade conveys an image of drowning in one's own excessive creation, which is exactly wrong for Proust's resolute molding of a free-standing narrative out of the available mass of materials. Let us not yield to the temptation to accept unthinkingly the prestige of the Pléiade collection.
>
> ("Looking Backward: Genetic Criticism and the Genetic Fallacy,"
> *French Literature Series 26* [1999]: 10)

The Challenge of Translation

Around 1907, before he had chained himself for good to a single lifetime novel, Proust wrote a letter to Robert de Billy to scotch a rumor that he was translating *Praeterita*. The rumor had merit. Ruskin's three-volume autobiography of a self constantly unwoven and rewoven in the writing is closer to *A la recherche du temps perdu* than any novel in English. Proust had already published two passionately annotated translations of Ruskin's essays. He had read *Praeterita*. The characteristic sinuosity of Proust's style and the remarkable concision of thought it embodies developed in great part during the five or more years he spent in the closest of all embraces with Ruskin's English. The whole complex problem, tactical and technical, of transmitting a work of literature from one language and culture to another was familiar ground to Proust.

By 1920, soon after he had miraculously won the Goncourt Prize following years of neglect, Proust was complaining to his editor, Gaston
Gallimard, that not enough was being done to arrange an English translation of the *Search*. He was wrong. A Scotsman of wide literary interests, employed as private secretary by Lord Northcliffe of the London
Times, had already discovered Proust's novel through the prize. He
began to translate it without authorization and was casting about for a
publisher. Considering the length and difficulty of the novel, we should
be grateful that Chatto and Windus and Random House soon agreed to
take on the whole project and that for the ten remaining years of his life
C. K. Scott Moncrieff gave up everything (except for an occasional binge
to translate Stendhal's short sentences and Pirandello's plays) to devote
himself to Proust. When he died, in 1930, Moncrieff was working on the
last volume. What he produced is widely considered a masterpiece of
twentieth-century translation into English.

Yet there was some carping. Many critics, myself included, pointed
out annoying bloomers and occasional excesses of style. And the near-
definitive 1954 Pléiade edition showed that Moncrieff had worked from
a partly faulty text.

For these reasons we were offered in 1981 a "reworking" of Moncrieff's translation that follows the Pléiade edition and has been thoroughly checked for soft spots and errors. On the dust jacket the
publishers called it "the definitive English version of one of the great
masterpieces of the twentieth-century." Terence Kilmartin, an experienced translator of de Gaulle and Malraux and longtime literary editor
of the *Observer*, spent four years on the task. Anyone in the business
knows how to make a preliminary check on him in about an hour of ri-
fling. Yes, he caught "o'clock" and "custom" in the opening pages and
changed them to "time" and "habit." He straightens out the tricky pronouns that duped Moncrieff into producing patent nonsense in the scene
where Swann first kisses Odette. Kilmartin has improved the mala-
propisms that fascinate Marcel in the speech of the hotel manager in
Balbec and even taken the trouble to find London street vendors' cries
that correspond to the Paris cries Proust quotes in *The Captive*. Moncrieff
simply left them in French without so much as a note.

Proust and Moncrieff:

Tam, tam, tam,
C'est moi qui retame,
Même le macadam,
C'est moi qui mets des fonds partout,
Qui bouche les trous,
Trou, trou, trou.

Kilmartin:
Tan, ran, tan, tan, ran, tan
For pots or cans, oh! I'm your man.
I'll mend them all with a tink, tink, tink
And never leave a chink, chink, chink.

After Moncrieff's labors and before Kilmartin's came three successive translators of the volume Moncrieff left unfinished: Sydney Schiff (signing "Stephen Hudson"), Frederick Blossom, and Andreas Mayor. Mayor, having displaced his rivals, also prepared notes for the revision of all Moncrieff's version. He died before he could do the work. Using Mayor's notes as well as comments garnered from critics who had discussed the translation, Kilmartin revised everything except Mayor's version of the last volume.

The following comments are based on extensive comparative soundings of the several versions. The "old" translation (unretouched Moncrieff followed by either Blossom or Mayor) works remarkably well. Moncrieff was a professional with staying power. The improvements average only a few words per page.

On the other hand, Kilmartin's "fix" of Moncrieff has not caused deterioration or inconsistency. He was wise enough not to tinker idly and to keep repairs to a minimum. Kilmartin peered at or listened to every line of the *Search*. Small readjustments turn up everywhere, not just in sudden clusters. Translations of slang, of course, usually work only for one culture. The American ear may not be happy with "loutish" for *voyou* or with "demirep" for *demicastor*. Slang allowed Proust to plunge far into the depths when he wished. Like a living creature, the *Search* has

a figurative and almost literal cloaca, its nadir. When Marcel's jealousy
of Albertine has reached its most intense stage, she growls to him a sentence that she stops in midpassage and that he has to complete later by a
leap of imagination. *"J'aime bien mieux que vous me laissiez pour une fois
libre pour me faire casser. . . ."* This may be the most obscene sentence in
the novel, and has quite naturally posed challenges for translators. Two
pages later Marcel finds the unutterable term, *"le pot."* Out of ignorance
or prudishness, Moncrieff left it all in French. Kilmartin does likewise
and explains in a note that Albertine has skirted "an obscene slang expression for anal intercourse (passive)." But notes are not translation.
Kilmartin could well have tried a rudimentary phrase like "get myself b.
. . ." French has no monopoly on sexual slang.

In the opening pages of *Cities of the Plain* where a comically disingenuous Marcel discovers the homosexuality of Baron de Charlus and
Jupien, Moncrieff did his job well in a difficult scene. Tone and pace are
both right. But Kilmartin was watching. Moncrieff has Jupien say to the
Baron, "Aren't you naughty!" Kilmartin restores the concreteness of the
original: "What a big bum you have!" It is also better to have Marcel's
eyes opened by "a transformation" in Charlus than by "a revolution."

Kilmartin makes many other improvements. I wonder, however,
whether in a version that systematically changes "shew" to "show" he
should have left Moncrieff's "I then bethought myself . . ." for *"J'avi-
sai . . ."* (it means simply "I noticed . . ."). And when Jupien says, *"Je vois
que vous avez le coeur d'un artichaud,"* Kilmartin changes only Moncrieff's
adverb and accepts "I can see you are thoroughly fickle." All my in-
stincts tell me that we should be given not an explanation but an equivalent of the artichoke heart. In another place *professeur* for some
unknown reason comes out "usher" in both versions. When Moncrieff
accurately though awkwardly renders *"Il m'arrive . . ."* as "It falls to my
lot, now and then . . . ," Kilmartin confuses things badly by modifying
it to "It occurs to me now and then. . . ." Most readers will wince when
they come upon the sentence that ends, ". . . used to couch with him at
the hour when Dian [*sic*] rose." Kilmartin takes it spelling and all from
Moncrieff. A second-year student would know enough to write, ". . .
used to go to bed with him at the hour when Diana arose."

There are more far-reaching questions. A translator must be particularly sensitized to certain buoy words or expressions that recur in a work and mark its channel. *Impression* and *croyance* (belief) are two such words for Proust. Yet on the very first page Kilmartin accepts Moncrieff's translation of *croyance* as "impression," a term Proust usually reserves for specially privileged, waking perceptions. Then there is the innocent, almost nonexistent word *pan*, meaning piece or side or section of something. As a child Marcel watches a ghostly *pan de château* on his bedroom wall projected by the magic lantern. Years later he can remember only a tiny *pan lumineux* or *pan tronqué* out of all his crowded childhood in Combray. Toward the end of the novel the writer Bergotte dies while muttering to himself, *"Petit pan de mur jaune"*—"Little patch of yellow wall." It is a symbol of Bergotte's whole art-idolatrous life, and he knows it. *Pan*, therefore, must be heard as a structural rhyme, a recurring eyelet through which one can thread the themes of perception, memory, and art. But in translation all is lost. *Pan* comes out as three different words—"wing," "panel," and "patch." The intended linkage disappears. It should be the same word in all cases. "Patch" would have served best.

Another structural rhyme closely related to *pan* forms out of two widely separated occurrences of the expression *"Mort à jamais?"* Moncrieff rendered it both times as "Permanently dead?" Kilmartin unfortunately changes the second instance to "Dead forever?" and weakens a vital connection.

Back on the first page, I accept Kilmartin's acceptance of Moncrieff's version of the opening sentence. The words "For a long time I used to go to bed early" seem now almost engraved in English. Unfortunately they do not accurately render the nebulous syntax and temporality of the French sentence. But no one has proposed a better version. (See Appendix III, page 265.) Three lines below Kilmartin omits the comma in the sentence that should have started, "And, a half an hour later, the thought. . . ." In some wonderful remarks on Flaubert's rhythmical use of *et*, Proust explains precisely why he wanted a comma after "And."

Since its appearance in 1970, Andreas Mayor's translation entitled *The Past Recaptured* has been judged the only one of the three to match Moncrieff's sustained performance. Inspection shows that Mayor worked with brilliance. His phrasing catches the abrupt shift in tone needed for the famous pastiche of the Goncourt journal. He also makes sudden and disconcerting leaps toward freedom. Moncrieff would never have changed a specifically literary and probably Baudelairean figure, *"ce qui forçait à changer de dictionnaire pour lire,"* into the vernacular expression "in which case I had been barking up the wrong tree." Brilliant, but out of place.

And Mayor needs close watching on other scores. I find it hard to believe that in the long passage on the inadequacy of pure aestheticism and connoisseurship Mayor can have intended to omit the two essential concluding words of the sentence in which Proust mocks them as "bachelors [of Art]!" At times he feels no qualms about inverting the order of sentences in the Pléiade.

Mayor also flubs another one of the subtle rhymes that pins the whole book together at a crucial juncture. As Marcel returns from a sanatorium to Paris years after the principal events of the novel, the train stops in the open countryside. Marcel is troubled by his lack of response to a special effect of sunlight on a line of trees. Mayor misinterprets the passage to refer to the contrast between the "luminous" side and the "shady" side of the trunks. But Proust's words carefully recapitulate two earlier scenes (in Combray and in the Bois) during which a church steeple and tall trees take on a heightened significance because their upper section lights up in the sun's rays while their base or trunk sinks into shadow. In the later passage in the train, the overall action of the book is at dead low tide, measured by Marcel's distance from his earlier responses to a contrast between a bright summit and a dark base. A translator must be aware of these interior correspondences in order to put them in relief.

The three-volume Moncrieff-Mayor-Kilmartin translation failed to reckon with the matter of titles. *Within a Budding Grove* comes close to euphemism for *A l'ombre des jeunes filles en fleurs,* in which it is unmistakably young girls who are budding or blossoming. *Cities of the Plain* has a similarly evasive tone as a version of the straightforward *Sodome et Gomorrhe*. However, the general title of the novel is more troubling than these two volume titles.

Proust knew English, had earned his spurs as a translator, and lived long enough to protest strongly against "Remembrance of Things Past." The phrase Moncrieff lifted from a Shakespeare sonnet has a soft, passive ring to it; Proust's title is resolutely active, and he chose it in preference to less dynamic possibilities like The Heart's "Intermittences." Kilmartin had the opportunity to rebaptize the novel properly in English as *In Search of Lost Time*. It did not happen. I understand that editors at both Random House and Chatto and Windus debated the issue and decided not to change a title already established in people's minds and in printed catalogs.

In 1981, nevertheless, Kilmartin made significant improvements on Moncrieff. It's a thankless job, cleaning up after a great translator; Kilmartin should have cleaned up after Mayor also. Kilmartin deserves great credit. He did not, however, produce the advertised "definitive" version.

Accordingly, the story has continued. James Grieve, an Australian scholar, published a reliable version of *Swann's Way* in 1982. In the late eighties Richard Howard, poet, critic, and prolific translator from the French, signed a contract for a new translation of the full novel. A few years later he lowered his sights to a projected volume of excerpts concerned with the Baron de Charlus.

Also in the eighties, the English critic, D. J. Enright, was commissioned to revise the Moncrieff-Mayor-Kilmartin version. Enright could benefit from criticisms and suggestions (including those you have just read) made in reviews and articles. The translation in currently available English and American editions, as adjusted by Enright, adopts many of the suggestions made above, including the title *In Search of Lost Time*. Above all, this six-volume version is physically inviting because of the type size and contains in the last volume "A Guide to Proust" with helpful synopses and indexes of characters, historical persons, places, and themes. Proust has finally become reader-friendly.

The next stage appears to lie not too far off. Penguin Books has an-

nounced a completely new translation of the *Search,* not by one person
but by a team. I hope its members take their time and coordinate their
work along the lines I have been suggesting.

In the eighty years since his death, Proust and his readers have been
well served in English. But all that activity should not discourage a bold
young translator—or an old hungry one—from starting afresh without
Moncrieff's inevitable Englishness. One might explore Proust's resource
of pastiche to get inside his labyrinthine syntax and psychology, and
even experiment with redesigning Proust's almost seamless pages into a
diagram-flowchart that reveals rather than conceals the undulations of
his thought. After all, Proust is now in public domain, as is the Moncrieff
translation. All the critical and editorial apparatus in the world cannot
lock back into copyright the text of the first edition. After a limited interval for author and heirs, intellectual property is meant to be free. It
then belongs to us all—particularly to translators, parodists, and film-
makers.

Filming the Unfilmable

We know now how inadequately we have been served by the traditional
metaphor for the novel, dear to Stendhal: that it "holds a mirror up to nature." The metaphor does not fail because there is no nature, no reality
out there to mirror. It fails because the novel offers us words, not the direct visual images that a mirror reflects. The reality those words reveal
is both there and not there. On the basis of widely shared cues and conventions, each reader's mind must to a large extent project and create that
imaginary reality. Thus literature may be both the most abstract and the
most personal of the arts.

When Flaubert heard of plans to issue an illustrated edition of
Madame Bovary, a kind of reading aid, he exploded.

> Never, as long as I live, shall I allow anyone to illustrate me, because:
> the most beautiful literary description is eaten up by the most

wretched drawing. As soon as a figure *[type]* is fixed by the pencil, it loses that character of generality, that harmony with a thousand known objects which make the reader say: "I've seen that" or "That must be so." A woman in a drawing looks like one woman, that's all. The idea is closed, complete, and every sentence becomes useless, whereas a written woman makes one dream of a thousand women. Therefore, since this is a question of aesthetics, I absolutely refuse any kind of illustration.

(To Ernest Duplan, June 12, 1862)

In 1874 Flaubert did finally permit an illustrated edition of *Madame Bovary,* but to his niece he wrote deprecatingly that the illustrations had as much to do with the book as with the moon. He was not objecting to their poor quality; he felt in his bones the contaminating, paralyzing effect that any particularized image can have on the suggestiveness of the word. An image short-circuits the reader's imagination and prevents him from conjuring up a character or a scene out of his own associations and fantasies. Flaubert provides a needed gloss on Conrad's words in the preface to *The Nigger of the "Narcissus"*: "My task . . . is before all to make you see." What we "see" in reading a novel arises from a collaboration between the author's words and our own imagination. We do not normally rely on an illustrator to do the work for us. A film version of a novel, in which everything is enacted, eliminates the reader's visual collaboration. I cannot conceive that either Flaubert or Proust would have welcomed films of their works, but their preferences have not prevailed.

Almost all the major masters of the twentieth-century novel before World War II have been translated into film. We have had at least one movie, in some cases several, based on the work of Conrad, Joyce, Mann, Faulkner, Kafka, and Woolf. Marcel Proust did not join that group until 1984. Before that, a procession of great directors and script writers had made various approaches to Proust's novel. Except for René Clément, the French directors quickly shied away. The non-French (Luchino Visconti, Joseph Losey, Peter Brook) all allowed themselves a lengthy dalliance with Proust, produced some form of script, and then

were either unable or unwilling to carry through. The full-length screenplay Harold Pinter wrote for Losey was published in 1977 in a gesture of
impatience and appeal. In 1982 when Peter Brook postponed filming his
own scenario, the German director Volker Schlöndorff stood ready to
take over Brook's version and begin production without delay. The list
of actors considered over the years for major roles in one adaptation or
another gives an idea of the variety we may still hope for: Laurence
Olivier, Marcello Mastroianni, Georges Wilson, Edwige Feuillère,
François Périer, Greta Garbo, Maria Callas. Meanwhile, the handsomely
made but somewhat overstated semibiography of Proust's final years,
Céleste (directed in German by Percy Adlon), contributes further evidence that the time for Proust on film has arrived.

There are three artifacts to consider in discussing Proust and film:
Pinter's *The Proust Screenplay,* Schlöndorff's feature film *Swann in Love,*
and Raul Ruiz's *Time Regained* (1999). Because they are profoundly different in form and approach, they reveal most of the attractions and pit-
falls associated with turning Proust's novel into a movie.

By publishing *The Proust Screenplay,* Harold Pinter and his associates
demanded a public response to what is usually a private and commercial
decision: Should this movie be made? There have been no takers. I would
answer the challenge as follows: yes, the film should be made, but not as
is. Like Moncrieff's translation, Pinter's remarkable screenplay needs
considerable revision. Still, his giant step from word toward image has
resourcefully shown the way.

In a two-page introduction Pinter describes his collaboration with
Losey and Barbara Bray, a BBC script editor. They decided to "distill the
whole work" by organizing the film around two basic themes: a narrative movement of disillusion, and a more intermittent movement rising
to the revelation of art. They also wanted to emphasize the circular, self-
reflexive structure of the book that links the opening and the close.
"When Marcel, in *Le Temps Retrouvé,* says that he is now able to start his
work, he has already written it." This sentence raises serious problems,
because the two *he*'s refer to two very distinct identities: a first-person
protagonist and a first-person narrator. I shall come back to this point.

Pinter has written a straightforward screenplay of 455 numbered shots in 170 pages with camera directions and sound effects. We are not very far from his plays. Many of the shots (e.g., 61, 104) are so extended and complex that they form a *plan-séquence,* as the French would say, and would probably break down in actual production into a series of shots. Many ninety-minute films contain more than 400 shots, but I believe that this ambitious screenplay would require at least three hours—and should be allowed all of it.

I have already gone to great lengths to show that the *Search* is written from two distinguishable points of view, which usually fuse stereo-phonically into one rich sound: the point of view of an aging Narrator who recalls the story of his growing up to become a writer, and that of the "same" person as a young man (conventionally called Marcel), who grows up thinking he will never write. Because he never appears on-stage, the Narrator remains disembodied, an all-pervading voice. Because Marcel's sensibility occupies the central space of the book (except in the extruded yet related episode of "Swann in Love"), Marcel's sub-jectivity saturates everything, including the most intimate sensations of sleeping, listening, and getting drunk. Yet we never learn what he looks like, how he dresses. At the center of the action hovers an absence. How can one convey this first-person absence in a film where all personages are shown in the flesh? In *The Lady in the Lake* (1946) Robert Mont-gomery made the camera represent the protagonist, who loomed up or peeked out infrequently from a mirror. This might have been an oppor-tunity to explore that device again in spite of its awkwardness.

Pinter and his collaborators did the safe and probably right thing in staying with the tradition of the objective camera. They acknowledge Proust's subjective point of view in two ways. First, with few exceptions Marcel remains a passive protagonist; he seems to do nothing but watch everyone else. Where everyone else is a character in every sense, Mar-cel merely witnesses what goes on. Second, Pinter has dramatically mod-ified the form of the story so that we begin at the end, not in an unspecified middle as Proust does. That way Pinter tells us that the events have already taken place and that, as we go through them, the

Narrator may intersperse shots and sequences that do not belong to Marcel's sequential experience. It leads to a very complex yet effective flow of interwoven, rhymed, and associated textures that both challenge and support the narrative line. Pinter seems to offer this crosscut technique as a translation of "involuntary memory." These two transpositions of Proust's fictional universe approach very close to the frontiers of cinematic art, sometimes risking boredom or incoherence. Yet I believe they consolidate in a beautifully appropriate context experiments that have been tried by Eisenstein, the French new wave, and Bergman.

Despite the mnemonic embroidery, Pinter's screenplay follows a basic outline. He miniaturizes the *Search* in what I discern as eight parts.

1. We begin with a figureless yellow screen plus the sound of a bell. Cut to a kaleidoscopic sequence of shots that preview scenes to come and slowly locate a middle-aged man moving through a grotesque reception of old people. The yellow motif is shown to belong to a patch of color in Vermeer's *View of the Delft*. (Pages 3–5)

2. A somewhat complicated exposition narrates Marcel's *drame du coucher* in Combray and the boy's distant relationship to the Duchesse de Guermantes and to Swann. Swann's long affair with Odette fifteen years earlier is presented in a fourteen-shot insert focused on jealousy. Marcel, in his teens, spies on his lesbian neighbor, Mlle Vinteuil, watches the amazing steeples of Martinville from a carriage, and (in Paris) suffers Monsieur de Norpois' scorn of his attempts at writing. (Pages 6–34)

3. Marcel now eighteen accompanies his grandmother to the seaside resort of Balbec. There he meets Saint-Loup and Charlus, two more members of the noble Guermantes family, and Albertine, an attractive and elusive young woman of uncertain origins. He tries disastrously to kiss her. (Pages 35–54)

4. In a lengthy section set in Paris, Marcel makes his entry into fashionable society through the Guermantes clan and discovers Charlus' homosexuality. His grandmother dies. Marcel cannot forget Albertine, who now virtually offers herself to him. (Pages 55–92)

5. Back in Balbec, this time with his mother, Marcel is consumed by

jealousy over Albertine's real or imagined lesbian relations. They attend dinners together where the rich hostess, Mme Verdurin, has Charlus bring a talented young violinist named Morel. (Pages 93–116)

6. Albertine moves into Marcel's apartment in Paris. But his jealousy becomes all the stronger every time she goes out; he cannot work. Without her he goes to a concert by Morel at Mme Verdurin's. The music is exquisite, yet it is the occasion for the dramatic humiliation of Charlus. (Pages 117–56)

7. A rapid series of sequences and landscapes represent the passing of twenty years for Marcel: Venice, Combray revisited, Paris during the war, Marcel "motionless as an owl" in a sanatorium. (Pages 156–64)

8. An expansion and modification of the opening section, with the reverse effect of our now recognizing images that were incomprehensible the first time. The links between key experiences emerge; memory has kept them intact. At the reception the forty-year-old Marcel meets the eighteen-year-old Mlle de Saint-Loup, Swann's granddaughter. A rapid montage of shots, symmetrical with the opening, ends with the camera panning into the yellow patch of the Vermeer painting. We hear Marcel's voice-over: "It was time to begin."

I may have done too much cuing and voice-leading, but the film takes shape in these loose clumps of narrative. Any Proustian will notice major omissions: Marcel's significant sleep and dream scenes, including the opening; Aunt Léonie and the daily round of life in Combray; the madeleine incident of involuntary memory; Elstir the painter and Bergotte the writer; all meditations on philosophical and psychological subjects. Their absence causes only temporary disappointment. A viewer unfamiliar with the novel would often have trouble making connections. For example, three times (in shots 35ff., 108ff., and 307ff.) Pinter begins a major sequence with an establishing shot or shots from the middle of the action and then has to use flashback to explain what is going on. The disruption seems gratuitous. It does not come out of the novel, nor does it belong to Marcel's or the Narrator's memory processes. Such cinematographic manipulation creates unnecessary obscurity. However, Pinter's principal transposition—the new opening that anticipates and rhymes with the end—is fully justified and establishes the deeply subjective nature of Proust's creation. The screenplay also performs some brilliant telescoping in order to salvage a few comic interludes (like the one about the Duc de Châtellerault and the footman) and highly visual incidents (like Saint-Loup's gymnastic trip around the café with Marcel's overcoat).

The two complementary themes of disillusion with life and the revelation of art do not emerge as clearly as they should from this version of Marcel's story. Pinter does not adequately show us that a large part of Marcel's disappointment springs from his early idolatry of art and from his procrastination over becoming a writer. For a variety of reasons, including the film medium itself and the elimination of the writer Bergotte, Marcel's obsession with registering experience in words remains in the background. Yet the excitement of the ending depends on our understanding that at last Marcel will get down to work as a writer. One place where Pinter misses a perfect opportunity to broach this literary theme comes at the end of the Martinville steeples sequence. Riding on top of the carriage and watching the three steeples perform their stately dance across the sunset sky, Marcel is inspired to write down his feelings. When he has finished, he cackles like a hen that has laid an egg. In the scenario both the writing and cackling disappear! Furthermore, this is the passage Marcel's father shows to Ambassador Norpois a few scenes later for an opinion. In this scene Norpois (or Marcel) could read the text not silently but aloud, the cinematic equivalent of its being quoted in the book. This literary incident is the necessary preparation for the return to writing at the end after so many barren years.

Inexplicably Pinter mutes the dramatic side of another important incident. Marcel aged thirteen sees Gilberte for the first time through a gap in the hedge. In the screenplay, we merely see "her black eyes, smiling." In the novel, Gilberte makes a gesture that Marcel cannot decipher. Years later he learns in conversation with her that it was an obscene gesture meant to express her desire for him. How could such an important visual image be left out of the film version, especially since the later conversation with Gilberte is included?

Because of the stripping away of connective tissue and philosophical disquisitions, Pinter's version of the *Search* seems to present Marcel as a precarious and somewhat forlorn heterosexual in the midst of a sea of homosexuals of both sexes. The effect is sometimes comic. I am troubled by the narrative or expository status of some of the intercalated shots that refer to the simultaneity of the entire action while it is transpiring. To whom or to what do we attribute the existence of these shots? Some seem to belong to Marcel's own associative memory. Others (e.g., 23 in its many recurrences, 275–78) can be attributed to the Narrator implied at the start who can anticipate and comment on the action. And a few seem to belong to the filmic imagination itself—seven consecutive close-ups of eyes (345ff.).

The subtle intermittent pace and the powerful use of color and silence in the scenario redeem its faults, many of which are correctable. It documents a fascinating cultural milieu. It catches a strong glint of Proust's haunting subjectivity. It enlarges the language of film in order to encompass a literary masterpiece. Even unproduced, Pinter's screenplay provides solutions for adapting the *Search* to a medium that will make new demands of the novel.

Schlöndorff and Brook paid no attention to Pinter. In order to give their film the "larger than life" feeling created by stars, as their publicity stated, they signed up the British actor Jeremy Irons to play Swann, and a number of respected French actors. Most people who saw the movie had barely heard of Proust.

Therefore I shall begin by describing and commenting on *Swann in Love* from the point of view of an occasional moviegoer unfamiliar with Proust. Afterward I shall introduce what might be the thoughts of a reasonably literate film critic who has read at least the first volume of the novel. Only then shall I allow the Proust scholar to say his piece.

MOVIEGOER: THE COSTUMES did the most for me. The movie follows Charles Swann, a Paris dandy with very English manners. He gets invited everywhere even though his parents were converted Jews. At a very elegant reception he gives the cold shoulder to a beautiful young duchess who has been panting after him for years, it seems. But he has other things on his mind. For months, maybe for years—it's hard to tell—he's been chasing a slippery little kitten called Odette. She's been around with everyone and knows how to excite Swann. She also makes him jealous of every other male or female who so much as sniffs at her. Swann is always smelling the flower she wears between her breasts. She has her own group of rich friends, and they don't much like Swann. Well, she finally lets him get into bed with her. He likes it from behind. The next day he tells his friend Charlus that it's all over after one night of love. Charlus knows better and asks him when he's going to marry her. In the last scene, which takes place about ten years later after their marriage, Swann is dying and pretty well shut out by the snobbish crowd that used to appreciate his cool wit. He and Charlus walk around the park trying to figure out what they have done with their lives.

The film has beautiful shots of Paris and furniture and costumes. But the action is hard to follow. The film is all cut up and put together fast like a modern film, but it really wants to be old-fashioned. The brothel scene hardly fits. Swann, with most of his clothes on and smoking a cigarette in a holder, takes one of the girls from behind, while he asks her about Odette. I suppose that's taken from the novel.

CRITIC: The film is about collecting, collecting things and memories. Schlöndorff and Brook have laid all the clues out nicely, at least at the beginning and the end. The first shot behind the credits—it's a visual riddle—turns out to be a close-up of the inside of the big secretary in which Swann keeps together in a kind of shrine his most precious and fetishistic possessions: some small Flemish paintings, the leather case that contains his cash reserve, and Odette's love letters. Very neat. Later he adds to the treasure a flower she has given him. Schlöndorff makes much of Swann being a rich man of exquisite taste who moves around in interiors laid out like a museum. Swann wants to collect Odette too, vulgar as she is, because she reminds him of a Renaissance painting. She drives him mad with jealousy, but he does finally collect Odette by marrying her. Meanwhile, he moves in and out of the various social circles from the book.

At the end as old men, Swann and Charlus are talking about death and the meaning of life. During the scene, Odette drives across the park in her carriage looking like the Queen of Paris. Just before the final freeze-frame Swann says, "All those old feelings are very precious to me now. It's like a collection. I can look back over my old loves and I say to myself it would be too bad to leave all that." Trivial sentiments, but they strike the right note. The film belongs to Swann (though Odette almost pushes him aside), and he comes off looking vapid. Just a collector, a dilettante in everything, and that's close to what Swann represents in Proust's novel.

Still, all kinds of things don't work or are obviously borrowed. Brook apparently had the idea of collapsing the action into one day of Swann's life, dawn to dawn. Not a bad idea, but the script makes it very difficult to follow the flashbacks unless you already know something about the story. For instance, in the book all the byplay around the cattleya orchid occurs on the night Swann first makes love to Odette. It's barely fifty pages into "Swann in Love." Most of the rest of the story—four times as much—is about his jealous pangs over the other men and women who may enjoy the same privilege, past, present, and future. Since the film doesn't make clear that he's been her lover for a long time, their one big scene in bed near the end appears to be his long-delayed reward. That's standing the plot on its head. Of course, the movie doesn't have to follow Proust exactly, but it is confusing.

In the movies *Danton* and *Céleste,* there are wonderful sequences when the coiffeur comes in to give a prolonged ritualized shave. Schlöndorff uses the device here not once but twice, and not so effectively. But he found true masters to do the sets and the costumes. All those chairs and corsets and veils and bric-a-brac everywhere—even a lot of the characters who are played not by actors but by "real French aristocrats"—they all fit the collecting motif. Schlöndorff is something of an ambitious hack. His taste for the perverse worked better in Günter Grass's *The Tin Drum* (1979) than in *Swann in Love.*

PROUST SCHOLAR: I have no quarrel with detaching "Swann in Love" from the rest of Proust in order to make a film of it. These 250 pages form a freestanding unit that relates a unified story with beginning, middle, and end. Every critic says all of Proust lies here in embryo. Since it's told in the third person, scriptwriter and director don't face the initial problem of first-person point of view.

The trouble with this version of "Swann" is that someone wanted to salvage the rest of Proust, as if all that wonderful literature just couldn't go to waste—or wait for another film. The very first sequence shows a man writing in bed. When we hear his words voice-over using the first person to analyze intimate feelings, we have been given a misleading allusion to the writer-narrator Marcel, or even to Proust. In the novel Swann keeps no journal, doesn't work in bed. Someone has to call a foul on Schlöndorff here. He needs the journal as a device to introduce some exposition of the action, which is already almost over in this truncated script. But the device is a red herring and evokes elements of the novel that are not pertinent to "Swann in Love."

Too many other items have seeped back into the film from the rest of the book: the boy-poet to whom Charlus makes homosexual advances; the Guermantes clan, whose elevated social status almost displaces the Verdurin *"noyau"* more central to Swann's story; the inappropriate brothel scene siphoned in from later stories about Albertine and about Charlus (I heard one earnest discussion at the critics' screening about whether Schlöndorff intended Swann to engage in sodomy or coitus *a tergo*); and the last ten minutes of the film that show Marcel in failing health a decade later. Brook and Schlöndorff imply classical unity with their twenty-four-hour structure and undermine it with these diversions.

If I had to write a screenplay for "Swann in Love," I'd try hard to be faithful to three aspects of the novel and allow the rest to fall into place according to the needs of the film medium. First, everyone in the story is afflicted with one or several strains of a hereditary and infectious disease: snobbery. It governs how they are placed in and move among distinct social strata: the demimonde of a fashionable cocotte; rich bourgeois with chic artistic tastes; and the landed aristocracy guarding their perimeter. Swann, having reached the top layers, succumbs to reverse snobbery and falls victim to a woman of the demimonde. The bourgeois Verdurin clan suppresses or at least camouflages its desire to rise socially. Proust's insights into human character and his constant comic perspective spring from his unrelenting scrutiny of snobbery at all levels. The film can't help catching some of this feeling; Jeremy Irons portrays Swann as a yawning fashion plate. I find him tense when he should be languid, and vice versa.*

The second essential element is the story of Swann's "love"—not sexual thralldom, quickly surpassed, not romantic love of an unobtainable ideal, but the obsessive stages of an illusion. The ill-fated timing, the perverse afterlife of attachment in the form of jealousy, and the ceaselessly shifting temporal sequences of "successive loves" almost disappear in the twenty-four-hour telescoping of the action. One loses what I would call the *Bolero* effect of the novel. In Proust, Swann's feelings go on and on, over and over, with gradual variations and changes in decor and tempo until he finally wakes from his dream. Schlöndorff comes closes to this obsessive quality of the action when he has Swann return alone to his house after watching Odette dress to go to the opera with the Verdurins. He wanders restlessly among the tastefully chosen paraphernalia of his life and recalls in convincing flashbacks Odette's first, tentative, almost girlish visit to his place. When he shows her the Botticelli

---

*I would trace some of the trouble to Irons' heroic effort to learn French for the part. His tutor, who remained with him during the shooting, did wonders. For prints of the film distributed in France, another actor dubbed Irons' voice in native French. For the version with English subtitles, Irons redubbed his own good but identifiably foreign French. (He apparently thought his fans would expect to recognize his voice.) Most non-French will not notice, but some viewers who know the language will find his longer speeches irritating, even comic. Obviously for some spectators and subtly for others who are unaware of the discrepancy, Irons' schooled French works against his role and the film. Voice is one of the principal instruments of snobbery, and in the redubbed version Swann is deprived of it. The actor whose carriage and voice best express the snobbery appropriate to his role is Jacques Boudet, who plays the Duc de Guermantes. A big bluff man, the Duke remains detached from everything he does and says, and carries his hand like a flabby fin at shoulder height for his male guests to touch. Boudet gives him a powerfully distasteful presence.

painting he thinks she resembles, her reply is perfect. "I'm not a museum piece." The drifting compulsiveness of Swann's mind comes out far better in this unhurried meditation than in the sequence where, unexpectedly hearing Vinteuil's melody, he gasps and leaves in the middle of an elegant concert.

Schlöndorff and his associates have done well by the third essential element: the idolatry of beautiful things. Swann epitomizes a culture of good taste, fashion, decorum, and art. He is a slave to the elevated social milieu to which he has been admitted. Every shot, exterior and interior, contains the outward and visible signs of an aesthetic point of view. For Swann, life must be certified by art; Odette is vulgar and "not his type" until she begins to look like a Botticelli.

Yes, this may be a film about its costumes. It also shows that Schlöndorff and Brook have read the rest of Proust, and they try to inject too much of it into this wonderfully self-contained story.

WHAT THESE THREE commentaries fail to bring out is the generally plodding quality of the film once you look beyond sets and costumes. Jeremy Irons acts primarily by abstaining from acting except when he gasps to express heightened emotion. A certain degree of stiffness is appropriate to Swann's character, but Irons creates neither an underlying humanity nor the powerful aura of a dandy who has mastered life by distancing it. Alain Delon does better in infusing a hammed-up intensity into the role of Charlus. I had the feeling that the only actor whom Schlöndorff really tried to direct was Ornella Muti as Odette. Having lived for several decades with my own half-particularized image of Odette (deeply influenced by a real woman who seemed to incarnate Odette socially and temperamentally), I needed a little time to fit this sultry, dark-complexioned lynx into my mental stereoscope. By evasion and posing and moments of apparent candor, Muti finally occupies the psychoerotic space necessary to bewitch Swann. The fact that her visage and body are far from stunning gives a certain reverberation to the magnificent sentence that closes the story but, unfortunately, not the film. "To think that I wasted years of my life, that I wanted to die, that I had my greatest love for a woman who didn't really attract me, who wasn't my type."

Moving pictures at their best offer us simultaneously the breathtaking freedom of dream and the convincing particularity of documentary. Proust's "Swann in Love," the novella, closes with a subtle, semicomic dream that recapitulates Swann's delusions and reverse snobbery. Brook and Schlöndorff generally keep their distance from the dream side of Proust. They go heavy on documentary.

The same is true of the sumptuous film *Time Regained*, directed in Paris by the Chilean Raul Ruiz and released in 1999. Ruiz revels in elegant receptions where liveried footmen in wigs pass champagne and petits fours. He uses lavish sets and costumes and curious customs (e.g., hand kissing) to demonstrate that aristocratic Europe was still strutting and preening during the most horrendous massacres of World War I. Whereas Schlöndorff chose to treat an early episode of the *Search* and couldn't resist throwing in morsels of later developments, Ruiz began at the end and supplied multiple flashbacks to suggest how it all comes to pass.

Time Regained succeeds on two scores. The social scenes capture the comic sense, verging on caricature, with which Proust treats the great social sequences. Ruiz picks up the latent hysteria in the *Search* and lodges it in the carefully differentiated voices, shrill laughter, and mugging faces of his actors. Saint-Loup (Pascal Greggory) delivers a withering sermon on the sacrifices of war while stuffing a succulent meal into his domineering face. At a few points, the film builds up to a situation of grotesque subversiveness that made me wonder if Luis Buñuel had taken over direction.*

The other successful aspect of *Time Regained* is the character of Marcel. Astutely made-up, the actor Marcello Mazzerella takes on an unset-

---

*That surmise is reinforced by a two-second insert shot early in the film, like an internal signature. We glimpse a grainy black-and-white clip of a horse writhing in its death throes, an oblique allusion to Buñuel's and Dali's film *Un Chien andalou* (1928). What is the connection? Ruiz, I infer, wanted to flash his surrealist credentials.

tling resemblance to Proust as seen in many familiar photographs. Marcel moves decorously, almost primly, through the social gatherings and portrays a comic, pathetic, yet sympathetic voyeur. He watches and abstains. His smiles are detached. His tears are utterly private, even in public. He hesitates to intrude. Opposite a whole cast of posers and gossips, Marcel, as directed by Ruiz, acts with the self-deprecation appropriate to his insecure role.

But it is impossible to follow this film. The viewer unfamiliar with the *Search* is simply lost among the self-possessed, endlessly talking women and the arrogant, monocle-sporting men. Someone who knows Proust's novel comes to feel one is taking an examination with endless identification items and subtly garbled questions. Chronology becomes very confused, as do the places where the scenes take place. Interludes of pure fantasy, not found anywhere in Proust, are interspersed with scenes faithful to his narrative. The opening sequence depicts the invalid Proust near death. He sighs and mutters over old photographs not of his past but of the fictional past of Marcel in the novel. The film closes equally enigmatically at the Balbec beach with a walk-out-to-sea sequence lifted from Thomas Mann's *Death in Venice*. Where are we? Ruiz offers us a generous handful of Proust materials. But Ruiz has also splintered the story line and scattered the major motifs. Without them, the movie *Time Regained* remains an opulent sampler.

Proust does not need illustration any more than Flaubert. Still, now that we have a full-length screenplay and ambitious inadequate versions of both the beginning and end of the *Search*, the exploration of how to adapt Proust to film should not cease.

Time and Space

The question of whether the *Search* will lend itself to film treatment is indirectly related to the dispute over what dimension, what mode of perception, dominates in Proust's novel. For many years the length and full title of the *Search*, its depiction of age, and its emphasis on memory convinced most readers that the book's essential subject is time and temporality. It conveys above all a sense of time deeply penetrated and linked back to itself in wide loops of recall and recognition. This approach lends weight to the order and pacing of events and endorses the conception of a story as basically linear, or perhaps circular, like time itself. In recent years, however, a number of critics have taken up their cudgels to make the opposite case. When one has finished the novel, they contend, when one can hold its parts together in the mind, its true character reveals itself as that of a single whole which stands free of temporal order and lies spread out before us in space, like a painting.

In this case, as usual, Proust speaks eloquently on both sides of the question. In the "interview" he supplied in 1913 for the journalist Elie-Joseph Bois, Proust justifies the still undivulged length of his novel by saying it will portray "psychology in time. It is this invisible substance of time that I have tried to isolate." And when the last volume appeared after his death, his words insisted all over again that the book was cast in "the form of Time" (III 1045; cf. III 1148/vi 526; cf. vi 532). The opening sentence of the entire work as well as its title indicate a constant cohabitation with time. The case would seem clear from the start. Yet, particularly in the decisive closing pages, Proust uses figures that describe a reaction against temporality. In the sentences that immediately precede the moment when the tide of the action turns and Marcel steps on the uneven paving stones, he complains that living to be a hundred would bring no reward. For it would mean nothing more than "successive extensions of a life laid out along one line" (III 866/vi 254). Images of height and architectural construction in the final pages seem to imply a new perspective. Proust had formulated the shift most tersely when speaking of architecture in an early draft of the novel: "Time has assumed the form of space" (*CSB*, Faillois edition, 285). A building in different styles displays time as simultaneous. To what degree does the *Search* aspire to the condition of architecture?

Now, time poses the crucial problem of how we know things, particularly how we know people, over a period of days or years. Proust never wandered far from this problem. Exasperated by his uncertainty over Albertine's and Andrée's unstable feelings toward him, Marcel tells himself in desperation that the only way to find out about their sentiments would be for him to "immobilize" them in order to examine the pattern of their behavior. But he could do so only by ceasing to desire them, for desire provokes change. Without desire he would no longer care about their feelings. The passage concludes glumly: "the stability we attribute to natural things is purely fictive and serves the convenience of language" (III 64–65/v 77). Immobility may permit knowledge, but it arrests life and love. Hence we can never know anyone we love. Such paradoxes of temporality permeate the incidents of the story.

Chronology itself raises parallel problems. Just how far does experience arise from or conform to the temporal order of events? While falling out of love with Gilberte, Marcel finds calendar time utterly meaningless. "Often (since our life is chronological to so small a degree and inserts so many anachronisms into the sequence of our days) I found myself living a day or two behind myself, going back through stages when I still loved Gilberte" (I 642/ii 299). Yet, in a later passage already quoted about what happens to Saint-Loup and Charlus as they grow older, the Narrator proclaims the opposite dogma: "Everything is a question of chronology" (III 737n/vi 68).

In the face of these contradictions, and with strong leads from Ortega y Gasset and Raymond Fernandez, two critics have taken a categorical position. In an essay called "Spatial Form in Modern Literature" (1945), Joseph Frank lumps Proust with Pound, Eliot, and Joyce as overdeveloped Imagists. They all incorporate in lengthy works Pound's original definition of an Image: to present "an intellectual and emotional complex in an instant of time." The length and temporal narrative of the *Search* should not deceive us, Frank argues. "Proust's purpose is only achieved, therefore, when these units of meaning [impressions and views of his characters] are referred to each other reflexively in a moment of time." A moment of time Frank interprets as not time at all but as space. Almost twenty years later the Belgian critic Georges Poulet defended the same thesis at greater length in *L'Espace proustien* (1963). Proust's narrative "juxtaposes" discontinuous images "exhibited side by side" as in a museum. "Thus time yields to space" (130).

Both these critics have much to say on Proust that is revealing. But how does a mind achieve this spatialization of time? The events and thoughts of Proust's novel, if they are genuinely spatial in Frank's sense, would have to conform to the principle that binds the units of meaning in Pound's *Cantos:* "...while they follow one another in time, their meaning does not depend on this temporal relationship." Poulet argues the same case in more homely terms. "Intact ... caught in their frames, the episodes of Proust's novel present themselves in an order that is not temporal, since it is anachronous, but which cannot be anything other than spatial, since, like a row of jam pots in the magic cupboards of our childhood, it sets out a series of closed vessels in the caverns of the mind" (134).

In order to persuade us that the order of events in Marcel's life has no significance, Poulet shows him storing those events in a kind of mental larder, with no temporal sequence. The figure applies fairly well to *Jean Santeuil* and to *Against Sainte-Beuve*. But in the final novel we are dealing with a linear story that Proust carefully and properly called a *search*. It could be compared to a climb to the top of a mountain. The view from the summit does indeed set out before one an arrangement of the landscape that allows one's gaze to move at will from feature to feature and to take it all in at once. That view is essentially spatial. But it does not and cannot abolish the climb that took one to the summit, and the temporal order of events in that climb. One cannot climb the last hundred feet before the first. Marcel could not have loved Albertine before Gilberte, nor could he have become a writer without the years of discouragement and disillusion that seemed to be leading him in quite another direction. Marcel remains the creature of a temporal order of events that obtains even in retrospect. "Just like the future, it is not all at once but grain by grain that one tastes the past" (III 531/v 716).

But we must go beyond isolated quotations picked shrewdly out of three thousand pages of waiting prose. If a spatial simultaneous vision of the past were Proust's fundamental purpose, then all the early pages would become strictly preparatory and subsidiary. They would in effect

drop off, and we would be left with an intense fifty-page essay on the rewards of memory and the nature of literature.* Everything I have written about Marcel's overcoming of idolatry and about the structure of
sheer length in the *Search* will weigh against this one-sided interpretation.

The *Search* affirms *both* perspectives. On the one hand, it insists on the
lived temporal order of things, which combines individual development
with a sense of the gradual modulation of reality itself. On the other
hand, it focuses on occasional resurrections revealing a glimpse of the
past outside of contingent time and creating patterns so convincing as to
be called essences. A mass of evidence, passed over by Frank and Poulet,
suggests that the temporal sequence dominates most of the narrative
and withdraws conditionally in favor of the spatial arrangement only at
the start and again as its end approaches. This close relation between time
and space in the novel as a whole parallels the art of description insisted
upon by the Narrator (I 653, III 379/ii 314, v 509). True description follows the temporal order of impressions—a kind of innocence reintro-
duced into experience otherwise encrusted by habit—before accepting
a ready-made concept or a word. The interchange never stops. The
Search creates a predominantly temporal perspective, scored through
deeply at crucial moments by arresting spatial insights. The only synthesis resides in the full dimensions of the work itself. Fifty pages of
theory on time, art, and memory near the end (III 865–916/vi 253–330)
cannot stand in for the whole book.

These concerns led Proust to give serious attention to music, an art
whose performance is entirely temporal, yet whose form may be spa-
tialized by repetition and memory. In two closely related passages, one
toward the beginning and the other toward the end of the novel, Proust

---

*I believe that Proust had such an expository, nonnarrative plan in mind when he
began to work on *Against Sainte-Beuve*. As I have already suggested, the Preface to that
project sets down his basic philosophical attitude with only a highly abbreviated version of how he reached it. He abandoned the plan almost as soon as he began writing.

describes that double experience. In the first, Marcel is listening to Odette play the piano.

> It was on one of those days that she happened to play for me the part of Vinteuil's sonata that contained the little phrase of which Swann had been so fond. But often, if it is a complicated piece of music to which one is listening for the first time, one listens and hears nothing. . . . That gives rise to the melancholy that clings to the knowledge of such works, as of everything that takes place in time. . . . Since I was able to enjoy the pleasure that this sonata gave me only in a succession of hearings, I never possessed it in its entirety: it was like life itself. But great works of art are less disappointing than life, for they do not begin by giving us the best of themselves. (I 529–31/ii 139–41)

The passage contains a tentative aesthetic. The experience of complex music is cumulative, subject to time, never exhaustive. It differs from life in that its greatest rewards come late and not early. The *Search* itself, we realize, observes this rhythm of delayed revelation. The time needed for gradual initiation to a work of art belongs to and forms part of its experience. An instant does not contain it, though art may contain exalted instants.

In the counterpart scene many years later, Marcel discovers in music an even deeper synthesis of temporal and spatial experiences. Albertine is selecting to play for Marcel on the pianola, not familiar works, but new pieces whose shape is still obscure for him. The Narrator distinguishes carefully between two experiences of these unfamiliar pieces. First comes a slowly built-up deposit of successive playings, which he describes as "a volume, produced by the unequal visibility of the different phrases." Later, Marcel can project and immobilize the different parts "on a uniform plane," open to inspection by his intelligence (III 373/v 501–2). The next sentence tells us not that one aspect is higher or more final than the other but that what brings a reward is the movement between the pathos of temporal experience and the immobility of analytic intelligence.

[Albertine] did not yet go on to another piece, for, without being really aware of the process taking place inside me, she knew that at the moment when my intelligence had succeeded in dispelling the mystery of a piece, it had almost always, in the course of its ill-fated work, discovered in compensation some profitable reflection. (III 373/v 502)

The shift from shadowy time to brightly lit space would be "ill-fated" *(néfaste)*, injurious to the sensibility, were it not for the fact that this shift in psychic levels brings a reward in some other realm of the mind.* Furthermore, the knowledge wrested by intelligence out of the flux sends Marcel continually back toward temporality and mortality. There is always another piece of music to listen to and understand. After the pinnacles of atemporal vision at the end, Marcel's reward comes in the form of the very down-to-earth discovery that "life was worth living" (III 1032/vi 507). Time and space do not try to elbow each other aside in the *Search* in order to dominate the scene. They perform an elaborate and moving saraband that leaves both of them onstage and in full possession of their powers.

Intelligence versus Sensibility:
Proust's Wager and "Experimental Faith"

Beginning with the earliest reviewers, there has been wide agreement that Proust's portrait of the writer in the *Search* (and, by implication, of

---

*If I understand Proust properly here, he is taking a step beyond the approach to art proposed by Ernst Kris in *Psychoanalytic Explorations in Art* (New York, 1962). Kris proposes that aesthetic experience entails a process by which we find pleasurable in itself a shift in mental energy, a change in psychic level, if kept under control of the ego. Proust seems to believe that the mental shift from temporal hearing to simultaneous understanding of music carries value not as an ascent to a higher level, and not as a pleasure in itself, but because it usually releases other mental insights. This undeveloped idea hints at a further argument against the idolatry of art, against art for art's sake.

himself) presents a man passively responding to experience. Georges Bataille refers to "the rigor with which he reduces the object of his search to *involuntary* discovery." Gilles Deleuze devotes his entire last chapter to Proust's thought as a form of abdication of will. "The great theme of *Time Regained* is that the search for truth is the characteristic adventure of the involuntary. Thought is nothing without something which forces and does violence to it." Most of these critics hunt out the Narrator's comments on sudden memories near the start of the final commentary. "I had not gone out looking for the two uneven paving stones in the courtyard which I had stepped on. But precisely the fortuitous and inevitable way in which the sensation had come about determined the truth of the past it resurrected and of the images it set in motion" (III 879/vi 274). *Fortuitous* and *inevitable*. Choice, will, and deliberation thus appear to have no role to play in provoking a reminiscence. Beginning with the madeleine sequence at the start of the novel, the Narrator insists on the involuntary nature of such experiences.

Do the original impressions, which provide the content of the reminiscences, conform to this pattern? Are they also untainted by any exercise of will? In its full freshness, an impression appears simply to impinge on Marcel's senses as an immediate and vivid whole. He never wills an impression, though his mental tonus clearly affects his receptivity. However, it is significant that Marcel does not record as major events—and often omits them altogether—the initial impressions that surge back later in the major reminiscences. He was mildly aware of the starched napkin at Balbec, of the whistles of pleasure boats, and of George Sand's novel *François le Champi;* but none of them struck him as anything more than an incidental part of the moment. He barely registered any taste or odor of the tea-soaked madeleine when his aunt Léonie offered him a piece (I 52/i 70). It merely formed a fragment of her world. He apparently took so little notice of the uneven paving stones in the baptistery of Saint Mark in Venice that he didn't even mention them at the time. When he saw the line of trees from the train (III 855/vi 238), he did not consciously hear the trainman's hammer tapping on the wheels. Yet later on it is precisely that sound that provides the open sesame for total recall of the scene (III 868/vi 257–58). Why this apparent absence of mind at presumably crucial moments?

In *Beyond the Pleasure Principle,* Freud speculates that the elements of experience that enter consciousness do not leave memory traces. Consciousness provides a "protective shield" against stimuli—or at least a kind of bypass for them. Only things we do not become conscious of make an imprint that may later be remembered. I find it a dismaying yet arresting theory. Is Proust saying something similar? Does the obscure mechanism or muse that activates our receptivity to impressions and reminiscences operate only when working surreptitiously, free of observation? Does any effort on our part to influence its working shut it off and float everything up into the desiccating air of consciousness? In this view the only acceptable activity of mind for the artist is a passive yielding to contingent forces around him. Many critics have read the *Search* as the case history of a man whose intense aesthetic experiences issue from complete surrender to the present moment and from a systematic stifling of focused attention. But Proust goes far beyond the absent-mindedness that Freud glimpsed at the root of memory. He shows consciousness not as a protective shield but as a mysterious vital process.*

---

*Another great restless mind ventured this far into this wilderness almost a century earlier. In the section of *Either/Or* called "The Rotation Method," Kierkegaard anticipated both Freud's doubts about the compatibility of memory and consciousness and Proust's resolve to surmount any such frailty through a form of psychic delaying action, a stopping to look. Here is Kierkegaard:

> Enjoying an experience to its full intensity to the last minute will make it impossible either to remember or to forget. For there is then nothing to remember except a certain satiety, which one desires to forget, but which now comes back to plague the mind with an involuntary remembrance. Hence, when you begin to notice that a certain pleasure or experience is acquiring too strong a hold upon the mind, you stop for a moment for the purpose of remembering. No other method can better create a distaste for continuing the experience too long. From the beginning one should keep the enjoyment under control, never spreading every sail to the wind in any resolve; one ought to devote oneself to pleasure with a certain suspicion, a certain wariness, if one desires to give the lie to the proverb which says that no one can have his cake

To limit the scope of Proust's literary accomplishment to mental passivity would be like accepting "negative capability" as the full measure of Keats's genius. Neither writer can be so confined. The force and reach of their sensibilities do not shun polarities. I have already insisted on the factor of willpower in Marcel's story. It reflects the choice that brought Proust to his full literary calling around 1909. At the beginning of the novel as at the end, the principal sickness afflicting Marcel attacks not his body but his will. The book hinges on the resolve Marcel wishes to discover in himself. One has little difficulty in finding quotations that paint a very different portrait of the artist from the one in the preceding paragraphs. The number of pages Proust devoted to Baudelaire leaves little doubt about the tutelary role the poet played in the development of Proust's sensibility and his theories of memory. There is nothing unintentional about the closing words of Marcel's final meditation before entering the Guermantes salon.

> In Baudelaire, finally, these reminiscences, more numerous even [than in Chateaubriand and Nerval], are less fortuitous and consequently, in my opinion, decisive. It is the poet himself who, with more choice than

---

and eat it too. The carrying of concealed weapons is usually forbidden, but no weapon is so dangerous as the art of remembering. It gives one a very peculiar feeling in the midst of one's enjoyment to look back upon it for the purpose of remembering it. (*Either/Or*, trans. David F. Swenson and Lillian Marvin Swenson, Anchor Books, 1:289)

Watching from behind several ironic masks, Kierkegaard has seen everything. Yet he never claims final truth for his insights in this deeply cleft and antithetical work that refuses synthesis in any form. What he cannot do so well as Proust is to write a novel. "The Diary of a Seducer," the following section, runs aground on the lame category of "the interesting." Proust works in a different form and tone. Instead of holding them apart in separate volumes, he mixes his Either and his Or into a composite narrative line. Repeatedly along the way we are obliged to "stop a moment" in order, almost, to have our cake and eat it too.

Walter Benjamin touches on this general subject in his essay "On Some Motifs in Baudelaire."

laziness, deliberately sought, in a woman's odor, for example, in her hair or her breast, the inspiring analogies that will evoke in him "the azure of a vast encircling sky" and "a harbor thick with flames and masts." (III 920/ vi 335)

Baudelaire's genius seems to have consisted in his capacity to apply choice and some kind of method to involuntary memory. In Marcel, Proust has created a figure in whose life the fortuitous and fleeting experiences of memory ultimately lead to a deliberately chosen self-dedication to literary art.

The passage quoted earlier on "the fortuitous and inevitable way" in which Marcel stumbled on the uneven paving stone (see above, page 213) is truncated. It belongs to a careful discussion of the sequence: impressions, reminiscences, art. The closing sentences correct many of the misconceptions I have been describing and speak not of passiveness but of *effort*.

> The impression is for the writer what experimentation is for the scientist, with this difference: that in the case of the scientist the work of the intelligence precedes, and in the case of the writer it comes after. Something we have not had to interpret, to illuminate by our personal effort, something that was clear before we arrived on the scene, is not truly ours. Only those things belong to us that we draw out of the obscurity inside us and that others do not know. (III 880/ vi 276)

In every instance of involuntary memory, from the madeleine through the multiple series at the end, Marcel tries at least briefly to find an explanation of the phenomenon. Otherwise, it would not be *his* experience. Often he succeeds. Pulsing beneath the rich textures of the *Search* and expressive of Proust's whole attitude, I detect a movement toward the mastery of life that is stronger than his complementary moods of passive resignation to it.

The last quotation and a few earlier ones have already slipped into this discussion a set of terms that define a closely related and equally important opposition of forces. In many contexts Proust names and assigns contrasting functions to two mental faculties: *sensibility* (or imagination, feeling, instinct) and *intelligence* (or reason). It will not be sufficient to label the former passive and the latter active, though a loose parallel of this nature can be discerned. Because Marcel moved through a series of positions about the separation of powers between these putative faculties, and because Proust was too canny to have stayed very long with any single schematic description of the human mind, one can demonstrate almost anything by quoting selectively from the *Search*. However, the topic is too important to evade.

The tradition that divides thought into reason and faith, logic and feeling, goes back a very long way and may well coincide with that partial alienation from ourselves we call civilization. We should beware of these divisions and of the way they are reflected in our language and institutions. In using the terms of this dualism, Proust was not so much approving a conventional division of mind as attempting to reach the seat of thought by any means at hand. His writing—both his style and his story—implies that sensibility and intelligence are not distinct faculties but gradations along a continuous spectrum of mental process.

Now, Proust never stops telling us that we can rarely possess or exercise all of our powers at once. According to the last quotation, the scientist leads with his intellect; the writer or artist leads with his feeling or instinct. But Proust put forward other proposals. In the early treatment of these ideas that he rapped out as the preface to *Against Sainte-Beuve*, he appeals less to a chronological order of priority than to a subtle and nearly sophistical order of value.

> And as to this inferiority of the intelligence, one must still ask the intelligence to establish it. For if the intelligence does not deserve the supreme crown, it alone can bestow the crown. And if the intelligence holds only the second place in the hierarchy of virtues, it alone is capable of proclaiming that instinct must occupy the first place. (*CSB* 216)

The authority to bestow is also the authority to withhold. I know of few passages in Proust that appears so forthright and remain so ambivalent. This "hierarchy of virtues" is compromised by divided sovereignty. Proust's confidence rings hollow and conveys his frustration over the knottiness of the problem. The novel he went on to write, and which he finally called the *Search*, dramatizes, among other things, his struggle to resolve the problem.

On the first page, barely twelve lines into the story, the Narrator describes a struggle in the sleeper's mind between reason and belief as to where and what he is. As Marcel grows up in Combray, he feeds on the mental nourishment of sensations and impressions. Yet he bemoans their lack of "intellectual value" and "abstract truth" (I 179/i 252). (See above, page 110.) He believes he should be raising his mind to a higher level. As a teenager in Balbec, Marcel hangs around Elstir's studio, where he begins to see that Elstir's intelligence resists painting intellectual images in order to seek out "true impressions" (I 835/ii 566) available to the innocent eye of sensibility.

As time goes by, the Narrator's account of Marcel turns to a different form of order. We hear often of "psychological laws" and even of "moral chemistry" (III 585/v 792), suggesting that human beings as much as things obey the workings of universal law. The entire apparatus of optical figures applied to our conscious and unconscious faculties as well as to social history implies that a set of laws forming a coherent science can describe these human processes. Certain passages in the *Search* sound more like the pronouncements of a nineteenth-century determinist than of a twentieth-century poet. "Thus it is useless to observe social behavior, for one can deduce it all from psychological laws" (I 513/ii 116–17). "Anything really important for a man can happen only in spite of him, by the action of some great natural law" (II 160/iii 211). For the most part Proust avoids sharp classifications in favor of generalizations that discover a regularity and coherence within a state of perpetual change. Still, he had the scientist's and moralist's sense of law as something exciting and alive. Proust's patient, probing intelligence seems to partake of the genius of La Rochefoucauld and Jean-Henri Fabre and Henri Poincaré.

In the final volume the tension between sensibility and intelligence surfaces again. During Marcel's long meditation in the library before entering the Prince de Guermantes' salon, several prominent passages line up on one side or the other of the debate. The truths abstracted by the intelligence from observation are less profound than impressions, because the latter are received through the senses (III 878/vi 273) and have the depth of our own experience (III 890/vi 290–91). On the other hand, only intellectual effort can make a thought truly ours (III 880/vi 275–76; see above, page 216) and "develop" it like a photograph (III 895/vi 299). In spite of the apparent standoff, Proust proposes a compromise in the same passage quoted on page 216. It's a matter of order of events. The artist and the writer, unlike the scientist and the intellectual, must start with impressions from their sensibility and appeal later to their intelligence. In this fashion both faculties are accommodated.

But is it really possible to make such distinctions in the bosom of our thinking? Is the mind divided into two parts? In an essay primarily about Leonardo da Vinci, "The Tortoise and the Hare" (in *The Innocent Eye*), I attempt to argue the shakiness of such a separation of thought. But a popular literary and philosophical tradition continues to distinguish systematic reason from looser and more personal forms of thought, and all of us are obliged to deal with it. Proust comes at the question more convincingly, I believe, in earlier pages spanning *The Captive* and *The Fugitive*.

In the midst of Marcel's debate with himself about breaking off his affair with and virtual captivity of Albertine (they fill four hundred pages), and while reflecting on the music she plays for him on the pianola, Marcel (backed by the Narrator) returns to his recurring examination of why he reacts so strongly to certain works of art and to certain impressions of the world and nature. Suddenly, midway in a four-page paragraph, we find ourselves presented with a choice between "two hypotheses." Either the strong pleasurable emotions of art and of "impressions" correspond to a spiritual and ideal reality belonging to a higher realm (III 374–75/v 503–5); or those emotions remain entirely material, their vagueness contains only illusion and no true depth, and our doubts should convince us of the "nullity" of any higher reality (III

382/v 513). We must choose one hypothesis or the other, spiritual or
material. The Narrator insists that this metaphysical challenge concerns
"all important questions: of Art, of Reality, and of Eternity of the soul"
(III 374/v 503–4).

In the novel this momentous philosophical decision is thrust on Marcel at a moment when he cannot collect himself sufficiently to make up
his mind whether or not to break off his elaborate psychological saraband—or charade—with Albertine. Accordingly, he dodges the bigger
decision by asking in regard to Vinteuil's music a rhetorical question
that admits both doubt and belief. But the metaphysical challenge to the
bases of Marcel's universe will not go away. After Albertine has left him,
the challenge returns to usurp his fretting over the reasons why she did
so. In the passage I shall quote now, it is the intelligence that defends the
second materialist hypothesis of doubt, and "other powers" that give
credence to a spiritual reality. The first two short clauses ask us to take
note of the close fit between the ideas expressed here and the flow of the
surrounding narrative.

> But—and what follows will make the situation even clearer, as many
> episodes have already suggested it—the fact that the intelligence is
> not the subtlest, the most powerful and appropriate instrument for
> grasping the truth, is only one more reason for beginning with the
> intelligence, and not with an unconscious intuition, not with an un-
> questioned faith in presentiments. It is life itself which, little by little,
> case by case, allows us to notice that what is most important for our
> heart, or for our mind *[esprit]*, is taught us not by reasoning but by
> other powers. And then it is the intelligence itself which, acknowl-
> edging their superiority, abdicates, by reasoning, in their favor, and
> accepts the role of becoming their collaborator and servant. Experi-
> mental faith. (III 423/v 569)

It is a stunning passage, studded with crucial words: *vie, esprit, foi, expérimentale*. It appears to reverse the order of events in a later passage already quoted (III 880/vi 276; see above, page 216). Now, our intelligence

must set our existential priorities not after but *before* the fact. On faith. *Reasoned faith*. The Narrator, backed by Proust, is here proposing a collaboration of intelligence and sentiment. We come inevitably to paradox, close to the paradoxes of theology. As it is reasonable to have faith in the impressions of childhood, it is reasonable to have faith in presentiments and other feelings that seek the truth. But that faith is experimental. It lies open to the examination and judgment of intelligence. We come back, then, to an alternation of states or stages, with the implication that reason has both the first and the last say. From his quest for the seat of thought, Proust returned with this short version of a long journey: *foi expérimentale*. Scientific belief. Faith-filled experiment. Intelligence and intuition working together, checking and encouraging each other.

The *Search* shows a man trying to find, among other things, his mind—his *whole* mind. Often it seems to have two opposed parts. But like Plato's charioteer, he learns to control his two steeds and make them pull as one. More than any other passage in the book, this one impels me to propose something called Proust's wager, *le pari de Proust*. When Pascal in the seventeenth century urged that we bet on the existence of God, he invoked primarily reasons of self-interest and absence of risk. One wonders if there isn't something crass or flippant about Pascal's reasoning in such a weighty matter. Before a comparable metaphysical question, Proust made a wager—but not like Pascal's. Proust wagered that he and we must surmount the choice between opposites and affirm the two mental faculties together as complementaries. We are all adults here, grappling with problems beyond our reach and our ken. Having come so far, we continue the debate as something significant and important, even if insoluble. I consider the fact that Proust closed this passage with so succinct and apothegmatic as formula as "experimental faith" to be an index of his conviction. He has made a double declaration of faith in the material and the spiritual, in the intelligence and in "other powers." Proust's wager.

But Proust was not writing a philosophical tract. What he has presented here in abstract terms inhabits, as he insists at the start of the passage, the characters and the episodes of his narrative. Examples abound,

beginning with Marcel's "intermittences." But a more unlikely and striking case concerns a personage painted as superstitious, stubborn, unre-
sponsive to reason, prejudiced, and overbearing. Yet that personage is
also deeply intelligent and a great artist. This person has never been
troubled by any opposition between intelligence and sensibility. For she
incarnates their collaboration, their natural hybrid. I am referring to the
only character who stays the whole course of the novel, Françoise.

   This servant of peasant stock, about whom one cannot use the word
"humble," has her own code of conduct and her own vision of the world.
Despite her limited education, Proust accords her full status as an artist,
in cuisine and in couture, and an almost perfect equanimity in maintain-
ing her place in society and before God. At one point, Proust seems to
want to explain to us that she illustrates a special case of the collaboration of intelligence and sensibility.

> One would not refer to thinking in respect to Françoise. She knew
> nothing, in that total sense in which "knowing" nothing means un-
> derstanding nothing, except the rare truths which the heart is capa-
> ble of attaining directly. The immense world of ideas did not exist
> for her. But under her clear gaze . . . one could wonder if there do
> not exist, among that humble stock, the peasants, some beings . . .
> who belong to the Holy Family, and are thus related, though
> remaining in childhood, to beings of the highest intelligence.
> (I 650/ii 309–10)

Proust here links Françoise both to *heart,* a term encompassing sensibility, feeling and intuition, and to *intelligence,* through a distinctly
evangelical connection.* In her, we see only simplicity and obtuseness toward sophisticated ideas, until we glimpse the deeper intelligence underlying her dignified behavior. Proust sets before us an immense cast
of characters, including some stunning wits and penetrating intelli-

---

*The term "heart" and the tenor of the passage allude to one of Pascal's most
quoted *pensées:* "The heart has its own reasons, which reason does not understand."

gences. But a passage like this one, reinforced by the overall movement of the narrative, which at the end leaves almost everyone else behind, allows one to conclude that, when it comes to character and to mental faculties, Proust bet on Françoise, for she is a member of the Holy Family. Among such beings, *heart* and *reason* work as one.

IX

READING FOR YOUR LIFE

T HE IMPOSING SCALE OF PROUST'S UNDERTAKING AND THE
suspense that builds in the last volume direct the reader's attention
toward the unfolding of the action itself. But there is room for many
other related questions. One is perfectly justified in asking if there are
any parallels to this narrative, any other major works to which it is linked
by any relation, from plagiarism to homage. We are as accustomed in the
twentieth century as were medieval commentators to connect great con-
temporary books to ancient forebears; thus Joyce resurrects the *Odyssey*
and Faulkner the Christ story and Mann the Joseph story, and every
playwright worth his salt has raided Aeschylus and Sophocles.

Even though Proust's work abounds in semimythical themes like
magical initiation and fetishism, and though it extends the highly conscious tradition of the literary memoir, he wrote what impresses one as
essentially a self-contained novel. The *Search* relies upon no exterior
counterpart to sustain or reflect its action; on the contrary, Proust set
about to create within the massive dimensions of his work the very parallels that would illuminate its meaning. The novel contains its own past
in the form of incidents forgotten and then recalled under special circumstances. The story resurrects only itself. In contrast to the linear

progression of a fairy story that immediately reveals its features in the opening formula, *Once upon a time* . . . Proust follows a compound rhythm of expression that might be partly conveyed in the expression *Twice upon a time*. Within the limits of the novel—limits, like those of Versailles, extended to encompass an entire countryside—Proust creates a form of double consciousness, which I have examined as stereologic or binocular vision in time. As our two pupils, when properly functioning, form one three-dimensional image in the mind, so the experience of two related events separated and connected by the proper interval of *oubli* forms one four-dimensional image in the consciousness—a *moment bienheureux* when it occurs fleetingly and without lasting effect on our life pattern, a self-recognition piercing of the veil of illusion when we are able to sustain our consciousness at this level.

In the chapter "Philosophy and the Novel" in *The Myth of Sisyphus*, Camus affirms this double consciousness as a central principle. "To create is to live twice. The anxious groping search of a man like Proust, his meticulous collecting of flowers and tapestries and states of anguish has no other meaning." The basic action of the *Search* is intermittent and constantly in decline until the close; the occasional references to a former life and to metempsychosis should be read figuratively as signifying levels of our own existence, the multiplicity of our states of awareness that we tend to spread out successively in time. Achieving its deepest insights and formal beauties by returning to and surpassing itself, the *Search* should be seen as reflexive in shape, a narrative that turns back upon itself and rises out of itself in a spiral.

Armed now with this sense of double consciousness in time, of living twice, we are ready to approach the question that has gone unanswered since page 155. Why, when only personal experience, only life itself can bring us to ourselves and to any kind of fulfilment, why do we value literature? As I argued in Chapter VI on idolatry, the most stalwart of writers, among them Proust and Tolstoy, affirm that literature cannot ever be a substitute for experience. But—and here is the point—literature is not therefore excluded from any role in shaping our experience.

Literature, as one among the arts, acquaints us with a special and intensified repertory of feelings and events and possibilities. Later, when we ourselves encounter an event similar to one of them, we may have a counterpart already at hand, forgotten, but available. And the movement of our mind is to say, "Here it is." For we have virtually experienced it once already.

Literature can foreshorten the complex, two-part process of full living; what we participate in through reading becomes the first half of that double process. Our own life, our personal experience, can then move directly into the second beat: recognition. The action I am trying to describe resembles the elaborate training pilots were put through in the Second World War in order to be able to recognize instantaneously all friendly and enemy aircraft. In a flash lasting one-hundredth of a second, a pilot could know, "That's a Zero." He could not be taught exactly how to bag the Japanese plane when he met one; but he could be taught, through this preparation, to concentrate all his powers on the task when the time came. Similarly, to read genuine literature is to accumulate within oneself a fund of possible experiences against which to achieve an occasionally intensified sense of what one is doing, to recognize that one is alive in a particular way. I remember the verb to "Proustify" that I traded with classmates in college when we first explored Proust's novel. The word referred to a certain kind of urgent, involuntary recollection that we all experienced from time to time and that now took on crucial significance because we had read Proust and accepted this experience as something no longer trivial. We were constantly on the alert with our inner spectroscopes.

Literature, then, like all the arts, plays a formative or preparatory role in training our sensibilities. In a limited way it supplies the first beat of a duple rhythm of existence. It offers not true life, but the potentiality of true life if we go on to complete that rhythm. The *Search* and *War and Peace* do not represent the wasted effort of authors who can offer us no more than skillful diversion. As Proust's optical figures insist, true literature does not divert but directs. The great books affect the economy of life for many individuals by allowing them to achieve personal experience sooner, more directly, and with less groping. This sense, this secret, is what allows certain people to live life at all times as an adventure. Others simply do not recognize that what they are doing, what is going on around them, has any significance as *life* at all. Literature is one of the keys. In the large sense, it is didactic. We learn from it.

This apparently simplistic explanation of the experience of literature holds up also in reverse. The person who has lived a full, varied life frequently fails to recognize its meaning or even to appreciate its qualities until encountering them afresh in a work of art—particularly literature. (In all this section "literature" must be read in the broad sense of any compelling account of experience—fireside story or epic, poem or play, biography, or maxim.) Whereas the young—in almost an optical sense—look forward to life through literature, the old look back at life through it. In both cases a metamorphosis occurs if the process finds its second term—either the event reencountered in the future after an interval of forgetting, or the event rediscovered in the past before it was forgotten. Thus Proust could speak of a reader as reading into his own self (III 911/vi 322).

This second experience commonly occurs accompanied by mixed feelings over having to acknowledge, "Yes, it was just like that and I never knew it." Roquentin in Sartre's *Nausea* looks back in amazement as he works on a biography and realizes that he has seen more of the world and of life than most people. The second beat of life comes to him after the living, and his "adventures" are discovered in retrospect until the terror of nausea plunges him into something more urgent. But I cannot help feeling that the reverse order of events leads to the more authentic experience: literature establishes the terms in which later events will be met. Literature itself contains a host of illustrations of this process—Paolo and Francesca reading romances together, Don Quixote reading tales of chivalry, Julien Sorel reading Napoleon, Emma Bovary reading novels, Tom Sawyer reading pirate stories. The precise equilibrium of forces between life and literature is one of literature's major themes. Proust makes it particularly urgent by the massive steadiness with which his novel directs our attention back at ourselves. On what level, in what rhythm, with what intensity are we alive as ourselves?

Even though the relation of the *Search* to the Western literary tradition is different from that of such masters as Balzac or Hardy or even Dostoevski, there still remain a certain number of comparisons that shed light on Proust's novel. Homer, for example, puts off Ulysses' homecoming almost to the point of his (and our) forgetting it—but never completely; then the long prepared return takes place in an elaborate series of disguises, unmaskings, and recognitions not unlike the close of Proust's novel. Long wandering followed by a homecoming, lost and found—few actions are more universal. French literature itself produced the three writers whose work turns most compulsively and searchingly back upon itself in order to find out the charm and the mystery of the past. Montaigne, Rousseau, and Chateaubriand strove to discover themselves as men and as writers through works of memory and reflection that engulf all their other writings. But the essay, the confession, and the memoir each faces in a different direction from the novel. More than any other modern novelist, Tolstoy in *War and Peace* conveys a sense of people's aging, losing and gaining in knowledge, circling around their own image of themselves. But where Tolstoy relied increasingly on a sense of family and progeny as the continuity of life, Proust held his universe tightly arrayed around one individual consciousness.

It is a slightly wider meaning of literary tradition that best accommodates itself to Proust's work: the tradition of legends and folktales we usually devour in our childhood. The *Search* is closer to *Arabian Nights* than to any other work. In his final meditation on the literary vocation and death, Marcel speculates that his book will demand many nights of work, perhaps a thousand. And then *A Thousand and One Nights* (along with Saint-Simon's memoirs) quietly appears to give its blessing to these closing pages (III 1043–44/vi 524–25). Of course, Proust-Marcel states that his book will be quite different. But the differences take root in several significant similarities. Both stories begin by presenting a secure and happy life soon shattered by a revelation of infidelity and depravity. The Sultan discovers his wife is deceiving him on a grand scale, and his eyes are opened to the unfaithfulness of all women. Marcel's innocent vision of Combray collapses beneath the weight of vice and duplicity that reveal themselves in every character outside his immediate family. Thus set adrift in a corrupt world, both stories move in apparently desultory fashion through magic powers, evil presences, cryptic events, and transformations in places and people. In the long middle reaches, everyone seems to be reduced to "passing time." But the beginning and end of the action stay firmly in place in the two books. The narrative, Marcel's or the Narrator's or Scheherezade's, is carried on in defiance of fate and time, and finally great persistence wins release and salvation for the two storytellers. Thus literature wins out day by day over death. Scheherezade gains pardon for herself and coaxes the Sultan back to mercy and benevolence by bringing to him the three children he has begotten during the thousand nights she has been his companion. Proust employs a similar incarnation of time lived in Mlle de Saint-Loup, the figure in whom Marcel finally recognizes himself and through whom he becomes reconciled to his world and his vocation as Narrator of his own tale. The parallels between the two stories are more than casual. I am inclined to think Proust took pleasure in considering himself, despite disclaimers, the legendary author of *Parisian Nights*.

An equally illuminating comparison, this one apparently unfamiliar to Proust, can be made with a story written in the New World and based on the folklore of the Old World. Few tales are at the same time so entrancing and so disturbing as that of the long sleep of the hunter who loses twenty years of his life in the depths of the Catskills, as Marcel loses long years in his *maisons de santé*. The real sleep of Rip Van Winkle confronts him, when he returns to his village, with a foreshortening of time and a scene of recognitions like the one at the close of the *Search*. Time, however, has bested Rip, passed him by and left him with nothing more than "his place on the bench at the inn door" and a good tale to tell any traveler who will listen to a garrulous old man. Marcel's literary sleep, on the other hand, has the opposite effect. It allows him to best time, to rise out of contingency. For it bestows on him, at last and for good, the sense of *la vraie vie*, which he only grazed earlier in the *moments bienheureux* and in the twilight consciousness on the edge of sleep. Marcel's long forgetting does not remain an unlikely tale of local legend like Rip's, but permits him the stereoscopic vision of time, the double consciousness of existence, which gives the *Search* its shape and its meaning. Rip's long sleep and Marcel's disappearance amount to a death in life from which they return to very different lots. Rip, for whom life is over, is content with his place on the bench by the inn door. In contrast, Marcel now begins his lifework, whose reading we have just finished and which, like a gigantic magic lantern, leaves us wiser than we were. The *Search* has the dimensions of a national, even an international, epic. Yet no book could be more personal, as if addressed to me alone. There are times when I seem to be reading for my life.

PROUST'S "MYSTERIOUS LAWS OF THOUGHT"

AUTHOR'S NOTE: I have come to believe that not all thinking is best expressed in expository prose. Some of the things I want to say about Proust emerged in a different form—in this case, an informal fictional dialogue. Several of these observations would not fare as well in the body of the book. Therefore, I include here as a "coda" pages written as a lecture and given at the University of Alabama at Birmingham. I should like to think that the marked change of tone will be more refreshing than jarring.

It is ten minutes after nine o'clock Friday morning in the rundown basement rooms of the Stentor Recording Studios in St. Louis. Sam Gates, fifty, owner and operator of the studio, is seated in front of his equipment in the control room and threading a reel. Callie Szonic, thirty-five, freelance radio journalist and producer, is reviewing a script at the studio table and referring to some books. They are waiting for Henry Fitzhugh, forty-five, professor of philosophy at Columbia University, and for Ned Price, graduate student in French at Washington University in St. Louis. Professor Fitzhugh, known among philosophers for his book on solipsism, has recently published another, Proust and Perverseness of Thought. *Yesterday he gave a lecture at Washington*

University sponsored by the Philosophy and Romance Languages depart-ments. His plane leaves today at noon.

Sound of knocking.

Callie: The door's open . . . Good morning, Professor Fitzhugh. I'm Callie Szonic. You brought your suitcase! That's fine. We'll have more time to talk before you have to catch your plane. Coffee?

Prof. F: Yes. Thank you.

Callie: This is Sam Gates. Professor Fitzhugh. Sam lets me use his place as my headquarters. I have no office.

Sam: Don't mind me. I have to go out in a few minutes. Why don't you two go into the studio? There's more space and better chairs.

Callie: Thanks, Sam. *(They move to the studio.)*

Prof. F: (Clearing his throat.) You can understand, Ms. Szonic, that I need to know a little more about what you're doing before I can de-cide whether to participate. Your letters say you have funding to do a series of programs on major authors in world literature. Do you mean to record a short talk on each author? And who are the authors?

Callie: No, not little lectures. More like conversations. We'll do an hour on each author. So far we've chosen Faulkner, George Eliot, Achebe, Goethe, Pascal, Lady Murasaki, and Proust. Not quite the standard run. First a discussion to place the author and describe his or her ge-nius. Then actors will read—really perform—selections from the work for the rest of the hour. Oral interpretation some people call it. We're hoping National Public Radio will air the programs. The point is to appeal to a wide audience. It's not a scholarly project.

Prof. F: I don't understand. Why did you pick me then? My books are very scholarly, particularly the one on Proust.

Callie: Yes, but you talk about subjects that . . . *(Knock)* Just a moment. Come in, Ned.

Ned: Excuse me, excuse me. My car wouldn't start today. Naturally. Pro-fessor Fitzhugh? Ned Price. I'm a graduate student in French at Wash-ington University. Did Callie tell you how we met? In a bookstore, where I was reading your book on Proust. She asked me what it was like. Now she calls me her adviser on Proust. I'm very pleased to meet you. The reviewers didn't do justice to your Proust book.

Callie: I was just starting to tell Professor Fitzhugh why we chose him to talk about Proust.

Ned: That's easy. Your chapter on perverseness of thought swept us away. Also the section on how the overall style of Proust's novel arises from gossip—malicious, loving, idle, compulsive gossip—the gossip of someone who cannot bear to let the wheel of words stop turning for fear that then everything else might disappear. You make your scholarship pretty lively.

Callie: Ned is an incorrigible Proust enthusiast. Which means he gossips too. But there's another reason why I invited you to do the Proust program. We're dealing with an author who took fifteen years to find his way to the novel and then, after the age of thirty-five, poured everything into one immense book, which he just barely finished in his last fifteen years. Story of a man obsessed. You know all this better than I do. Hundreds of characters, complex subplots, hilarious scenes of people's behavior in social situations, lengthy meditations on the major philosophical questions of life. In the last stage just before he got started on the *Search*—incidentally, I agree with you that the old title must go—Proust wrote an essay on the French romantic author Gérard de Nerval. It's in *Against Sainte-Beuve*. The essay contains a passage I've always wanted to hear a Proust scholar comment on. A philosopher more than anyone else. Proust has been talking about . . .

Prof. F: Ms. Szonic, this is beginning to sound like an oral examination. I thought we were going to confer about ways of doing the program.

Callie: Yes, yes. Exactly. I want to know if you think this would make a good lead-in for the discussion. Proust has been discussing *Sylvie*, Nerval's haunting story about three women, all of whom the hero loves and loses. The hero is pretty close to Nerval himself speaking in the first person. Proust, who deeply admires Nerval, tells us that everything is colored purple in the story, especially the name Sylvie with its two *i*-sounds. Rimbaud has the same color for the *i*-sound in his "Sonnet of the Vowels." Then in one complex and unforgettable sentence—I have it marked right here—Proust states that Nerval's story contains "the mysterious laws of thought which I have often wanted to express—I'd count up to five or six of them." But that's all. Proust doesn't tell us what they are and closes the discussion by saying that there may even be a little too much intelligence in *Sylvie.* Five or six laws of thought—the idea fascinates me. But there's no follow-up. What can we do with the passage?

Prof. F: I've read those pages on Nerval, but I don't remember the specific passage. Five or six laws . . . There's a challenge for every Proustian alive, philosopher or not. Of course, Proust talks about laws all the time. In *Within a Budding Grove* (another title that should be abandoned), the narrator blurts right out that "it's useless to observe people's behavior because you can derive it all from psychological laws." Now, the Nerval passage you quoted doesn't sound ironic or playful. I think Proust gives you the first of his laws right there in the purple *i*-sounds. He's affirming Baudelaire's *correspondances,* synesthesia, analogies. That law of association of impressions through similarity and proximity leads directly into the great echo chamber of involuntary memory: association in time. How's that for a first law? When you attend to them carefully, things mysteriously connect. The other laws may take a bit longer.

Ned: You make it sound easy. Callie, do you expect Professor Fitzhugh to do all the work? No. Then I'll suggest one. This may be more a principle than a law. I mean the double, the doppelgänger, the identical Other. It doesn't seem to me that Proust necessarily borrowed this device from anyone else—Hoffmann or Poe. It was the natural consequence of his decision to write an autobiographical novel. He lays it right out for us in the madeleine sequence. The second and third mouthfuls of tea and cake do not fill him again with the original precious essence. Marcel, who at that age may be about halfway to becoming the narrator, puts down his cup and turns toward his mind, his spirit, as the source of the essence that surpasses mediocrity and contingency. But—all this is close to verbatim quotation—the mind is in a quandary because "it, the seeking mind, is also the dark countryside where it must do the seeking." The endlessly fruitful dilemma of autobiography consists in the fact that the prey lies inside the hunter. Proust enacts this dilemma by making this principal character a double: the Narrator and Marcel, seeker and sought, one character at different ages, two virtually identical characters distinguishable only by chronology, by the contingency of time. But style and syntax conspire to bind us to this crucial bifurcation inside the endlessly recurring *I*. Proust's *je* in all its inflections sounds like just one person.

You know what has happened as a result. Almost all of Proust's critics have become fastidious purists. Since author must never be confused with narrator, the name Marcel has virtually disappeared— too close to Proust's name. The editors of the three massive new French editions of the *Search* say "the Narrator" for *both* persons of the double. They spurn the name that Proust himself twice tentatively gave to his principal character: Marcel. Yet that name is truly appropriate in a work of fiction displaying a subtle and unmistakable relation to autobiography. In the enacted scenes of this bildungsroman "the Narrator" is a patently inaccurate term to designate a slowly maturing prospective writer, one of whose principal traits is, by all the evidence, including his own declarations, the incapacity to settle down to write or narrate anything at all. Critics should reconsider their skittishness and return to "Marcel" to refer to the hero and principal character. Even a Kafkaesque "M" for certain roles of Proust's *I* would be better than a blanket "Narrator" to cover every aspect of the first person.

Well, I hope I haven't botched my point completely. I see the law of the double as essential to everything Proust wrote. A first-person singular tracking itself until . . .

Callie: Ned! I can't let you go on. You agreed not to get off on a rant.

Ned: I'm sorry. I'll try to be quiet.

Prof. F: You must be writing your dissertation on first-person pronouns in Proust. I'm not sure you need me here. Now we have two laws out of five. What about you, Ms. Szonic? You should answer your own question. Surely you have an answer.

Callie: Don't forget I'm just a radio journalist. But yes, I may. A couple of pages before the passage about laws in Nerval, Proust describes *Sylvie* as a "dream of a dream" or "a dream within a dream." I feel certain he's alluding to some kind of law. But I can't put my finger on how it works in the *Search*.

Prof. F: In *Aurélia,* another of Nerval's stories, he talks about "the spreading of dream into real life." It's really an analogy for Nerval's incipient insanity. Proust has hidden away in the *Search* far more dreams than we usually remember on first reading. After Albertine is killed in a riding accident, "the *da capo* effect" of Marcel's dreams prevents him from forgetting her, and the narrator describes dreams as "passing intervals of insanity." Proust was never swept away completely by dream or insanity as Nerval was. But the possibility is there always, a law held in abeyance, the threat of the abyss of unreality, of dreams taking over everything.

Callie: You see? I told you a scholar would help me. Now we have three laws: things connect, we are all doubles, and dream encroaches on reality. Where do we go now? More coffee?

Prof. F: Yes, please. You are relentless. I'll try once more. There's a psychological law that applies in many domains of Proust's novel. I wish I had a good name for it. Since I don't, I'll have to borrow a phrase from a critic I have my reservations about, Roger Shattuck. In his second book on Proust, Shattuck himself borrows an expression from Montaigne, *erreur d'âme,* soul error. The term refers to the condition that makes it so difficult for us to cherish what we have and leads us to see mystery and prestige in what we do not possess. Anyone who has read a single volume of Proust can sense the operation of this law in the domain we call romantic love. We say possession is nine-tenths of the law. Marcel's extended capture and imprisonment of Albertine demonstrate that in attachments of the heart, possession is one-tenth of the law. But soul error, which wants what it does not or cannot have, also explains Proust's rejection of friendship. He presents friendship as a false and distracting personal relationship in which we seek "hospitalization" in another individual instead of cultivating the true life of the mind in ourselves. Shattuck fails to see how essential a role soul error plays in the great driving force of all social relations: snobbery. There's a superb comic page in the second volume about a rich and titled old lady—it's Mme de Villeparisis—arriving at the Grand Hôtel in Balbec. All the guests in the dining room are consumed with curiosity about her and the desire to make her acquaintance—a desire they then half-successfully suppress by convincing themselves that she is ugly and not worth knowing. Proust has written a subtle modern version of Aesop's fable of the sour grapes. All these constantly readjusted states of mind turn on the axis of soul error. Of course, now we have come back around to what I discuss in my chapter on "perverseness of mind" in Proust. I cannot judge whether soul error has equal sway in Nerval, an author I don't know as well as the two of you.

Ned: Yes. Yes. Everything in *Sylvie* and *Aurélia* depends on keeping the ideal at a distance in order to sustain the illusion and the emotion. But . . . going through a set of laws like this . . . If I can remember accurately . . . Just a minute. Borges. That's who it is. Somewhere I read about Borges stating in a lecture the principles of fantastic art. They are almost the same ones that we have pulled out of Proust and Nerval. I think I can remember Borges's four devices. The work within the work, the contamination of reality by dream or unreality, the voyage in time, and the double. The voyage in time may be Borges's version of memory and association. But what does it all mean? Should we believe that these are four great universals of all thinking and all art? I'm not sure I want to be told that there are just so many laws that cover all cases.

Callie: They're not so different from one another if you look carefully. I think there may be an almost infinite number of laws of this kind all representing one principle: *interference.* The interference of one domain with another, one sense with another, one time with another, one place with another, one state of mind with another, one social level with another, and so on. Proust blurs everything, all our classifications, even our sense of character. Still, the *Search* represents a deep and strong faith in something—in the life of the mind, I suppose.

Prof. F: Perhaps you can group all the laws so far under the heading of interference. But there's at least one more major law that does not belong with the rest. I think of it as the principle of self-determination. At three different stages in his career—in 1904 writing about Ruskin, in 1908 writing on Saint-Beuve, and then some ten years later quoting Elstir in his studio—Proust states his conviction that "we cannot receive the truth from anyone; we have to create it for ourselves." Here we have the opposite of interference. In another place he describes every writer as having to start out from scratch, like Homer. Each time Proust seems to be reaffirming that ontogeny recapitulates phylogeny—not just in the embryo but in life itself. He had his own monadology.

Ned: Isn't this what all the critics refer to as radical subjectivity? The impossibility of true communication between human beings? All the extended social occasions in the *Search,* which is full of them, and all the scenes driven by some form of appetite or love for another person, describe only the most superficial form of exchange between individuals. As you write yourself, gossip drives out all other forms of exchange. Marcel cannot even kiss Albertine properly, because her face gets in the way. And in the opening scenes of "Combray," Marcel and his mother cannot converse easily with one another, even alone. Her goodness and tenderness reach him, unalloyed, only when she begins reading George Sand aloud to him in a voice whose lack of affectation expresses true "moral distinction." But there is a yawning dilemma here. If we must learn everything for and by ourselves, if we cannot communicate essential trusts to one another, why write books? Why read them? Isn't literature a hoax exposed in the very pages we are reading?

Callie: Andy why are you in graduate school scrutinizing these contradictions and digging yourself into an intellectual hole?

Prof. F: That may be what graduate school is for. But now you two are going to have to let me talk about what's on my mind instead of asking me questions as if this were an interview or examination. After receiving your letters, Ms. Szonic, I tried to . . .

Callie: Please forgive me, Professor Fitzhugh. We've been impolite. What are your ideas for the program?

Prof. F: No need to apologize. A discussion like this accomplishes more than a monologue. Ned just said the word I have on my mind. Reading. Are you aware how many scholars and critics have published about reading in Proust? At least two full-length books and scores of articles in French, English, German, Japanese, and other languages. It's true that one of the essential subjects of the *Search* is reading and writing. But most of the criticism I've read leaves me deeply dissatisfied. One of the most carefully written scenes in the novel concerns Marcel reading in the garden in Combray. It comes near the opening; any reader of Proust should know it. Marcel is persuaded by his grandmother to leave his bedroom, where darkness, stray rays of light, street sounds, and other distractions prevent him from reading. With an unidentified book he takes shelter in the depths of a canopied cane-and-canvas chair under a chestnut tree in the garden. Here Marcel is solitary and hidden enough to read. The Narrator devotes five pages to describing and narrating the act of reading a novel. I see you have the English translation of the *Search* there. Pass me the opening volume, would you.

The narrator moves in four carefully distinguished steps from the innermost recesses of Marcel's consciousness to the real world outside that surrounds him. Remember? First comes the striking metaphor of an incandescent object. It evaporates anything in its path and therefore can never touch a substance it approaches. The scene starts with a version of our last fundamental law: the incapacity of the consciousness to make contact with any other consciousness. "A narrow spiritual border" always separates us from the real world of other beings and other things. But: one precious mental activity can transcend this limit, this law. Reading. Proust explains this everyday miracle by examining the next level of Marcel's mind. While he reads, Marcel's consciousness is released by his *croyance,* his "belief in the philosophical richness and the beauty of the book." And the book offers a very special kind of material for his emotions to deal with. The novelist sets

before us not the material opaqueness of real beings but transparent
images evoked by words, images "which our soul can assimilate,"
which our consciousness can make contact with. These immaterial
images have the further advantage of not being subject to contingent
human time. They can move at an accelerated speed that reveals
changes we fail to notice at the pace of ordinary living. The novelist's
images have the privileged status of a prolonged, clarified dream.

   The third level of phenomena described by the narrator in Marcel's
mental state of reading consists of the imaginary landscape in which
the imaginary characters move, a countryside that seems to belong to
"true Nature" with a capital N, Nature "worthy of being studied and
explored." And here the narrator or Proust places a paragraph that
sets the tone for the rest of the book, its essential action and its intellectual life. Let me read the paragraph. There's no other way to convey the pace and the rhythm of Proust's style. The prison image in the
second sentence recasts the earlier image of an incandescent filament
that cannot make contact with anything. And notice how insistently
he uses the word "soul." I've checked; it's in the original. *Ame* means
our entire mental, emotional, and spiritual equipment. The passage
describes how an irresistible force—later Proust calls it "that immense desire to know life"—meets an immovable object—the inac-
cessibility of material, opaque beings. Just listen. I'll go slowly. It's
less than a page:

> Had my parents allowed me, when I read a book, to pay a visit
> to the region it described, I should have felt that I was making an
> enormous advance towards the ultimate conquest of truth. For
> even if we have the sensation of being always enveloped in, sur-
> rounded by, our own soul, still it does not seem a fixed and im-
> movable prison; rather do we seem to be borne away with it, and
> perpetually struggling to transcend it, to break out into the world,
> with a perpetual discouragement as we hear endlessly all around us
> that unvarying sound which is not an echo from without, but the
> resonance of a vibration from within. We try to discover in things,

which become precious to us on that account, the reflection of what our soul has projected on to them; we are disillusioned when we find that in this natural state, they are devoid of the charm which they owed, in our minds, to the association of certain ideas; sometimes we mobilize all the forces of that soul in a glittering array in order to bring our influence to bear on other human beings who, we very well know, are situated outside ourselves where we can never reach them. And so, if I always imagined the woman I loved in the setting I most longed at the time to visit, if I wished that it were she who would show it to me, who would open to me the gates of an unknown world, it was not a mere chance association of thoughts; no, it was because my dreams of travel and of love were only moments—which I isolate artificially today as though I were cutting sections at different heights in the jet of a fountain, iridescent but seemingly without flow or motion—moments in a single, undeviating, irresistible outpouring of all the forces of my life.

What can I say about such a passage? There's nothing to add. Yet one could talk endlessly about how much philosophy, how much feeling, is packed into every sentence. We want to know precisely what we cannot know—the universe of beings that lies outside us. Our soul pours itself out by a kind of fate—entirely in vain. We live a tragicomic paradox. Near the end of the passage you can hear the Narrator, "moments . . . which I isolate artificially today," speaking in the present tense, separating himself from Marcel in the past and cozying up to Proust in the present writing this book, these words. The narrative goes on to . . . What is it, Ned? You want to say something?

Ned: Is it that obvious? Yes, just a parenthesis about the fountain analogy. I've thought a lot about it. The fountain belongs to a special set of images that affirm both flux and stasis. There aren't many. Heraclitus' river, the one you cannot step into twice. In our time, Wordsworth's "standing waterfalls" and Pater's "candle flame." Each one a streaming stillness. Proust's whole paragraph echoes Heraclitus' balance of opposites.

Prof. F: You're right. I never thought of that link. Well, the fourth stage
of Marcel's reading is the immediate, his Sunday afternoon world of
a chair sheltered in the silent garden. At regular yet unpredictable intervals that hushed scene is invaded by notes striking the hour from
the Saint-Hilaire bell tower. This outer layer of familiar circumstances
contains the other layers going back to Marcel's soul or consciousness.
They form a kind of multiple capsule or monad. Now, all kinds of images in these five pages on reading tell how cut off Marcel remains
from the real world he yearns desperately to reach, to touch. Yet the
last significant substantive of the scene is "crystal," reinforced by the
adjective "limpid." These two words characterized the magical, transparent hours of reading, our closet approach to communication, to
getting out of ourselves.

Ned: What do you say about the transparency we find through reading
makes me think of another word Proust uses from time to time to describe the ordinary state of life without transparency. The word in
French is *trouble,* which doesn't mean "trouble" the way we use it in
English. It means a troubled, a disturbed, a confused state of mind. I
began to keep a list. Toward the end of the *Search* the pages Marcel
reads from the Goncourt journal cause a *"trouble"* in his mind because they seem to describe transparently people he has himself
known and never grasped so clearly in life. If reading is our crystal
ball, we live in a state of *trouble*—cloudiness, uncertainty.

Callie: You said earlier, Professor Fitzhugh, that you are dissatisfied by
what the critics have written about reading? Why is that? Whom do
you mean?

Prof. F: (Looking at his watch.) I think the cab I ordered may be here now.
I'll have to be brief. There's one critic who seems to have led most of
the others in the wrong direction. Do you know Paul de Man's essay
on Proust in *Allegories of Reading?* He spends half his time discussing
metaphor and metonymy in the two paragraphs just *before* the garden
reading scene—paragraphs in which Marcel essentially fails to read.
Then he quotes at length from the paragraph I just read and examines
what he calls a "reversal." Consciousness is captive within us, yet it

chooses "to submit itself to the test of truth" in the outside world. De Man says that Proust's novel leaves no doubt that the test must fail, and that this failure is affirmed right here "in a passage whose thematic and rhetorical strategy it reduces to naught." Proust's passage never attains the desired "totalization" or synthesis.

Now, de Man's Hegelian vocabulary is difficult enough to follow. But the principle flaw is that de Man has read the passage wrong. The Narrator—here very close to Proust—is not trying to synthesize or "totalize," anything. He is presenting a contrast, an opposition between *real life*, in which our attempts to communicate with other beings are inevitably thwarted, and the special activity of *reading*, relying on transparent images, which permits a closer approach to the conquest of truth, to knowledge. Far from deconstructing itself by an inner contradiction or a failure to "totalize," this passage presents the special rewards of reading as an activity complementary to living, not replacing it but opening up its potential spaces. The earlier lessons about reading from "Journées de lecture" hover close by. Although time spent reading is "fully lived," it brings us only to the threshold of spiritual life, provides incitements to it. De Man fails to take account of the close symbiotic relation Proust describes between reading and living.

There's one more step. As a philosopher I have to take it, even at my peril. Near the beginning of these pages on reading, the narrator speaks of Marcel's "belief" in the philosophical richness and the beauty of the book he is reading. Belief. It may be the key to everything. At the end of "Combray," the Narrator undertakes to explain why the two "ways"—Swann's way and the Guermantes way—have provided the essential structure and the most significant episodes of his intellectual life. Belief, a child's belief in the beings and things it lives among, lends them unforgettable reality and meaning. A kind of transparency without *trouble*. The child's belief in its world corresponds to the belief that we can provisionally reassemble and direct toward the book we are reading. In the *Search*, Proust casts doubt on many of our treasured values—love, friendship, social attainment, idolatrous forms of art. Beneath it all remains a startlingly invincible *faith*—faith in childhood experience and in reading.

Sam: (He has come in and waited during the last sentences.) Sorry to interrupt. The cab driver out front says he's come for you, Professor.

Callie: How did it go? Did you get it all?

Sam: Perfect. This is one of the best tapes yet. You have a pretty good voice for radio, Professor. I could even follow a lot of what you said. And I've never read a word of Proust—*Prowst*, I probably would have said. Maybe I'll have a look at his book.

Prof. F: (Incredulous, a little peeved.) You mean you recorded all this? *(To Callie.)* You said we were going to plan a program. I never agreed . . .

Callie: Don't worry, Professor Fitzhugh. We taped some material this morning. In a formal interview, thinking about how they sound, people often freeze up. You were fine. Believe me. And I promise you, nothing will leave this studio without your permission. We'll clean up the tape a little, make a few cuts, and send you a cassette copy. Then you'll tell us what you think. If you insist, we can do it over, or parts of it. But wait till you hear what we send you. You even did a reading for us!

Prof. F: I'll be damned. Does everyone walk into your trap as innocently as I did? All right, I'll wait to hear the results.

References for Coda

Page 235, "the mysterious laws": *CSB* 239/*OAL* 156

Page 236, "it's useless": I 513/ii 116–17

Page 236, "it, the seeking mind": I 45/i 61

Page 238, "dream of a dream": *CSB* 237/*OAL* 153

Page 238, "the *da capo* effect": III 538/v 725

Page 238, "passing intervals": III 540/v 727

Page 238, "hospitalization": II 394/iii 541

Page 239, There's a superb: I 678/ii 349

Page 239, Borges: James E. Irby, introd. to Jorge Luis Borges, *Labyrinths* (New York: New Directions, 1962), xviii

Page 240, Proust states: *CSB* 177; see also *CSB* 220/*OAL* 97 and I 864/ii 605–6

Page 240, "moral distinction": I 42/i 56–57

Page 241 to 243: I 84–87/i 115–18

Page 242, "that immense desire": III 553/v 745

Page 244, De Man: Paul de Man, "Reading (Proust)," in *Allegories of Reading* (New Haven: Yale University Press, 1979), 71

Page 245, "fully lived": *CSB* 160

Page 245, Belief, a child's belief: I 184/i 259–60

APPENDIXES

THE WONDERS OF OPTICS

(See page 107.)

S OME READERS WILL WELCOME A FEW SUPPLEMENTARY observations about optics—about light and space, about the human eye, about previous uses of optical imagery in art, and about Proust's familiarity with optical science. Optics as an independent discipline has tended to lose its identity under the shadow of astronomy, atomic physics, and the theory of relativity. But the unity of optics as a field and a mode of thinking is too great to abandon.

Light is the most rapid and miraculous means we know by which one part of the universe can impinge on another across space. We know its behavior, but are less sure of its composition and means of propagation. At the same time light is one of the familiar elements of our environment; specifically, it is the most regularly changing condition we experience and therefore the basic source of our sense and measurement of time. Shifts in lighting yield hours and days, seasons and years. Rays of light can be refracted or reflected into an image of their source; thus optical instruments, the eye as well as those constructed by man, become our primary source of information on near and remote objects. In science the speed of light, having been accurately measured, has become an important and useful physical constant, with the unique advantage

that it does not vary with the motion of its source or of its observer. The
science of optics has been deeply involved in all modern advances in
the fields of electromagnetism, quantum mechanics, and relativity. Light
is the most important single factor in our knowledge of the universe. Yet,
as is clear on every page of Proust, this medium of observation ultimately becomes a barrier to final knowledge. Light incorporates the
limits of its own revelations. Heisenberg's indeterminacy principle affirms that in the observation of infinitesimally small phenomena, the
very light energy by which we see them affects their velocity. And the
light by which we observe distant heavenly bodies arises out of a vast ex-
penditure of energy that, by the time their light has reached us millions
of years later, may have led to the total modification or disintegration of
those bodies. Such technical terms as "light years," "red giants," "white
dwarfs," and "black holes" take on an almost metaphysical meaning.
Light, then, is the source of our truth and our error—and equally of our
poetry.

The eye, which registers light for us, has characteristics that we ordi-
narily forget or take for granted. In its relaxed state the lens of the eye
focuses on infinity, and it requires muscular tension to accommodate it
to close vision of our immediate environment. With increasing age, our
ability to accommodate declines, producing the state of presbyopia, the
farsightedness of the old. Similarly only darkness can relax the iris, for
light causes an immediate contraction of its aperture. All the finest adjustments of the eye are reflex; only the gross actions of opening and di-
recting the eye fall under predominantly voluntary control. And when
our vision has adjusted itself to an object, the accurate interpretation of
its twin inverted images in our eyes depends upon habit, memory, and attention. The optical image disappears entirely into consciousness and life
process. Finally, even though all the events of vision occur in the few
inches of tissue between the eye and occipital lobe at the back of our
head, we see objects incontrovertibly out *there*, reassembled in space.
Our principal knowledge of the third dimension of space results not
from the exactness of the two dimensional images of it which we receive
but from the discrepancy between the two slightly different versions of

space that reach our consciousness from two separated eyes. The binocular nature of human vision (which requires that we see double and cross-eyed) introduces into the seat of our consciousness the principle of essential difference, of meaningful error. This projection of relief in three dimensions would scarcely suffice if we could not move through space and explore the nature of that error in order to make sense of it.

It would be worse than foolish to try to trace the role of optical imagery in art. It is universal. One of the most ancient and haunting symbols of the magic of vision is the single schematic eye that pervades Egyptian art, both in the eternal profile of figure drawing and in haughty isolation on one side of many sarcophagi. Resuming the researches of late Greek painting, it was the Renaissance with its science of Albertian perspective that established optics as the central discipline of art. It becomes not only the method but the matter of Uccello's studies and paintings, and of Piranesi's drawings. This rational construction of space was not to be systematically broken down until the nineteenth century, when an optical revolution of new instruments and new theories of color and light provided expressive technique for the restlessness of modern sensibility. It was then that Impressionism, like the nineteenth-century novel, developed an art of instantaneous fragments, not of eternal poses.

I am not trying to suggest that all these significant aspects of optics were consciously present in Proust's mind as he came to compose his novel. But we must not forget that the science of optics, under its own name and without the fancy dress of relativity theory and wave mechanics, played a dominant role in the scientific advances of the period. It was during the last three decades of the nineteenth century and the opening of the twentieth, exactly coincident with Proust's career that Helmholz fully described the physiology of the eye; that Edison invented the incandescent lamp; that Abbe and Schott perfected optical glass; that Maxwell established the relationship of light and electricity; that Michelson and Morley performed their masterly experiment to test the ether; that the mathematician Henri Poincaré, a friend and colleague of Bergson, was lecturing at the University of Paris on celestial mechanics and geometric optics (Proust mentions him twice in the *Search*);

that the Lumière brothers invented the *cinématographe,* which replaced
Edison's kinetoscope (and it will remain a mystery how Proust missed
exploiting the magic name of Lumière); that the magic lantern, the stereoscope, and the kaleidoscope had their greatest vogue; and that illumination of public buildings was first tried out on the Eiffel Tower for the
exposition of 1889. At the end of the nineteenth century the optician's
shop in every French town offered a display of optical instruments and
toys that constituted the most advanced collection of scientific devices
in the community. Even the pharmacies could not rival this exoticism.
Marcel refers four times to the *opticien* in Combray, to the exact location
of his shop and to the contents of his window. And in the closing pages
of the novel he compares himself as writer to the optician with his magnifying glass (III 1033/vi 508). Proust studied optics as a part of his
physics course at the Lycée Condorcet in the 1880s; he knew the *romans
d'anticipation* of Jules Verne and the literate science fiction of Villiers de
l'Isle-Adam, who wrote about Edison as "the sorcerer of Menlo Park."
Like many others, Proust collected photographs of all his friends and
studied them as new revelations of character. Optics figured in Proust's
environment as space exploration and genetics figure in ours, and he
sensed its symbolic significance. With the exception of acoustics, which,
with its derivatives of music and the inflections of the human voice,
yields the next most important corpus of images in Proust's work, optics is the only discipline that spans the fields of physics, physiology,
psychology, and aesthetics. By being "celestial" as well, it lent itself to
the tremendous demands Proust made of his material. In the long passage quoted on pages 105–6, it is this perspective of "human astronomy" that allows Proust to write, ". . . what we have forgotten that we
ever said, or indeed what we never did say, flies to provoke hilarity even
in another planet."

When the critic Vettard wrote an article comparing Proust and Einstein as "analytical visionaries" with an intuitive understanding of the
great natural laws (*NRF,* August 1922), Proust stated with enthusiasm
that he "found the article accurate" (*Lettres à la NRF,* 259). Literally
from his deathbed he wrote Vettard one of the most revealing of all his

letters on his artistic intentions, a letter developing the microscope-telescope comparison already incorporated into his novel (III 1041/vi 520). Considering the numerous and familiar applications of the science, and the aptness of its laws and terminology to describe artistic processes and human perception, it is not surprising that optics became the controlling metaphor of Proust's fiction.

TABLE OF THE
MOMENTS BIENHEUREUX

(See page 125.)

I HAVE TRIED TO CONVERT SEVERAL PAGES OF DETAILED analysis on the *moments bienheureux* into an outline whose schematic nature emphasizes several neglected points. Each of these *moments bienheureux* (also referred to as resurrections and reminiscences, here numbered to eleven by counting as one the five successive recurrences in the last volume) follows or partially follows a uniform pattern.* The pattern itself and the deviations from it give these moments their particular feeling and significance.

First, Marcel is always in a dispirited state of mind—bored, usually tired, alone (or if not, annoyed by the presence of others interfering with his solitude), and entangled in the *train-train* of habitual living. Second, he experiences a physical sensation, which comes unexpectedly and by chance through any one of his senses or a complex of them, with no one sense predominating throughout the book. Third, the sensation

---

*Samuel Beckett counts eleven "fetishes" plus a few incomplete instances. Howard Moss counts eighteen "mnemonic resurrections." Neither tried to discern a basic pattern.

is accompanied by a clear feeling of pleasure and happiness that far surpasses anything explained by the sensation alone. These three components, which occur together in the present, combine in the fourth step to
lift Marcel steeply out of the present and raise him high enough to see
what he has lost sight of: an analogous and forgotten event in the past.
That event is now remembered and recognized and assimilated into the
same binocular field of vision with the present event.

The fifth part of this pattern is a little more subtle and has generally
escaped notice even though it is essential to the full interpretation of
these "landmarks" in Marcel's life and to the form of the novel itself. In
the complete pattern, the first three components reach out to form a link
not only with the past but also with an event or development *in the future*. At the close of the madeleine sequence "the whole of Combray"
takes shape out of Marcel's teacup—not just the memory of the place but
the yet to be composed narrative that completes that recollection. The
clochers de Martinville look forward to the three trees near Balbec and to
the line of poplars Marcel sees from the train on the way back to Paris.
The musty odor in the little pavilion in the Champs-Elysées foreshadows
the death of the grandmother. And the multiple sequence of *moments bienheureux* near the end reaches out, as a group, toward Marcel's final
self-recognition as a person and writer. Proust's words *réalité préssentie*
(I 179/i 253) explicitly state that in addition to backward-looking recollection, these moments may look forward by presentiment to a related
state of affairs in the future. Through this twin eyepiece Proust-Marcel
can look out of the present at Time itself.

Depending now on the extent to which these five elements have combined in an episode—and frequently the pattern remains incomplete or
goes astray—a sixth element follows: some response to the experience.
Four times the experience aborts and produces no results (V, VI, VII, X).
Twice Marcel senses something he should reach out for beyond his present sensation, but he resigns himself to postponing the attempt (III, IV).
Three times the Narrator responds to the urging of the moment by a
lengthy meditation on the nature of time, experience, life, and the most
essential features of reality (VIII, IX, XI). Once the experience leads

him to produce on the spot a literary fragment celebrating the moment, thus attaining an exhilarating sense of accomplishment (II). Once the experience is complete and convincing enough to project its sustaining power forward across the meanderings of the narrative until the renewal of forces at the close (I).

VII. TABLE OF THE *MOMENTS BIENHEUREUX* OR REMINISCENCES OR RESURRECTIONS

Basic Pattern

1. *state of mind*	4. *recognition of*	*none*
2. *sensation*	*past* (souvenir)	*postponement*
3. *inner feeling*	5. *presentiment* 6. *result*	*reflection*
	of future	*creation-vocation*
	(avenir)	*entire book*

I. Madeleine sequence (I 44–48/i 60–64)

    1. "I was cold"; "weary";   4. "Sunday morning "out of the ordinary"   in Combray"; "the vast structure of recollection"

    2. "taste of tea and cake";   5. the entire book—   6. _____ "I shuddered"   "face to face with   ("The whole of something that does   Combray and not yet exist"; "I   its environs") have to start ten times over"

    3. "exquisite pleasure"

*II. The steeples of Martinville (I 179–82/i 252–57)

    1. "Having taken an   4. _____   6. "I composed unusually long walk";   the following "we went like the   little fragment" wind"; "in the absence of other company"

    2. "sight of the twin   5. "reality foreshadowed" steeples"; "lines   (cf. IV, X)

          moving in the
          sunshine"
      3. "special pleasure"

III. Smell in the little pavilion (I 492–94/ii 87–91)
      1. "I was in despair"   4. Uncle Adolph's   6. "I could not
      2. "chill and fusty smell"   little room   understand and
      3. "pleasure . . . rich with   (I 72/i 99)   postponed the
         a lasting truth";   attempt to
         "exaltation"   5. (grandmother's attack) discover why"
                                    (II 309–11/iii 419–22)

*IV. Three trees in Hudimesnil, near Balbec (I 717–19/ii 404–8)
      1. "I should have to   4. Martinville (cf. II)   6. (the happiness
         be alone"   5. "presentiment"; "if,   "remained
      2. "three trees made   in time, I should   incomplete"; "I
         a pattern"   discover"   seemed to die
      3. "happiness like that at   unto myself")
         Martinville"

V. Hawthorn bush, near Balbec (I 922/ii 685–86)
      1. (with Andrée)   4. Hawthorn in bloom   6. _____
      2. "fretted and glossy   at Combray
         leaves"   5. _____
      3. "touched to the heart"

*VI. "Congealed memory" with Saint-Loup in Paris (II 396–98/iii 542–45)
      1. "if I had remained   4. "vast patches of   6. ("wasted
         alone"   oblivion";   years through
                                   (Doncières,   which I was
                                   Combray,   yet to pass
                                   Rivebelle)   before that
      2. "going down the stairs"; 5. _____   invisible
         foggy night   vocation
      3. "enthusiasm"   was to reveal
                                                           itself")

*VII. "Kind of exaltation" after dinner at the house of the Duc de Guer-
     mantes (II 547–49/iii 750–52)
      1. "melancholy";   4. _____   6. "my exaltation

"carriage taking me to M. de Charlus's house" — subsided quickly"

2. "boring conversa-
   tions . . . stories"
3. "I marveled at my
   happiness"

5. _____

VIII. "Disruption of my entire being" in the hotel at Balbec (II 755–60/iv 210–17)

1. "cardiac exhaustion"

2. "touched the top
   button of my shoes";
   "sobs . . . tears"

3. "felicity"; "grief"

4. "the face of my
   grandmother"; "I had
   just grasped that she
   was dead"

5. Marcel's own death;
   "I would be nothing"

6. _____
   ("For the
   heart's
   intermittences
   are closely
   linked to
   disturbances
   of memory")

IX. Septet by Vinteuil (III 248–65/v 331–53)

1. "I was in an unknown
   country"

2. "a tender phrase,
   familiar and domestic,
   of the septet"; "the
   particular accent of that
   phrase"

3. "magic apparition";
   "substantial joy";
   "beginnings of a true
   life"

4. "sonata by Vinteuil"

5. "presentiment . . . of
   joy in the hereafter"

6. _____
   (reflections on
   art and genius)

*X. "The train had halted out in the open country" (III 854–56/vi 253–86)

1. "the thought of my
   lack of literary gifts"

2. "the sun . . . fell on a
   line of trees"

3. "not the slightest
   elation"; "absolute
   indifference"

4. _____

5. _____

6. _____

XI. The reception at the house of the Prince de Guermantes (III 865–86/vi
253–86)
1. "Lassitude";
"boredom": "the
moment when all
appears lost"

a. 2. "unevenly cut 4. Venice (III 623ff./
flagstones" v 844ff.)
3. "felicity"; "A deep
azure intoxicated my
sight" 5. _____

b. 2. "servant struck a 4. "hammer of a
spoon against a plate" trainman" (cf. X)
(III 868/vi 257)
3. "felicity" 5. _____

c. 2. "wiped my mouth 4. "first day of my stay
with the napkin" at Balbec" 6. reflections on
(III 868/vi 258) the novel to
3. "fresh vision of azure" come (III
5. _____ 888–920/vi
279–336)

d. 2. "harsh noise 4. "calls" from
from a water pipe" "pleasure boats off
(III 874/vi 266) Balbec"
3. "ecstasy"; 5. _____
"ineffable vision"

e. 2. *François le Champi*, 4. "book my mother
book in the library read aloud in Combray"
(III 883–86/vi 281–86)
3. "disagreeably stuck" 5. _____
(II 1004–5/vi 463–65);
"mystery of literature";
"a child arises"

*Marcel is in motion: carriage, train, flight of stairs, etc.

Although they follow one basic pattern, therefore, the *moments bien-heureux* are by no means repetitions and do not resemble identical eye-lets through which to thread an unvarying experience of unconscious memory. The fluctuations themselves take on unusual significance. After a promising start, the *moments bienheureux* fall off rapidly both in fre-quency and in intensity, until, at the end, a new impulsion revives them. A graph would look like this:

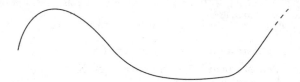

In the simplest of possible terms it represents the action of the book in profile. The low point in the curve, the dead point of all Proust's ma-chinery, at which it seems incapable of moving again in spite of any force applied to it, comes at X when Marcel coldly confronts his lack of "any kind of elation" watching the line of obliquely lit poplar trees from the train (III 856/vi 240). But only thirty pages later the sight of a novel by George Sand carries him beyond his mere memory to the power to recognize himself in the past. "That stranger was myself, he was the child I was then . . ." (III 884/vi 283).

This last of the *moments bienheureux* stands out in two respects among the five moments that come in rapid succession in these pages. It reaches all the way back to the beginning of the book, to the beginning of time in *la première abdication* at Combray. And second, the literary nature of this particular memory out of earliest family experiences gathers up and directs the flood of speculations about the novel that rises around the in-cident (III 870–917/vi 261–332). In these magnificent pages on memory and forgetting, on death and the literary vocation, Marcel almost but not quite comes to final terms with himself. Proust might have closed the novel with Marcel's certainty (in quiet retreat in the Prince de Guer-mantes' library) that he now possesses the secret of recapturing the past and with his still unchallenged plan to apply this secret to a "new life" and the composition of a novel.

But it is not to be so. Marcel comes to terms with himself only 150 pages and about an hour later, not in the evanescence of a sensation re-calling his past, but in confronting the lovely figure of a girl who by her exceptional birth reincarnates all the major characters of the story. Mar-cel's highly complex act of recognizing Mlle de Saint-Loup demands as both its past and its future the novel itself—the one we have just read and the one Marcel will straightway set himself to write. This event alone, amplifying the feebler signal of the madeleine passage, establishes the pitch for the entire work of art, its living and writing.

THE OPENING SENTENCE

(See pages 136 and 189.)

W HAT I HAVE SAID ABOUT THE NATURE OF THE *MOMENTS bienheureux,* and how they are finally surpassed by recognition and binocular vision in time, can now be traced back to the opening of the book and one of the great enigmas in Proust. Just how does one explain the syntax of the opening sentences?

No writer was ever so sensitive as Proust to the sheer tonus of tense in literary discourse. Marcel bursts into tears when he realizes he has spoken of his feelings for Gilberte in the past tense (I 633/ii 287), just as in one of his few known love letters Proust focuses his passion on the tense in which he has to refer to the person he loves (*Disque vert,* 1953). And above all he spoke of the bewitching qualities of the imperfect tense. In Flaubert it "entirely changes the aspect of things and people, like a lamp which has been moved," and elsewhere: "I admit that a certain use of the imperfect indicative—of that cruel tense which presents life to us as something at the same time ephemeral and passive, which, in the very act of retracing our actions, turns them into illusion, buries them in the past without leaving us as does the perfect tense the consolation of activity—has always remained for me an inexhaustible source of mystery and sadness" (*CSB* 170).

Proust wrote his own novel predominantly in the imperfect tense, a condition that makes the pervading tone of sadness and illusion untranslatable into English. For we have no simple tense between the past (aorist) and the unwieldy progressive. Against the long, lush undulating stretches of imperfect, the actions in Proust's novel requiring the *passé simple* stand out in startlingly clear silhouette. Marcel acts comparatively rarely, but his actions assume monumental proportions, raised as they are out of that vast plateau of the imperfect—monumental, and sometimes so trivial and contrived as to carry us far into the domain of the comic. Through these two basic tenses, the present weaves a thread of generalized observation and permanent "truth" or "law."

What, then, is one to make of the opening sentence, especially when one comes back to it after reading through the rest of the novel? Once one begins to consider the other possible versions of the same sentence, it appears deliberately to avoid the characteristic tenses of the novel, the imperfect, the *passé simple,* the present.

Longtemps, je me suis couche de bonne heure.

Why did Proust not clarify his meaning with a temporal preposition or follow conventional syntax?

Depuis longtemps, je me couche de bonne heure.

Depuis longtemps, je me couchais de bonne heure.

Longtemps, je me couchai de bonne heure.

Longtemps, je me couchais de bonne heure.

There are arguments against all four. The first, moving directly into the present, begins to sound confessional and familiar. The second tends to anticipate a specific event coming along to break the routine suggested by the imperfect. The third throws the whole action into the remote past. The fourth—probably the least distorted and the version that is usually understood (and translated) instead of the inscrutable sentence Proust actually wrote—yields too quickly to the pull of reminiscence. Is the sentence, as written, merely conversational and casual in its choice of tense? I doubt it. May we conclude that Proust wanted to keep this opening sentence free of any exact location in time and to begin in a temporal free zone? In part this is surely the effect, whether deliberate or not. *A la recherche* begins outside of time, or hovering above it, and it will end by climbing back up to this altitude.

But if we look and listen long enough, this sentence reveals a deeper secret in the heart of its verbal construction. *Longtemps:* a period of indefinite duration at any point in time. Then: *je me suis couché. Passé composé.* Not a simple tense but a compound tense composed of two other tenses, or times (*temps* meaning both "tense" and "time" in French). The French language, like English, contains a verb form that crosses the present of the auxiliary with the past of the participle to form what we curiously call the perfect—a past action still working its effect in the present and not yet separated from us by insignificance or temporal remoteness. *Two* times, then, past and present, locked in the compound verb form, a fact that allows us to perceive in this, the first verb of the novel, the double time sense of the entire work. Marcel is in bed both literally in the past and symbolically-grammatically in the present as he tells of it—an indefinite time spanning past and present, *passé indéfini,* as it is also called. Without this interpretation, the first sentence remains annoyingly vague and amorphous; with it, these eight words embody the mood and significance of the three thousand pages to follow, because of the fact that they do not employ one of the simple tenses out of which the rest of the book is gradually constructed. We can read fully into the depths of this opening sentence only when we have finished the novel and have plumbed Marcel's past and present here, crossed in a syntactic equivalent of stereoscopic vision in time. He has gone to bed forever. His past and his present are one.

The syntax of Proust's opening sentence (with its two words for time) subsumes the movement of the novel in another way. Neither transitive, bringing its action to bear on another part of the universe, nor intransitive, arresting any direct effect in midflight, the verb is reflexive. The subject turns softly around to discover itself in a new guise: the "accusative"! Extending from here, the action of the book takes place within Marcel himself multiplied into different reflexive and accusative persons. The reflexiveness, the monumental circular subjectivity of the *Search,* as a whole, philosophically and psychologically and even syntactically, forms a subject unto itself, beginning with the first sentence. The passage quoted on pages 105–6 reproduces the circular movement on the scale of a lengthy paragraph turning back to surprise itself: "This is you!" And the self-recognition I have proposed as the central theme of the book constitutes a reflexive action. What the full novel unfolds is the experience and the *oubli* that come to separate the *je* from the *moi* before they reunite—what lodges between I and me. Most written languages contain an equivalent of the revealing expressions: "I forgot myself," and "I came to myself." Proust's "A long time, I have laid me down to sleep at an early hour," begins a self-forgetfulness that will last until a coming-to, a novel and a lifetime later.

One further time, Proust requires his syntax to embody his double time sense in this precise fashion. In the madeleine sequence, after Marcel's vain attempts to identify the source of his pleasurable sensations, the denouement of the incident comes unexpectedly in a sentence parallel to the one I have been examining. *"Et tout d'un coup le souvenir m'est apparu"* (I 46/i 63). And then the final sentence of this opening section: *". . . tout Combray . . . est sorti . . . de ma tasse de thé"* (I 48/i 64). Here, forty pages later, the effect is reinforced. We sense that the memory is with him as he writes, conferring on him the power to compose the novel. Such a device, however, cannot be used often without extinguishing its effect. The *passé composé* does not occur again with this binocular and stereoscopic significance.

SELECTED BIBLIOGRAPHY

Beckett, Samuel. *Proust*. New York: Grove Press, 1931. Seventy of the most probing and succinct pages ever written on Proust's work.

Bersani, Leo. *Marcel Proust: The Fictions of Life and of Art*. New York: Oxford University Press, 1965.

Bowie, Malcolm. *Proust among the Stars*. London: HarperCollins, 1998. Seven fine chapters on the major themes in the *Search*.

Brée, Germaine. *The World of Marcel Proust*. Boston: Houghton Mifflin, 1966.

Bucknall, Barbara J. *The Religion of Art in Proust*. Urbana: University of Illinois Press, 1969. A useful study of a much debated subject.

Carter, William C. *Marcel Proust: A Life*. New Haven: Yale University Press, 2000. The most comprehensive biography written in English.

Descombes, Vincent. *Proust: Philosophy of the Novel* (1987). Translated by Catherine Chance Macksey. Stanford: Stanford University Press, 1992. Essentially a study of how the narrative in Proust carries philosophical significance more telling than the expository passages.

Deleuze, Gilles. *Proust and Signs* (1964). Translated by Richard Howard. New York: George Braziller, 1972.

Maurois, André. *Proust: Portrait of a Genius*. Translated by Gerard Hopkins. New York: Harper, 1950. A readable early biography.

Painter, George D. *Proust: The Early Years* and *Proust: The Later Years*.

2 vols. Boston: Atlantic–Little, Brown, 1959 and 1965. The first major biography.

Pugh, A. R. *The Birth of "A la recherche du temps perdu."* Lexington, Ky.: French Forum, 1987.

Rousset, Jean. *Forme et signification*. Paris: Corti, 1962.

Tadié, Jean-Yves. *Marcel Proust: Biographie*. Paris: Gallimard, 1966. A monumental study, soon to appear in English translation.

Wilson, Edmund. *Axel's Castle: A Study in the Imaginative Literature of 1870–1930*. New York: Scribner's, 1931. Chapter 5 offers a brilliant sixty-page essay on the *Search* as a Symbolist novel—the perfect complement to Beckett's study published the same year.

ACKNOWLEDGMENTS

During all stages and at all levels, Sarah Raff has helped me with the composition of *Proust's Way*. I am grateful for her critical acumen and her extensive knowledge of Proust.

Portions of several of my published writings have been recast and adapted in sections of the present book:

Proust's Binoculars. Random House, 1963.

Marcel Proust. Modern Masters. Viking, 1974.

"The Proust Screenplay by Harold Pinter." *Partisan Review* 46, no. 4 (1979).

"Kilmartin's Way." *New York Review of Books*, June 25, 1981.

"Not Swann's Way." *New York Review of Books*, August 16, 1984.

"Searching for the True Text" (with Douglas Alden). *Times Literary Supplement*, June 10–16, 1988.

"Trouble and Transparency in Marcel Proust." In *The UBA Marcel Proust Symposium*. Summa Publications, 1989.

"Looking Backward: Genetic Criticism and the Genetic Fallacy." French Literature Series 26 (1999): 10.

"The Threat to Proust." *New York Review of Books*, May 6, 1999.

"Sheer Length." *Literary Imagination*, Spring 2000.

INDEX

Note: Names followed by an asterisk* refer to fictional characters.